KU-379-313

ADOPTION OF CHILDREN
IN SCOTLAND

A. J. DRUMMOND & CO.
SOLICITORS
4 PANMURE ST.
DUNDEE
DD1 2BP
18295

ADOPTION OF CHILDREN IN SCOTLAND

PETER G. B. McNEILL,
M.A., LL.B., Ph.D., Advocate

*Sheriff of Lothian and Borders
at Edinburgh*

SECOND EDITION

EDINBURGH

W. GREEN & SON LTD.

St. Giles Street

1986

First published in 1982
Second edition published in 1986

©
1986
P. G. B. McNeill

ISBN 0 414 00779 4

PRINTED IN GREAT BRITAIN BY
The Eastern Press Limited
SPECIALIST LAW BOOK
AND JOURNAL PRINTERS
LONDON AND READING

To

M.F.M.

Preface to Second Edition

At the time of the first edition of this book, some of the provisions of the Children Act 1975 which related to adoption in Scotland had already been brought into force. The remaining adoption provisions were brought into force in 1984, and at the same time the Adoption (Scotland) Act 1978 came into force, thereby repealing and re-enacting the adoption provisions of the 1975 Act and consolidating them with such parts of the Adoption Acts of 1958, 1960, 1964 and 1968 as were still in force. Thus in Scotland, there is in the Adoption (Scotland) Act 1978 a consolidated statute dealing with adoption; but between the passing of the act and its commencement, some parts have been amended, such as the provisions relating to nationality; and some other parts of the law of adoption are to be found outside the 1978 Act, such as section 53 of the 1975 Act which empowers the court in an adoption petition to treat the petition as if it were an application for custody.

(In England the adoption law has also been consolidated in the same way—in the Adoption Act 1976; but in England that consolidating statute has not been brought into force; and the law has to be found in the unrepealed parts of the Adoption Acts of 1958, 1960, 1964 and 1968 and Part I of the Children Act 1975.)

The principal change which has now been brought into force is the new procedure of freeing a child for adoption, whereby the question of the agreements of the natural parents may be disposed of in advance of any actual adoption. In addition, the statute and the rules of court have made hearings compulsory in all cases, even where there is no dispute, whereas, formerly, in undisputed matters no hearings were required unless the court felt that a hearing was necessary. Also, whereas formerly the court was only concerned with one officer—the curator *ad litem*—there is now, in addition, the new reporting officer. In the past, the court relied upon a single report: now the legislation provides for nine types of report. New regional panels of curators *ad litem* and reporting officers have been created; and the fees of these officers in most cases is borne by the local authority and not the petitioners as was the case formerly.

The terms of the adoption rules of the sheriff court and the Court of Session were at one time the same, and thereafter substantially identical: now, in form they are significantly different, but despite these verbal differences, the total information which will be given to each court will in substance be the same. Indeed, generally, the changes brought about by the 1978 Act and the subordinate legislation are more apparent than real. There has been no significant change in the conditions precedent nor in the merits; and even the agreements of the natural parent and the consent of the child in a freeing application are the same in a freeing application as in a petition for adoption, but with some elaboration in procedure: thus, the duties of the reporting officer merely provide a more elaborate method of esablishing the agreement of the natural parents which, formerly, was executed in most cases before a justice of the peace.

The size and nature of the problem of adoptions can to some extent be illustrated by reference to the statistics. For the last few years the number of adoptions which have been granted are of the order of 1600 per year. In court, the proportion of parent and step-parent adoptions on the one hand and non relative adoptions on the other hand is about equal; and the total of them is well over 90% of the whole number. Almost all adoption petitions are presented in the sheriff court: only a tiny number are presented in the Court of Session. (It is unlikely that petitions to free a child for adoption will show any difference.) Surprisingly, almost all appeals from the decision of the sheriff are made to the Court of Session rather than to the sheriff principal. Almost all petitions for adoption are by married couples rather than by a single person. And probably most significant of all, almost every adoption is unopposed most throughout the proceedings and the rest eventually. In these cases, if the court is otherwise satisfied that all the requirements have been met it will, no doubt, grant the adoption order after the hearing.

I have taken into account the further implementation of the 1975 Act, section 53 of which allows the court in an adoption petition to deal with custody instead of adoption, and the modifications of the regional panel of curators *ad litem* and reporting officers. The Law Reform (Parent and Child) (Scotland) Act 1986 received the Royal Assent on 26 March 1986; but the Act shall only come into force on such day as the Secretary of State may appoint by order made by statutory instrument.

Edinburgh   P. G. B. McN.
9 May 1986

Preface to First Edition

Adoption of children was introduced into Scotland over 50 years ago: yet there is no Scottish textbook on the subject such as there is in England in the form of J. F. Gosling, *Adoption of Children* (9th ed.), Oyez Practice Notes. It is hoped that the present work will go some way towards filling the gap in Scotland. The book arose out of lectures which were given to the panel of curators *ad litem* in Glasgow Sheriff Court and to a conference of solicitors; and it has been expanded to include additional aspects of procedure in the sheriff court where all but a tiny handful of petitions are presented. The result may be of interest to those who are professionally involved in adoption in or out of court and also to lay people.

I have only dealt with the extant law, that is, chiefly the residue of the 1958 Act together with those parts of the 1975 Act which relate to adoption and have been brought into force in Scotland. At the same time, I have included references to the corresponding provisions of the 1978 Act which prospectively consolidates the Scottish law of adoption. I have taken into account the changes in the law which came into force on 15 February 1982 and which are contained in the Children Act 1975 (Scotland) (Commencement No. 3) Order 1982 (S.I. 1982 No. 33) and Adoption Agencies (Scotland) Regulations 1982 (S.I. 1982 No. 34). I have also noted the prospective changes effected by the British Nationality Act 1981 in so far as they affect the adoption of children.

In 1930 there were 339 adoption petitions in the sheriff courts of Scotland; in the late 1960s there were over 2000; and in the late 1970s there were about 1600 and decreasing. In England the decline is even more marked. The recent fall in numbers is probably due to several causes: the increase in use of contraception, the greater resort to abortion and the fact that more unmarried mothers are willing to bring up their children themselves in a moral and economic climate which is less harsh than formerly. The figures come from the Civil Judicial Statistics and the Reports of the Registrar General for Scotland.

For lay people and the profession also an ideal outline of adoption procedure before and after the case comes into court is to be found in *Adopting a Child* (1981), a booklet of the British Agencies for Adoption and Fostering, 11 Southwark Street, London SE1 1RQ: (01) 407 8800. The booklet also contains a list of adoption agencies throughout Britain with their addresses and telephone numbers. The addresses and telephone numbers of the courts and the Keeper of the Records of Scotland which respectively hold the more recent and older adoption processes can be found in the telephone directories. Local authorities also produce their own leaflets directed to those inquiring about adoption, for example, *Thinking about Adoption?* which is produced by Strathclyde Regional Council.

Glasgow   P. G. B. McN.
1 February 1982

Acknowledgments

I would like to acknowledge with thanks the assistance and encouragement which I have received in many ways from Mr Colin Armstrong, Sheriff Clerk Depute, Glasgow, Mr A. McLure Campbell, Principal Clerk of Session and his staff, Mr Peter Gillam, solicitor, Edinburgh, Mr Donal Giltinan of B.A.A.F., Edinburgh, Sheriff I. D. Macphail, Sheriff Neil MacVicar, Sheriff J. J. Maguire, Statutory Publications Office, Social Work Services Group, Social Work Department of Lothian Regional Council, Sheriff Marcus Stone, Mr Colin Urquhart, Sheriff Clerk Depute, Edinburgh and Mr David White, Sheriff Clerk, Edinburgh, and his staff.

Once again, Sheriff D. B. Smith read the typescript and the proofs and made innumerable helpful suggestions. Miss Iris Stewart, the General Manager of the publishers, and her colleagues gave me much help. Lastly, I must acknowledge the help of my wife who read all the proofs: without her assistance this edition would not have appeared.

Table of Contents

Table of Cases

[All references are to paragraph numbers]

Table of Statutes

[All references are to paragraph numbers]

Table of Statutory Instruments

[All references are to paragraph numbers]

List of Abbreviations

AS	Act of Sederunt (Adoption of Children) 1959
RC	Rules of Court of Session
1926 Act	Adoption of Children Act 1926
1930 Act	Adoption of Children (Scotland) Act 1930
1950 Act	Adoption Act 1950
1958 Act	Adoption Act 1958
1968 Act	Social Work (Scotland) Act 1968
1975 Act	Children Act 1975
1976 Act	Adoption Act 1976
1978 Act	Adoption (Scotland) Act 1978

CHAPTER 1

Adoption

1.01 Adoption defined

Adoption is the legal process whereby a new status of parent and child is created by the order of a court[1] between an adult and a child, whether they are related to each other or not. The statutory definition of an adoption order is " an order vesting the parental rights and duties relating to a child in the adopters, made on their application by an authorised court."[2] Notwithstanding the procedure of Roman law for adoption, and the former Scottish practice of legitimation by Church or state,[3] the law of Scotland has never recognised any private contract of adoption; and attempts to achieve adoption in this way have been regarded by the courts as unenforceable.[4] Adoption in Scotland and England is the creature of the legislation of the last half century.

1.02 Adoption legislation

Adoption was introduced into England and Wales by the Adoption of Children Act 1926, and into Scotland by the Adoption of Children (Scotland) Act 1930. Subsequent amendments and the consolidation Acts of 1950 and 1958 were Great Britain measures—although in many respects there were quite separate Scottish and English provisions contained within each statute. The Children Act 1975 added to the complication in respect that not only was it a Great Britain measure, but it dealt with both adoption and custody of children; and in addition the parts of the Act which had been brought into force had been enacted piecemeal in both countries and large and significant parts of the Act—such as the power to make a custody order in an adoption application: sections 37 (England) and 53 (Scotland) which constituted an important part of the report of the Houghton Committee which preceded the legislation—have only been brought into force on 1 April 1986.[5] Formerly until the end of 1984 it was necessary to refer to the residue of the 1958 Act and to such parts of the 1975 Act (as were Scottish and as related to adoption) as well as the 1960 Act, the 1964 Act and the 1968 Act. The fragmented state of the law came to an end in Scotland only in 1984 when the 1978 Act was brought into force[5a]; but in England and Wales the corresponding consolidating statute, the 1976 Act, has not yet been brought

---

[1] *J. & J.* v. *C.'s Tutor*, 1948 S.C. 636 at 641.
[2] 1978 Act, s. 12 (1).
[3] Green's *Encyclopaedia* (1st ed.), i, 134 and viii, 32.
[4] *Kerrigan* v. *Hall* (1901) 4 F. 10.
[5] Children Act 1975 (Scotland) (Commencement No. 6) Order 1985 (S.I. 1985 No. 1557), para. 3: in England, s. 37 (as amended by Health and Social Services and Social Security Adjudications Act 1983, s. 9 and Sched. 2, para. 23) came into force on 1 December 1985: Children Act 1975 and Domestic Proceedings and Magistrates' Courts Act 1978 (Commencement) Order 1985 (S.I. 1985 No. 779), reg. 2 (1) and Sched. 1.
[5a] Adoption (Scotland) Act 1978 Commencement Order (S.I. 1984 No. 1050), para. 3.

into force: accordingly, the fragmented state of the law remains in England and Wales. However, although the 1976 Act is not in force in England and Wales, it has application to Scotland by virtue of references to it contained in the 1978 Act:[6] and the 1978 Act has also repealed parts of the 1976 Act in so far as they apply to Scotland.[7] Yet the situation remains anomalous: since the 1976 Act is not in force in England, it appears that there cannot presently exist an adoption society approved under section 3 of that Act, or a freeing order under section 6, or an adoption order under section 18[8]; and there are no references to the corresponding extant legislation in England and Wales—principally the 1958 Act and the 1975 Act. It may be that the references are to be treated as prospective. In one case the Scottish legislation refers to adoption orders " effecting an adoption " made *inter alia* in England and Wales,[9] but without reference to any statute.

The Scottish procedural rules which govern petitions presented in the Court of Session are contained in Act of Sederunt (Rules of Court, Consolidation and Amendment) 1965 (S.I. 1965 No. 321), rules 219–230L. They are printed in Appendix I of this book; the corresponding sheriff court rules are contained in Act of Sederunt (Adoption of Children) 1984 (S.I. 1984 No. 1013) which also appears in Appendix I. The current regulations governing adoption agencies approved under the 1978 Act came into force on 1 September 1984.[10]

In adoption there are differences between the laws applying in Scotland and in England and Wales. The procedural provisions are quite distinct and are contained in separate statutory instruments applicable to each of the courts of each country.[11] However, many of the important provisions in the statutes are expressed in the same language. In this respect Lord President Clyde said in *A. B. & C. B.* v. *X.'s Curator*[12]: " In a matter of this kind it would be unfortunate if the Courts of these two countries arrived at different constructions of the same statutory provision equally applicable to both, and I see no reason in the present case for reaching a different interpretation from that arrived at in England." Yet the impression may be got from some of the statutory provisions and certain dicta of the judges that in England there is a bias against adoption and in favour of custody, particularly in relation to adoptions by a parent and a step-parent. Thus, there is a provision, which does not apply to Scotland, that where the application is by a married couple and they consist of a parent and a step-parent of the child, " the court shall dismiss the application if it considers the matter would be better dealt with under section 42 (orders for custody etc.) of the Matrimonial Causes Act 1973."[13] This provision does not allow the court in an adoption petition to grant a custody order; such an alternative remedy

---

[6] *e.g.* 1978 Act, s. 65 (1).
[7] *e.g.* 1978 Act, s. 66 and Sched. 4. S. 74 of 1976 Act had been brought into force on 27 May 1984: Children Act 1975 and Adoption Act 1976 (Commencement) Order 1983 (S.I. 1983 No. 1946).
[8] 1978 Act, s. 65 (1).
[9] 1978 Act, s. 38 (1) (c).
[10] Adoption Agencies (Scotland) Regulations 1984 (S.I. 1984 No. 988).
[11] In the High Court and County Court Adoption Rules 1984 (S.I. 1984 No. 265), and Magistrates' Courts, Magistrates' Courts (Adoption) Rules 1984 (S.I. 1984 No. 611).
[12] 1963 S.C. 124 at 135.
[13] 1975 Act, s. 10 (3).

has been in force in England and Wales since 1985 and in Scotland since 1986.[14] Further, the " well and firmly " expressed observations of the judges in *Re B.*[15] which included the phrase "the statutory guillotine" were expressed in a case in which there was a protesting parent—which is not a common situation—and it was in the same context in that case at page 145 that Bagnall J. said:

> "The disadvantages of adoption are perhaps too obvious to be stated. It is an irrevocable step constituting a change in status and also involving not only cutting the child off from his father as a matter of law, but also from the grandparents and any other relevant members of the father's family. The child is thereby deprived of any opportunity, as he grows up in later life, to decide whether he wishes to remain with his father."

Those remarks can at most only apply to an adoption by a parent and a step-parent with a still protesting father, and no doubt depend on the facts of the particular case; and although the remarks just quoted cannot be regarded as an unqualified and general statement of the law, they may be taken as such even to the extent of dissuading potential adopters from embarking on proceedings or solicitors from so advising a client: and the statistics indicate that proportionately the number of adoption petitions in England is now less than that in Scotland.[16] Yet there has never been any suggestion that in matters other than procedure there is any difference in the law between the two countries: indeed, appeals to the House of Lords from both countries appear to have equal acceptance.[17]

1.03 Adoption order and other orders

The legislation dealing with adoption provides for several different kinds of order.

(a) An *adoption order* is the most common: indeed the overwhelming majority of petitions seek an adoption order, and the present book is almost wholly concerned with them. Briefly, an adoption order is appropriate where the child is in Scotland and (generally) where the petitioners are domiciled in Scotland or elsewhere in the United Kingdom or the Channel Islands or the Isle of Man, and in most cases have their usual residence in Scotland or England.[18]

(b) A *freeing order*, which was introduced by legislation which came into force in 1984,[19] may only be sought by an adoption agency. A petition to free a child deals with the agreement of the natural parents in advance of an adoption petition, which deals with the remainder of the matters in issue. If this procedure is used, in the subsequent adoption process it is unnecessary

---

[14] 1975 Act, ss. 37 and 53; see above, para. 1.02.
[15] [1975] Fam. 127.
[16] The Office of Population Censuses and Surveys have produced figures of the annual number of adoptions in England and Wales, Chart 2.22, and the large decline shown in step-parent adoptions since 1976 is attributed to the effect of s. 10 (3). *Social Trends*, No. 11 (1981 ed.), Central Statistical Office, p. 39.
[17] *Cf. Re W.* [1971] A.C. 682; *A.* v. *B. & C.*, 1971 S.C.(H.L.) 129; *Re D.* [1977] A.C. 602, all of which cases were decided on the law as it stood before s. 10 (3) was in force. See also below, para. 9.02.
[18] *Cf. Re W.* [1962] Ch. 918; App. II, 6.
[19] 1978 Act, s. 18; see below, para. 5.12.

to deal again with the agreement of the natural parent. Before the final adoption order is granted the natural parent can seek to revoke the freeing order.[20] In most cases there will be no freeing order in force before the adoption petition is presented.

(c) An *interim order* is an alternative to an adoption order: it is not an adoption order, but merely an interim order giving the custody of the child to the petitioner for a period of up to two years by way of a probationary period. Thereafter the court may grant or refuse an adoption order.[21] Before an interim order can be made there must be the agreement of the natural parents (or their agreement must have been dispensed with); but the other matters do not apply until the time of granting the adoption order itself. Although an interim order may be made for a fixed period, with or without conditions, the court could, if the interests of the child demanded it, vary the conditions or bring the order to an earlier end on the motion of parties, or *ex proprio motu*. Since an interim order vests custody of the child in the petitioners, they are entitled to have an extract decree[22] for the purposes of schooling, income tax, state benefits or medical services as well as to vindicate the right to custody against anyone seeking to resist it. In order to preserve confidentiality, the interlocutor need not mention the word " adoption," or one interlocutor can postpone determination of the petition and the other can grant custody.[23]

(d) An *order to adopt a child abroad* (formerly referred to as a *provisional adoption order*[24]) is appropriate where the petitioners are usually resident in Scotland, but in any event are *not* domiciled in England or Wales or Scotland, and an authorised court is satisfied that they intend to take the child out of the country with the intention of adopting the child under the law of or within the country in which the applicants are domiciled.[25] Petitions to adopt a child abroad are most common in those courts within whose jurisdiction there are substantial numbers of servicemen of visiting forces. Except under the authority of an order to adopt a child abroad it is not lawful for any person to take or send a child who is a British subject or a citizen of the Republic of Ireland out of Great Britain to any place outside the British Islands with a view to the adoption of the child by any person not being a parent or guardian or relative of the child.[26] The order authorises the petitioners to remove the child out of the country for the purpose of adoption; and the order only gives the petitioner the right of custody but does not create the relationship of adoptive parent and child[27]; and there is no change brought about in relation to succession or citizenship.[28] As will be noted,[29] a longer period of care and possession of the child by the petitioners applies in a petition to adopt a child abroad than an adoption petition.

---

[20] See below, para. 5.14.
[21] 1978 Act, s. 25. See below, para. 8.05 (m); App. II, 5.
[22] See below, para. 11.04.
[23] See Appendix II, No. 1 (adoption order). Confidentiality is discussed later; see para. 5.02.
[24] 1958 Act, s. 53.
[25] 1978 Act, s. 49.
[26] 1978 Act, s. 50 (1).
[27] *Re M.* [1965] Ch. 203 at 210, *per* Buckley J.
[28] 1978 Act, s. 38.
[29] See below, para. 3.02.

Otherwise, the provisions of the legislation apply equally to petitions to adopt a child abroad and an adoption petition[30]; and the style of the petition in the two cases is substantially similar[31]; but the petitioners must adduce evidence of the law of adoption in the country in which the child is domiciled[32]; and the form of the order to be transmitted to the Registrar General for Scotland will also be the same as in an adoption order, but with such variations as the case requires.[33]

(e) *Convention adoption orders* were introduced in substance but not by that name by the 1968 Act: in that Act they were merely referred to as "adoption orders,"[34] and this nomenclature served to show that what are now called "Convention adoption orders"[35] are with certain variations the same as adoption orders: a Convention adoption order is an adoption order made in accordance with section 17 (1).[36] The purpose of the 1968 Act was to implement the Hague Convention on the Adoption of Children 1965 (Cmnd. 2613), hence the name Convention adoption order. The current provisions have been in force since 23 October 1978.[37] A Convention adoption order can only be granted by the Court of Session, for which provision has been made in Rules of Court 230A-230L. An application is appropriate where there is a foreign element in relation to the child or the petitioners—apart from domicile, which is not relevant[38]: indeed the provisions are an alternative to the case where the petitioners are domiciled in the United Kingdom, the Channel Islands or the Isle of Man. The court may make a Convention adoption order where:

(i) the petitioners
    (a) (1) are nationals of the United Kingdom or a Convention country, and
        (2) are habitually resident in Great Britain; or
    (b) (1) are United Kingdom nationals, and
        (2) are habitually resident in British territory or a Convention country; and
(ii) the child
        (1) is a national of the United Kingdom or a Convention country, and
        (2) habitually resides in British territory or a Convention country, but
        (3) is not a United Kingdom national living in British territory if both petitioners are; and
        (4) must not be or have been married.[39]

Those conditions must be satisfied both at the time that the application is made and when the order is made.

---

[30] 1978 Act, s. 49 (2).
[31] A.S. 16 (1) and Forms 7 and 8 (R.C. 222 (1) and Form 36).
[32] A.S. 17 (1) (R.C. 224 (3) (*b*)).
[33] 1978 Act, s. 49 (3). See App. II, 6.
[34] s. 1 (1).
[35] 1978 Act, s. 17.
[36] 1978 Act, s. 65 (1).
[37] 1975 Act, s. 24 and Children Act 1975 (Scotland) (Commencement No. 2) Order 1978 (S.I. 1978 No. 1440); 1978 Act, s. 17.
[38] 1978 Act, ss. 14 (2) (*b*) and 15 (2) (*b*).
[39] 1978 Act, s. 17.

The 1978 Act also covers adoptions which have been made outwith the United Kingdom. These are of two categories:

(i) *Convention adoption* means an overseas adoption—but restricted to those adoptions of a description designated by the Convention Adoption (Miscellaneous Provisions) (Scotland) Order 1978[40] and made under section 53 (1) of the 1978 Act as an adoption regulated by the Convention.[41]

(ii) *Overseas adoption* means an adoption of such a description as the Secretary of State may by order specify. The only order which has so far been made is the Adoption (Designation of Overseas Adoptions) Order 1973.[42] Overseas adoptions form a wider group than Convention adoptions. There are provisions for recognising overseas adoptions,[43] and for the annulment of Convention adoptions.[44] Further, where an overseas adoption of a child who was born in Great Britain is recognised here, the Registrar General for Scotland will if he is satisfied that the order relates to an entry in the Register of Births record the adoption in the Adopted Children Register.[45] In the first six years of the operation of section 8, an average of 23 overseas adoptions per year have been recorded by the Registrar General for Scotland.[46]

(f) *Custody* arises in adoption procedure in several ways:

    (i) in England and Wales, but not in Scotland, in step-parent adoptions, the court must dismiss the application for adoption, if it considers that the matter "would be better dealt with" under the Matrimonial Causes Act 1973, section 42 (which deals with orders for custody)[47];

    (ii) in a petition to adopt a child abroad, the order of the court vests in the petitioner the parental rights and duties relating to the child[48];

    (iii) in a petition for adoption the court may make an interim order "vesting the custody of the child in the petitioners"[49]; and

    (iv) from 1986 in Scotland[50] (and from 1985 in England and Wales[51]) the court must, in certain circumstances, in a petition for adoption, direct that the petition for adoption be treated as if it had been made for custody (and where such a direction has been made the court does not cease to have jurisdiction by reason only that it would not have had jurisdiction to hear an application by the applicant for custody of the child). It is thought that such a direction would only be likely in very limited

---

[40] S.I. 1978 No. 1441.
[41] 1978 Act, s. 65 (1).
[42] S.I. 1973 No. 19.
[43] 1978 Act, s. 53(1).
[44] 1978 Act, s. 47.
[45] 1978 Act, s. 45 and Sched 1, para. 1(2).
[46] Report of the Registrar General for Scotland, 1978.
[47] 1975 Act, s. 10 (3) (1976 Act, s. 14 (3)).
[48] 1978 Act, s. 49; see above, para. 1.03 (d).
[49] 1978 Act, s. 25 (1); see above, para. 1.03 (c).
[50] 1975 Act, s. 53; 1978 Act, ss. 14 (1) and 15 (1).
[51] 1975 Act, s. 37; s. 37 came into force in England on 1 December 1985: Children Act 1975 (Commencement) Order 1985 (S.I. 1985 No. 779); and Domestic Proceedings and Magistrates' Courts Act 1978: s. 53 came into force in Scotland on 1 April 1986; Children Act (Scotland) (Commencement No. 6) Order 1985 (S.I. 1985 No. 1557), para. 3.

circumstances. The petitioner in the adoption proceedings must be a person qualified to apply for custody of the child, which includes any relative, step-parent or foster parent of the child.[52] The court is required to make a direction under section 53 in one of two situations where the court is of the opinion

> " (a) in the case of an applicant who is a relative of the child or a husband or wife of the mother or father of the child (whether applying alone or jointly with his or her spouse)—
>
> > (i) that the child's welfare would not be better safeguarded and promoted by the making of an adoption order in favour of the applicant than it would be by the making of a custody order in his favour; and
> >
> > (ii) that it would be appropriate to make a custody order in favour of the applicant; or
>
> (b) in any other case, that the making of a custody order in favour of the applicant would be more appropriate than the making of an adoption order in his favour."

Formerly, the court could either make an adoption order or refuse to do so; now, under this section, a third possibility is open to the court. But the court would clearly not consider this issue in isolation: in terms of section 6 of the 1978 Act, in reaching " any decision relating to the adoption of the child " it has to have regard not only to the welfare of the child but also *all* the circumstances. It is thought that only in a very small number of cases would the court be of the opinion that the adoption petition should be treated as a custody application, and these few would almost all be step-parent adoptions, but only where there has been a significant and continuing contact between the other parent and the child, and that other parent does not agree to the making of the adoption order. If all the parties—the petitioners, the natural parent and the child—are at one that an adoption order should be granted, it is unlikely that the court would *ex proprio motu* direct that the adoption petition be treated as an application for custody. Even if the information in the case did persuade the court that custody was a likely alternative to adoption, the court would obviously not consider directing that the petition for adoption should be treated as an application for custody until the parties had been heard on their own motion or *ex proprio motu*. The parties might persuade the court that in terms of section 53 the direction should not be made. Indeed, the very fact that the attitude of the parties was that even if a direction were made, one or both of the petitioners would in no circumstances seek a custody order might well be a circumstance which the court would have to take into account in deciding whether to make a direction.

However, in a custody action in the Court of Session decided 30 years ago,[53] the court granted warrant to the sheriff clerk at Falkirk to transmit to

---

[52] A person qualified to apply for custody of a child is defined in 1975 Act, s. 47; but see also *S. v. S.*, 1967 S.C.(H.L.) 46; 1967 S.L.T. 217.

[53] 1955 S.C. 378.

the Deputy Principal Clerk of Session an adoption process in respect of the same child in that court. Thereafter, the court having heard counsel, found that there was contingency between the two processes—which contingency was doubted by the reporter who had been appointed by the court to investigate the facts of the case and to report. The court subsequently refused the Court of Session petition for custody and without further reference to Falkirk Sheriff Court (as far as is disclosed) granted the adoption order in the sheriff court action. At present, in England and Wales, but not in Scotland, "where an application is made to a court . . . and the married couple consist of a parent and a step-parent of the child, the court shall dismiss the application if it considers that the matter would be better dealt with under section 42 (orders for custody etc.) of the Matrimonial Causes Act 1973 "[54]; but this provision does not allow that court itself to make an order for custody.

1.04 Effect of adoption orders and other orders

It has been the purpose of the legislation dealing with adoption to put as far as it is possible the adopted child into the same position in law in relation to his adoptive parents as he would be with natural parents. In relation to the 1926 Act, Lord Atkin observed:

" that the Act does not put the adopter and the child into the position of natural parent and child for all purposes. But, as to the matters enumerated in sub-s. 1, custody, maintenance and education, it does in the plainest language transfer from the natural parent to the adopter the whole rights and obligations that flow from parenthood; and places the child in the same position as though he were the lawful natural child of the adopter "[55]; and Vaisey J. said:

"normally, an adoption presupposes a complete and final separation between the child and its natural parents. The child looks thenceforth to the adopters as its parents, the natural parents, relinquishing all their parental rights and duties, step as it were forever out of the picture of the child's life."[56]

The making of the order vests the parental rights and duties relating to a child in the adopters.[57] The change in the status of a child which occurs on the making of an adoption order has several aspects.

(1) *Legitimation.* Generally, from 1 January 1976, or from the date of any later adoption, the adopted child is treated in law

    (a) as the legitimate child of the marriage where there are two adopters, or

    (b) as the legitimate child of the adopter where there is one adopter and as if he were not the child of any person other than the adopters or adopter.[58] However, where an illegitimate child has been adopted by one of his natural parents as sole adoptive parent, and the adopter thereafter

---

[54] 1975 Act, s. 10 (3) (1976 Act, s. 14 (3)).
[55] *Coventry Corporation* v. *Surrey County Council* [1935] A.C. 199 at 205.
[56] *Re D. X.* [1949] Ch. 320, a single judge decision in an interlocutory application.
[57] 1978 Act, s. 12 (1).
[58] 1978 Act, s. 39 (1) and (*prosp.*) Law Reform (Parent and Child) (Scotland) Act 1986, s. 10 (1) and Sched. 1, para. 18 (2).

marries the other natural parent, these provisions do not affect any enactment of rule of law whereby, by virtue of the marriage, the child is rendered the legitimate child of both natural parents.[59] Further, where the natural parents of an illegitimate child, one of whom has adopted him in Scotland, have subsequently married each other, the court by which the adoption order was made may, on the application of any of the parties concerned, revoke that order.[60]

(2) *Adopted Children Register*. Every adoption order must contain a direction to the Registrar General for Scotland to make in the Adopted Children Register an entry recording the adoption which will include the date and place of birth as determined by the court and the names and surnames of the child.[61] Generally, the Adopted Children Register as far as the child is concerned takes the place of the Register of Births and an extract relating to him would be of an entry in the Adopted Children Register. Thus, for example, in an application for a passport, an adopted person is not required to disclose his former names.

(3) *Forbidden degrees*. The provisions relating to legitimation on adoption do not apply in determining the prohibited degrees of consanguinity and affinity in respect of the law relating to marriage, or in respect of the crime of incest, except that, on the making of an adoption order, the adopter and the child are deemed, in all time coming, to be within the said prohibited degrees in respect of the law relating to marriage.[62] In *H. M. A. v. R. M.*[63] which was a decision on the now repealed analogous provision which had excluded reference to the law of incest,[64] it was held that sexual intercourse between a man and his adopted daughter is not a crime by the law of Scotland.

(4) *Domicile*. The new status of parent and child which is created by an adoption order " must be validly created by the law of the domicile of the adopting parent. You do not look to the domicile of the child: for that has no separate domicile of its own. It takes its parents' domicile. You look to the parents' domicile only."[65] In Scotland, a girl can acquire an independent domicile at 12, and a boy at 14. By statute, the domicile of a child (which includes an adopted child) who is incapable of having an independent domicile and whose parents are living apart may have the domicile of his mother.[66]

(5) *Citizenship*. Where an adoption order is made in respect of a child who is not a British citizen, then, if the adopter, or in the case of a joint application one adopter, is a British citizen, the child becomes a British citizen as from the date of the order[67] but the status of legitimacy conferred by adoption[68] does not apply for the purposes of any provision of

---

[59] 1978 Act, s. 39 (2).
[60] 1978 Act, s. 46. A style of petition for revocation of an adoption order appears in App. II, 22.
[61] 1978 Act, s. 45 (9) and Sched. 1, para. 1.
[62] 1978 Act, s. 41.
[63] 1969 J.C. 52.
[64] 1958 Act, s. 13 (3).
[65] *Re Valentine's Settlement* [1965] Ch. 831 at 842, *per* Lord Denning.
[66] Domicile and Matrimonial Proceedings Act 1973, s. 4.
[67] British Nationality Act 1981, s. 1 (5) and (6).
[68] See above, para. 1.04 (1).

(a) the British Nationality Act 1981,

(b) the Immigration Act 1971,

(c) any instrument having effect under an enactment with these two statutes, or

(d) any other law for the time being in force which determines British citizenship, British Dependent Territories citizenship or British Overseas citizenship.[69]

This provision does not affect the nationality of persons who are adopted by those who are not citizens of the United Kingdom and Colonies: generally, even if a British child is adopted by an alien, he will remain British.

(6) *Parent and child.* As has been indicated the adoptive parent has vested in him the parental rights and duties relating to the adopted child. As in the case of a natural parent, he will have custody of the child; he will be bound to aliment the child; and he will have to ensure the education of the child and give such advice and guidance as a parent should. Generally, the duties between the natural parent and the child in these respects are extinguished.[69a]

(7) *Succession, etc.* For all purposes relating to

(a) the succession to a deceased person (whether testate or intestate), and

(b) the disposal of property by virtue of any *inter vivos* deed,

an adopted person must be treated as the child of the adopter, and not as the child of any other person.[69b] However, where the adopter has died before the commencement of that Act the adopted person shall be treated for the purposes of succession to the estate of a natural parent who dies after 3 August 1966, as the child of that parent.[70] However, titles of honour are not affected and where the terms of any deed provide that any property or interest in property shall devolve along with a title, honour or dignity, these provisions shall not prevent that property or interest so devolving.[71] A few minor rights are preserved to the child notwithstanding the adoption order, such as entitlement to a pension and funeral benefit.[72]

(8) *Title to sue.* An adoptive child has the same title to sue as a natural child and by statute a right to claim damages in respect of the death of his adoptive parents and vice versa.[73]

(9) It is provided in terms that a resolution of a local authority assuming parental rights shall cease to have effect when the child becomes the subject of an adoption order.[74]

Generally, the provisions as to the effect of an adoption order on the status of an adopted child apply to:

(i) an adoption order under the 1978 Act, s. 65 (1)[75];

---

[69] 1978 Act, s. 41 (2).
[69a] 1978 Act, s. 12 (3) and (4).
[69b] Succession (Scotland) Act 1964, s. 23 (1).
[70] Law Reform (Miscellaneous Provisions) (Scotland) Act 1966, s. 5.
[71] Succession (Scotland) Act 1964, ss. 23 (3) and 37.
[72] 1978 Act, ss. 42 and 43.
[73] Damages (Scotland) Act 1976, s. 1 and Sched. 1, para. 1 (*b*); 1978 Act, s. 39 (1).
[74] Social Work (Scotland) Act 1968, s. 16 (11) (*a*) as substituted by 1975 Act, s. 74.
[75] 1978 Act, s. 38 (1).

(ii) an adoption order under the 1975 Act, the 1958 Act, the 1950 Act or any enactment repealed by the 1950 Act;

(iii) an order effecting an adoption made in England and Wales, Northern Ireland, the Isle of Man or any of the Channel Islands;

(iv) an " overseas adoption " as defined in the 1978 Act, s. 65 (2); or

(v) any other adoption recognised by the law of Scotland.[76]

The provisions do not apply to the orders which are in essence custody orders, that is to say, an interim order[77] and an order to adopt a child abroad[78]; nor do they apply to an order following on an adoption application which is treated by the court as if it were an application for custody.[79]

Where an order freeing a child for adoption is made, the parental rights and duties relating to the child vest in the adoption agency, and the former rights and duties between the child and his natural parents are extinguished.[80] To that extent only, a freeing order has the same effect as an adoption order.

---

[76] 1978 Act, s. 38 (1) and Succession (Scotland) Act 1964, s. 23 (5).
[77] 1978 Act, s. 25.
[78] 1978 Act, s. 49.
[79] 1975 Act, s. 53.
[80] 1978 Act, ss. 12 (2) and (3) and 18 (5); see below, para. 5.13.

CHAPTER 2

Who May Adopt

2.01 Generally

An adoption order may only be sought by two classes of petitioner:

   (a) a married couple[1]; or
   (b) a single person[2]; but that single person must not be married, or if married the court must be satisfied that his spouse cannot be found, or is separated, or is incapable of making an application for an adoption order. Presumably, if in the course of proceedings by a married couple, they were divorced from each other the petition would be thereby rendered incompetent, unless one of the petitioners dropped from the action.

The same provisions apply to Convention adoptions; and they are applied to an order to adopt abroad.[3] If petitioners are otherwise eligible to adopt a child their relationship to the child does not by itself render them ineligible, except in so far as that relationship does not enure to the benefit of the child. To assert that a particular relationship such as grandparent and grandchild or step-parent and step-child should inhibit the granting of an adoption order would be not only to do violence to the rule that each case must be decided on its merits but also to fly in the face of the law. The statutory provisions envisage adoptions by relatives, which term "means a grandparent, brother, sister, uncle or aunt, whether of the full blood or half-blood or by affinity and include, where the child is illegitimate the father of the child and any person who would be a relative within the meaning of this definition if the child were the legitimate child of his mother and father"[4]; and the court must have regard to "all the circumstances,"[5] of which the relationship between the child and the petitioner is only one. Decisions in particular cases have indicated a variety of unexceptionable relationships between adopters and children, many of which are now commonplace, including adoption

   (a) by two spouses of a child who has already been adopted by one of the spouses[6];
   (b) by one parent of his or her illegitimate child[7];
   (c) by both natural parents now married to each other of their own

---

[1] 1978 Act, s. 14 (1).
[2] 1978 Act, s. 15 (1).
[3] 1978 Act, s. 49 (2).
[4] 1978 Act, s. 65 (1).
[5] 1978 Act, s. 6; cf. Re W. [1971] A. C. 682 at p. 699, when Lord Hailsham referred to "the totality of the circumstances."
[6] A.S. 25.
[7] D., Petitioner, 1938 S.C. 223; H. & H., Petitioners, 1948 S.L.T.(Sh.Ct.) 37; 1978 Act, s. 46.

illegitimate child born to the female petitioner during the subsistence of a former marriage[8];

  (d) by a husband and wife of the legitimate child of the wife by a former marriage[9];

  (e) by a mother of an illegitimate child and her husband who was not the father of the child[10];

  (f) by the grandparents of a grandchild.[11]

However, in other cases the court refused to grant adoption orders in petitions

  (a) by a married man living in adultery with a married woman of their illegitimate child, because to grant the order would be contrary to public policy[12];

  (b) by married parents of their own legitimated child.[13]

2.02 Matrimonial status of petitioners

Different rules apply depending on whether the petitioners are married or not:

  (a) In the case of an application made by a married couple

    (i) at least one of them must be domiciled in a part of the United Kingdom, or the Channel Islands or the Isle of Man; or

    (ii) the application is for a Convention adoption order.[14] Convention adoption orders have been discussed earlier.[15]

  (b) In the case of an application by a single person[16]

    (i) where that person is not married, and

      (1) is not a natural parent, there is no specialty,

      (2) is a natural parent, the adoption can be made only if

        (a) the other natural parent cannot be found, or

        (b) there is some other reason justifying the exclusion of the natural parent (which reason must be recorded by the court)[17];

    (ii) where that person is married and

      (1) his spouse cannot be found, or

      (2) the spouses have separated and are living apart and the separation is likely to be permanent, or

      (3) his spouse is incapable of making an application by reason of ill-health, whether physical or mental,[18] then the adoption order can be made;

---

  [8] *B. & B., Petitioners*, 1936 S.C. 256; *H. & H., Petitioners*, 1948 S.L.T.(Sh.Ct.) 37.
  [9] *I. & I., Petitioners*, 1947 S.C. 485.
  [10] *A. & B., Petitioners*, 1932 S.L.T.(Sh.Ct.) 37.
  [11] *T. F. & H. F., Petitioners*, 1949 S.L.T.(Sh.Ct.) 48; *C. D., Petitioners*, 1963 S.L.T.(Sh.Ct.) 7, where the court refused to pronounce an adoption order on other grounds; *cf. A. B., Petitioners*, (1962) 78 Sh.Ct.Rep. 148; and in England: *Re W.* [1980] 10 Fam. 190; [1981] C.L.Y. 1751.
  [12] *J. S., Petitioner*, 1950 S.L.T.(Sh.Ct.) 3.
  [13] *M. & M., Petitioners*, 1950 S.L.T.(Sh.Ct.) 3; *cf.* 1978 Act, s. 46(1).
  [14] 1978 Act, s. 14 (1).
  [15] See above, para. 1.03 (e).
  [16] See below, paras. 3.01 (d) and 8.05 (k).
  [17] 1978 Act, s. 15 (3).
  [18] 1978 Act, s. 15 (1).

(iii) (1) the person must be domiciled in the United Kingdom or in
the Channel Islands or the Isle of Man, or
(2) the application must be for a Convention adoption order.[19]

2.03 Age of the petitioner

A petitioner must have attained the age of 21: this general rule has
replaced the former law under which the age of the petitioner depended on
the relationship between the petitioner and the child.[20] Thus, although
persons may marry at 16 and have children, and are able to vote at 18, they
cannot adopt a child—even their own child—until each petitioner is 21.
There is no upper age limit for a petitioner at which a petition would be
incompetent; but since 1966 the court must have a report on the
considerations arising from the difference in age between the petitioners and
the child if such difference is more or less than the normal difference
between parents and their children.[21] No doubt any considerable difference
between the age of the petitioners and the child would be taken into account;
but in many cases where such differences exist the child has been with the
petitioners for a long time and no matter what happens in the adoption
proceedings is likely to remain in the care and possession of the petitioners.
As to " grandparent adoptions," they are discussed elsewhere.[22]

2.04 Domicile

In each case the domicile in the United Kingdom, the Channel Islands or
the Isle of Man of the petitioner where there is only one and of one of them
where there are two is an overriding condition of granting the adoption
order.[23] If neither petitioner is so domiciled, then according to an English
decision on the former United Kingdom provisions relating to domicile[24] it
would be incompetent to grant an adoption order: only a provisional
adoption order under the 1958 Act, s. 53 (now an order to adopt a child
abroad), could competently be granted.[25] Now in addition it is competent to
apply for a Convention adoption order.[26] Under the former law it had been
held that the ordinary residence of the petitioners need not be within Great
Britain,[27] and the present requirements do not appear to render that
situation impossible.[28]

2.05 " Authorised court ": Remit to the Court of Session

Formerly the criterion for jurisdiction was the residence of the child[29];
now, generally, if the child is in Scotland when the application is made the
authorised courts are
(a) the Court of Session;

---

[19] 1978 Act, s. 15 (2).
[20] 1950 Act, s. 2 (1); *cf. H., Petitioner*, 1960 S.L.T.(Sh.Ct.) 3.
[21] A.S. 21 (2) (*q*) (R.C. 222 (7) (*p*)); see below, para. 8.05 (*q*).
[22] See above, para. 2.01; and below, para. 4.02.
[23] 1978 Act, ss. 14 (2) (*a*) and 15 (2) (*a*).
[24] 1958 Act, s. 1 (1).
[25] *Re R.* [1962] 3 All E.R. 238.
[26] 1978 Act, ss. 14 (2) (*b*) and 15 (2) (*b*).
[27] *Re W.* [1962] Ch. 918.
[28] See below, para. 8.05 (n).
[29] *e.g.* 1930 Act, s. 8 (1).

(b) the sheriff court of the sheriffdom (not merely the sheriff court district)[30] within which the child is.[31]

In the case of an application for an adoption order or for an order freeing a child for adoption, where the child is not in Great Britain, or for a Convention adoption order then the authorised court is the Court of Session.[32] These rules are not affected by EEC Rules on jurisdiction.[33] Presumably, the rule that the child must be present at the time that the petition is presented does not extend to a requirement that the child should also reside in Scotland at the time of granting the order: the former provisions[34] to that effect have been repealed.[35] However, after the authorised court has been ascertained, the child must at all times immediately preceding the date of the order have had his home with the petitioners or one of them: that phrase is the obverse of the petitioners having the care and possession of the child.[36] It would appear to be incompetent to prorogate the jurisdiction of a court other than the authorised court.[37] The power to remit a case from one sheriffdom to another in ordinary actions and summary causes[38] would no doubt be applicable to adoption procedure also.[39] It has been held by a single judge that the ordinary residence of the petitioners need not be within Great Britain.[40] In addition, in the case of any action in the sheriff court in relation to the custody or adoption of a child, the sheriff may of his own accord at any stage remit the action to the Court of Session; and a decision " to remit or not to remit " is not subject to review.[41] New rules following upon this and similar changes in procedure have been made in the Court of Session[42] and in the sheriff court.[43] And from a date yet to be appointed by the Lord Advocate, the Court of Session will have power in relation to any action before it which could competently have been brought before a sheriff to remit the action (at its own instance or on the application of any of the parties to the action) to the sheriff within whose jurisdiction the action could have been brought where, in the opinion of the court, the nature of the action makes it appropriate to do so.[44]

---

[30] But the sheriff has a discretion whether to grant warrant to cite a defender who is resident in another district: Dobie, *Sheriff Court Practice*, pp. 52–53; *Tait* v. *Johnston* (1981) 18 R. 606; *Davidson* v. *Davidson* (1891) 18 R. 884.

[31] 1978 Act, s. 56 (2).

[32] 1978 Act, s. 56 (3) and (4).

[33] Civil Jurisdiction and Judgments Act 1982, s. 2 (2), Sched. 1, Article 11.

[34] 1958 Act, s. 1 (5); *cf. X. Y.*, *Petitioners* 1954 S.L.T.(Sh.Ct.) 86.

[35] 1975 Act, s. 108 and Sched. 4, Pt. IV; Children Act 1975 (Scotland) (Commencement No. 1) Order 1977 (S.I. 1977 No. 227), para. 3 and Sched. 1.

[36] 1978 Act, s. 13.

[37] *G. & G.*, *Petitioners.*, *S. & S.*, *Petitioners* and *R. & R.*, *Petitioners*, Edinburgh Sheriff Court, E50/85, E49/85 and E51/85 (unreported).

[38] Sheriff Courts (Scotland) Act 1907, Sched. I, r. 19; Act of Sederunt (Summary Cause Rules, Sheriff Court) 1976 (S.I. 1976 No. 476), r. 22.

[39] *Central Regional Council* v. *B.*, 1985 S.L.T. 413; *Magistrates of Portobello* v. *Magistrates of Leith* (1882) 10 R. 130.

[40] *Re W.* [1962] Ch. 918 at 926, *per* Wilberforce J.

[41] Sheriff Courts (Scotland) Act 1971, s. 37, as amended by Law Reform (Miscellaneous Provisions) (Scotland) Act 1980, s. 16.

[42] R.C. 274 and 275.

[43] Sheriff Courts (Scotland) Act 1907, Sched. 1, r. 95.

[44] Law Reform (Miscellaneous Provisions) (Scotland) Act 1985, s. 14.

2.06 Health of petitioner

There is no statutory requirement that prospective adopters be of good health. Indeed, in the case where one of the petitioners is a parent of the child, there is no need to have a medical certificate as to the health of either petitioner. No doubt, however, if the court was told of a significant medical condition of the petitioner which might affect the welfare of the child, it would make such further medical inquiries as seemed appropriate. Even in the case of petitioners of whom neither is a parent of the child, all that the rules require is that there be medical certificates as to the health of the petitioners lodged in process with the petition itself.[45] No doubt the doctor will adapt the report to meet the state of the petitioner's health; and if he gives a reason for his opinion that the petitioner is not a suitable person to adopt the child, the court can decide what weight to give to that reason with or without the assistance of an expanded report or other medical evidence or the views of the petitioners. Having decided what the medical state of the petitioner is, the court must decide what weight to give to it. There appears to be no good reason why the lack of good health in a petitioner should of itself preclude the granting of an adoption order: it is merely one of the circumstances to which the court shall have regard, " first consideration being given to the need to promote the welfare of the child throughout his childhood."[46] In *G. & G., Petitioners*[47] an adoption order was refused because of the possible danger of infection of the child by the female petitioner who was suffering from a chronic tuberculosis condition. The circumstances of the case might require other medical evidence about a petitioner or a parent who was not a petitioner, for example, as to the mental condition of a parent who has neglected or ill-treated the child[48]; or who is incapable of giving his agreement[49]; or is incapable of making an application for an adoption order or falls to be excluded from an application.[50]

---

[45] A.S. 16 (3)(*c*); but in the Court of Session the requirements are somewhat different: there must be a medical report on the health of the child, but only when the child was not placed by an adoption agency: R.C. 222 (4) (*d*).
[46] 1978 Act, s. 6.
[47] 1949 S.L.T.(Sh.Ct.) 60.
[48] 1978 Act, s. 16 (2) (*d*) (*e*) or (*f*).
[49] 1978 Act, s. 16 (2) (*a*).
[50] 1978 Act, s. 15 (1) (*b*) (iii) and 15 (3) (*b*).

CHAPTER 3

The Child

3.01 Child defined

(a) Since 1969 only a child who has not attained the age of 18 can be adopted.[1] A child can only be adopted after it is at least 19 weeks old (and 32 weeks old where the petition is to adopt the child abroad[2]) and has had his home with the petitioners at all times during the 13 weeks preceding the making of the order[3] (and 26 weeks where the petition is to adopt the child abroad[4]). Where the child is not being adopted by a parent, step-parent or relative or is not being placed for adoption by an adoption agency, the child must be at least 12 months old and at all times during the 12 months preceding the making of the order have had his home with the petitioners or one of them.[5]

(b) A child who is or has been married cannot be adopted.[6]

(c) A child who is a minor—that is a girl over 12 and not yet 18, and a boy over 14 and not yet 18—must consent to the making of the adoption order, except that where the court is satisfied that the minor is incapable of giving his consent it may dispense with that consent.[7] This is the only ground for dispensing with the consent of the minor, whereas there are several grounds for dispensing with the agreement of the parent.[8] The *punctum temporis* for dispensing with consent is the making of.the adoption order, not the lodging of the petition.[9] In England and Wales the consent of the child is not required. Apart from the question of such formal consent to the making of an adoption order, the court in reaching any decision relating to the adoption of the child must so far as is reasonably practicable ascertain the wishes and feelings of the child regarding the decision and give due consideration to them, having regard to the age and understanding of the child[10]; and in sheriff court cases the curator *ad litem* must report to the court on these matters,[11] but this is not presently required in the Court of Session.[12] In addition the local authority or the adoption agency must

---

[1] 1978 Act, s. 65 (1); *cf. M., Petitioner*, 1953 S.C. 227.
[2] 1978 Act, s. 49 (2).
[3] 1978 Act, s. 13 (1); *e.g. O. & O., Petitioners*, Edinburgh Sheriff Court, E54/85 (unreported), where the child had been found abandoned in Delhi and had been given into the guardianship of the petitioners by the Indian courts.
[4] 1978 Act, s. 49 (2).
[5] 1978 Act, s. 13 (2).
[6] 1978 Act, s. 12 (5).
[7] 1978 Act, s. 12 (8).
[8] See below, para. 10.09.
[9] 1978 Act, s. 12 (8).
[10] 1978 Act, s. 6.
[11] A.S. 21 (2) (*s*); see below, para. 8.05 (s).
[12] R.C. 222 (7) (*d*).

investigate and report on " matters relevant to the operation of section 6 "[13] which would include the welfare of the child.

(d) Until 1958 an adoption order could not be made in respect of a child who was a female where the sole applicant was a male unless there were special circumstances " which justify as an exceptional measure the making of an adoption order."[14] In one case, which was decided while that section was in force, a policeman and his wife received a month-old female child into their care and possession with the intention of applying for an adoption order. On the death of his wife, the policeman went to reside with his wife's mother who looked after the child. He applied for an adoption order, and it was held, after hearing evidence, that in the special circumstances the adoption order should be granted.[15] That provision of the 1958 Act has been repealed[16] and it has not been re-enacted. However, notwithstanding the repeal of that subsection, in the case of a sole male petitioner who is seeking to adopt a female child the welfare of the child would still be a very important consideration in the decision whether to grant the adoption order as would be the case of a sole male seeking to adopt a male child in so far as it affected the welfare of the child.[17]

3.02 Care and possession

(a) Generally, before a child can be adopted it must have been continuously in the care and possession of the petitioner. Before 1978 the *de facto* custody which the petitioners had of the child which they intended to adopt was called " care and possession "; and it was essential that before an adoption order could be granted the child should have been continuously in the care and possession of the petitioners for at least three months preceding the date of the order.[18] The phrase " care and possession " is still used in some aspects of the new law,[19] but in the provisions dealing with the child being with the petitioners, the child must have " had his home with " the petitioners for a probationary period.[20] The two phrases are different views of the same thing—from the point of view of the child, and of the petitioners. Accordingly, the former law is applicable to the child having his home with the petitioners. Using the new terminology, the present position is

(a) generally, before a child can be adopted he must have at all times during the preceding 13 weeks had his home with the petitioners or one of them, and the child must be at least 19 weeks old immediately preceding the making of the order[21];

(b) in the case of a petition to adopt a child abroad the period is 26 weeks and the child must be 32 weeks old[22]; and

---

[13] 1978 Act, ss. 22 and 23; see below, para. 8.09.

[14] 1958 Act, s. 2 (3).

[15] *H., Petitioner*, 1960 S.L.T.(Sh.Ct.) 3.

[16] 1975 Act, s. 108, Sched. 4, Pt. IV, and the Children Act 1975 (Scotland) (Commencement No. 1) Order 1977 (S.I. 1977 No. 227), art. 3 and Sched. 1.

[17] This is discussed below, see para. 8.05 (k).

[18] 1958 Act, s. 3 (1).

[19] *e.g.* 1978 Act, s. 30 (1).

[20] 1978 Act, s. 13.

[21] 1978 Act, s. 13 (1).

[22] 1978 Act, s. 13 (2).

(c) in the case of a child which has been placed for a purpose other than adoption the period is 12 months.[23]

Formerly, where one of the petitioners was a parent they did not need to give notice to the local authority of the intention to adopt the child, whereas in other cases the petitioners had to give such notice.[24] Now the positions have been reversed and are made more elaborate: if the child was *not* placed by an adoption agency, the petitioner must give notice to the local authority within whose area he has his home of his intention to apply for an adoption order.[25] On receipt of such notice the local authority must investigate and report on the matter.[26] (Formerly, where arrangements were made by a registered adoption society for the adoption of a child by an adopter resident in Great Britain, no application to the court could be made until after the period of care and possession had expired.[27]) The giving of notice to the local authority brings into play the provisions relating to a protected child[28]; and while an adoption petition is pending where the parent or guardian has agreed to the making of the adoption order (whether or not he knows the identity of the applicant), the parent or guardian is not entitled, against the will of the person with whom the child has his home, to remove the child from the custody of that person except with the leave of the court.[29]

(b) The former provisions which applied have been modified in the case where an application for an adoption order was made jointly by spouses who were not, or one of whom was not, ordinarily resident in Great Britain[30] and the situation is now governed by the generality of section 13. This aspect is discussed later.[31]

(c) The fact of care and possession has been held to have been satisfied where the child was a nurse in residence in hospital,[32] a child was in hospital as a patient,[33] but not where a child was serving in the R.A.F. but in that case there were other reasons for refusing the adoption order.[34] However, the requirements were satisfied where a regular soldier spent his leaves with his family in the house of the female petitioner's parents.[35] Now the child will require to have his home with the applicants or one of them at all times during the appropriate period.[36] In England, "home" has a statutory definition: the 1975 Act[37] provides that in the Act, unless the context otherwise provides, references to the person with whom a child has had his home refer to the person who, disregarding absence of the child at a hospital

---

[23] 1978 Act, s. 49 (2). *e.g. O. & O., Petitioners,* Edinburgh Sheriff Court E54/85 (unreported).
[24] 1958 Act, s. 3 (2).
[25] 1978 Act, s. 22 (1).
[26] 1978 Act, s. 22 (2).
[27] Adoption of Children (Regulation) Act 1939, s. 6 (2).
[28] 1978 Act, s. 32.
[29] 1978 Act, s. 27. This is discussed below, para. 5.06.
[30] 1958 Act, s. 12 (3).
[31] See below, para. 8.05 (n).
[32] *A., Petitioners,* 1953 S.L.T.(Sh.Ct.) 45.
[33] *G., Petitioner,* 1955 S.L.T.(Sh.Ct.) 27.
[34] *M., Petitioner,* 1953 S.C. 227, also cited as *S., Petitioner,* 1953 S.L.T. 220; see also *F., Petitioners,* 1955 S.L.T.(Sh.Ct.) 12.
[35] *A., Petitioners,* 1958 S.L.T.(Sh.Ct.) 61.
[36] 1978 Act, s. 13.
[37] s. 87 (3).

or boarding school and any other temporary absence, has actual custody of the child. The existence of care and possession is a question of fact. Obviously, the child will have had his home with the petitioners and that situation will not alter merely because the child or a petitioner is out of the home for schooling or employment or the like. A further requirement has now been added: the court must be satisfied that sufficient opportunities to see the child with the petitioners or the petitioner in their home environment have been afforded to the adoption agency which placed the child and to the local authority in other cases.[38]

(d) As has been noted, the *terminus ad quem* in the running of the period of care and possession is the granting of the adoption order not the lodging of the petition. It may be, however, that at the time when the curator *ad litem* visits the home of the petitioners, such a short time will have elapsed from the beginning of the period of care and possession that no satisfactory report can be made: then the curator *ad litem* may wish to make a later visit to the home, or the court may deal with any outstanding matters arising from the care and possession by interviewing the petitioners. On the other hand, in many cases, the child has been in the care and possession of the petitioners for considerably longer than the minimum period long before the petition has been lodged.

(e) Apart from the case of a petition for a Convention adoption order, the domicile and nationality of the child do not matter.

3.03 Health of the child

There is no requirement that the child be of good health at the time of adoption. At the earlier stage of placement for adoption by an adoption agency there must be a report on the child's medical condition.[39] In the Court of Session, but not the sheriff court, on presentation of the petition for adoption, where the child was not placed for adoption by an adoption agency, the petitioners must lodge three copies of a medical report showing the physical and mental health of the child.[40] The regulations merely provide that no child shall be placed by an adoption agency in the care and possession of a person proposing to adopt him until the agency has " obtained a report prepared within the previous 12 months by a fully registered medical practitioner as to the health of the child . . . ." It would appear that one reason for requiring such a report is to safeguard the interests of the proposed adopters. No doubt the nature of any medical condition which the child may suffer from—such as a condition which required special medical attention on the part of the petitioners—would be a matter which the court would have to take into account in considering the welfare of the child; and if such a condition came to the knowledge of the court, it would undertake such further inquiries as seemed necessary. Pre-existing ill-health which only becomes apparent subsequently is not a

---

[38] 1978 Act, s. 13 (3).
[39] Adoption Agencies (Scotland) Regulations 1984 (S.I. 1984 No. 988), para. 17 (1) (*b*).
[40] R.C. 222 (4) (*d*).

ground for reduction of the adoption order[41]; and there is no provision for cancellation of an adoption order.[42] In *M. & M.* v. *Glasgow Corporation*,[43] where there was supervening manifestation of brain damage to a child which had been caused at birth, it was held that a local authority which had placed the child with the pursuers had been under a duty to take reasonable care to avoid placing for adoption a child who was medically unsuitable.

3.04 Foundling

It is not an impediment to the adoption of a child that the child is a foundling. If the parents cannot be found their agreement can be dispensed with.[44] No doubt the petitioners can lodge any police report as to the circumstances of the finding of the child and the efforts made, for example by local inquiry, advertisement in the press and on television or the like, to trace the parents. In these circumstances the child is usually given an artifical name: in one case the child was given as its first name the Christian name of the matron of the home to which the child had been taken by the police, and as its surname the name of the street in which the child had been found. Similarly, in the case of a child found abandoned in Delhi, in which situation the authorities did not issue a birth certificate, the date and circumstances of the birth were attested by an affidavit of the person responsible for the care of the child and who had been appointed as guardian by the High Court of Delhi.[45] If need be the court must determine the probable date and country of birth of the child.[46] If the correct place and time of birth of the child emerge later, these particulars can be entered in the Adopted Children Register by amendment or rectification.[47] Amendment of the registers is dealt with later.[48]

3.05 Subsequent adoptions

A child who has formerly been adopted may be adopted again.[49] In that case the agreement of the adoptive parents—not the natural parents—to the making of the adoption order is required.[50] Instead of an extract in the Register of Births an extract in the Adopted Children Register will be produced when the petition is lodged. A second adoption was refused where the sheriff-substitute was of the opinion that it was designed to meet the situation where a headstrong child was rebelling against her adoptive mother.[51] In terms of section 24 of the 1978 Act, where the petitioner has made a previous application for a British adoption order in respect of the same child, the court must not proceed to determine an application for an

---

[41] *J. & J.* v. *C.'s Tutor*, 1948 S.C. 636.
[42] *Skinner* v. *Carter* [1948] Ch. 387 at 395, *per* Lord Greene M.R.
[43] 1976 S.L.T.(Sh.Ct.) 45.
[44] 1978 Act, s. 16 (2) (*a*).
[45] *C. & C., Petitioners*, Edinburgh Sheriff Court, E77/85 July 1985 (unreported).
[46] 1978 Act, s. 45 and Sched. 1, para. 1 (3).
[47] 1978 Act, s. 45 and Sched. 1, para. 4.
[48] See para. 12.01.
[49] 1978 Act, s. 12 (7).
[50] *E. & E., Petitioners*, 1939 S.C. 165 (where the earlier adoption order had been made in England); *Re M.* [1941] W.N. 244.
[51] *B., Petitioner*, 1952 S.L.T.(Sh.Ct.) 48.

adoption order in relation to that child where the previous application has been refused by any court unless

(a) in refusing the previous application the court directed that section 24 should not apply, or

(b) it appears to the court that because of a change in circumstances or for any other reason it is proper to proceed with the application.[52]

These restrictions on the making of a subsequent application do not apply where the earlier petition was withdrawn. Where the earlier petition was refused it would appear to be necessary to produce the process in that earlier petition or otherwise prove the former circumstances. The process in a petition which was not granted does not require to be sealed up,[53] and accordingly there will be no difficulty in producing the process.

---

[52] 1978 Act s. 24. See below, para. 11.02.
[53] See para. 11.04.

CHAPTER 4

Placement of a Child for Adoption

4.01 Parent adopting own child

Generally, placement of a child for adoption may arise in two ways:
(a) a relative of that child may adopt that child;
(b) otherwise, only an adoption agency may make arrangements for the adoption of a child, or place a child for adoption.[1]

These provisions only relate to placement for *adoption*: if a child had been placed with persons for a purpose other than adoption,[2] such as for fostering, these persons could later seek to adopt the child without breaching these rules; but as in the case of other adoptions which do not involve placement by an adoption agency, the petitioners must intimate to the local authority their intention to adopt.[3] In this context "relative" is defined as a grandparent, brother, sister, uncle or aunt, whether of the full blood or half-blood or by affinity; and includes, where the child is illegitimate, the father of the child and any person who would be a relative within the meaning of this definition if the child had been the legitimate child of his mother and father.[4] The class of relatives cannot be enlarged to include remoter relatives, such as great-aunts; and it would appear that a testamentary placement would be illegal.[5] These provisions not only prohibit placements contrary to their terms but impose criminal sanctions; and where a person is convicted of such a contravention the court may deal with the care of the child.[6]

A substantial group of these adoptions in most courts is the one where the child is a natural child of one of the petitioners: the commonest situation is where a mother seeks to adopt her own child along with her new husband on marriage or on remarriage after divorce or widowhood. Occasionally the petition is presented by the natural father and the stepmother of the child.[7] In Scotland this group of petitions has amounted to about 46 per cent. of adoptions.[8] Usually such cases present little difficulty where the natural father has died or was not married to the natural mother (in which case his agreement to the making of the adoption order is not required) or where the natural father gives his agreement or his agreement is dispensed with by the court. On the other hand, in the much rarer case, where, for example, after divorce the natural mother has been awarded custody of the child and the natural father has been granted access to the child and has kept in touch with

---

[1] 1978 Act, s. 11 (1).
[2] 1978 Act, s. 13 (1).
[3] 1978 Act, s. 22.
[4] 1978 Act, s. 65 (1).
[5] 1984 S.L.T. (News) 73.
[6] 1978 Act, ss. 11 (5) and 26.
[7] *e.g. H. & H.*, *Petitioners*, Edinburgh Sheriff Court, E72/85 and E73/85 (unreported).
[8] First Report on the Children Act 1975 (7 March 1980).

the child, "it is quite wrong to use the adoption law to extinguish the relationship between the protesting father and the child, unless there is some really serious factor which justifies the use of the statutory guillotine "[9]; " an adoption order (which is irrevocable) should not be used to deal with practical questions concerning custody, or care and control of the child, or access to the child. These can, and should be flexibly dealt with by the court exercising matrimonial jurisdiction."[10] The provisions whereby in a petition for an adoption order the court may direct that the application be treated as if it were made for the custody of the child have been discussed earlier.[11]

4.02 Other relatives adopting a child: adoption by grandparents

Another small but significant group of cases consists of those where the child to be adopted is related to the petitioners but is not a child of the petitioners. A common relationship is that of grandparent and grandchild. The situation often arises where the mother of the child has died or has abandoned the child or for some reason—such as extreme youth or shiftlessness—is unable or unwilling to look after the child properly.[12] Cases have also arisen where a married couple do not wish to keep their child and are quite content that it be adopted by an aunt or other relative. The constant practice of the courts over the years is sufficient authority for the competence of adoption by grandparents or other relatives.[13] However, there are differing views on the desirability of such adoptions, particularly adoption by a grandparent. One of the objections put forward is that it would conceal from the child that the adoptive parents are not his true parents. However, that objection has sufficient answer in the former practice: in *A., Petitioner*[14] the court required that the child was made acquainted with the whole circumstances set forth in the petition. In addition, the present statutory requirements make it mandatory that the child should, if he is a minor, consent to the making of the adoption order; and in any event the court must ascertain the wishes and feelings of the child; and the curator *ad litem* must report on these matters as well: this is discussed elsewhere.[15] Again, it is said that such adoption orders should only be made in the special circumstances of a given case, as there may be no final separation between the child and its natural mother.[16] It is also said that such adoptions distort the natural family relationship, and in the case of adoption by grandparents often result in the adoptive parents being somewhat older than would be the case with natural parents. These considerations are often not capable of exact proof and are only part of the whole circumstances which must be taken into account.[17] The curator *ad*

---

[9] *Re B.* [1975] Fam. 127 at 143.
[10] *Re D.* [1977] A.C. 602 at 627, *per* Lord Wilberforce.
[11] See para. 1.03 (f).
[12] *e.g. L. & L., Petitioners*, 1965 S.L.T.(Sh.Ct.) 66; *Re W.* [1980] 10 Fam. Law 190; [1981] C.L.Y. 1751, a decision of the Court of Appeal, where the grandparents were in their middle sixties and the child was seven.
[13] See above, para. 2.01.
[14] 1936 S.C. 255.
[15] See paras. 3.01 (c) and 8.05 (s).
[16] *Re D. X.* [1949] Ch. 320, a single judge decision; *cf. C. D., Petitioners*, 1963 S.L.T.(Sh.Ct.) 7.
[17] See above, paras, 2.01, 2.03; below, para. 8.05 (k).

litem and the court are frequently faced not with a choice between a good adoption and a less good adoption, but between the adoption which is before the court and no adoption at all. In most cases of adoptions of this kind the granting of the order does give legal approval to a *de facto* family; and whether the adoption order is granted or not, the child is almost certain to remain in the same family without the benefits which adoption can confer. It is doubtful whether the court should *ex proprio motu* seek to counsel the petitioners to drop a petition for adoption which is otherwise in order merely because the petitioners stand in a particular relationship to the child: indeed if the petitioners were not dissuaded and the court refused to grant the order on that ground, it might be difficult to formulate findings in fact and reasons to support such a decision, unless the proposed adoption was not in the interests of the child, as in *H. & H., Petitioners*,[18] where the separation of the natural parents was not final; but in *L. H. & L. H., Petitioners*[19] the separation of the natural parents was final. There does not need to be a "compelling reason" before an adoption order can be granted.[20] In *H. & H., Petitioners*,[21] which was a step-parent adoption in which the natural father had "washed his hands" of the child, the sheriff had dismissed the petition. The court allowed the appeal, and at its own hand dispensed with the consent of the natural father and granted the prayer of the petition. In the course of its opinion the court said,

> "On the merits of the petition and upon the question of whether discretion should be exercised to dispense with the father's consent, we are satisfied that the sheriff misdirected himself in the approach which he took. From his note it is clear that he had no regard to the advice of the curator to the effect that the proposed adoption was consistent with the child's welfare. He appears further to have given undue weight to the custody order without fully appreciating its limitations as a means of safeguarding the child's position in an established home, and the effect on a child at the beginning of a school life of bearing a name different from that of the persons who to all in the locality would appear to be her mother and father. In addition, notwithstanding the competency of the application and in spite of the fact that the father had 'washed his hands' of his daughter, the sheriff has, it seems, questioned the propriety of adoption by a parent and a step-parent and has been influenced in that view by a working paper and the report of a departmental committee which he mentions in his note. In the result he refused both the motion and the crave because no 'compelling reason' for adoption by the petitioners had yet been shown. The true question in all such cases which is relevant to both the merits of an application and to the motion to dispense with consent, is whether the making of an order or refusing to make it is more likely to enure to the welfare of the child (see *A.B.* v. *C.D.*, 1970 S.C. 268, the opinion of Lord President Clyde at p. 269). What is required is a balancing of advantages from the

---

[18] 1951 S.L.T.(Sh.Ct.) 17.
[19] 1951 S.L.T.(Sh.Ct.) 46.
[20] See the opinion of the court in *H. & H., Petitioners*, 1976 S.L.T. 80 at p. 83.
[21] 1976 S.L.T. 80.

point of view of the welfare of the child. What is not required is a search for a compelling reason to grant the order, the propriety of which the court chooses to question upon the ground that the order is sought by a parent and a step-parent of a legitimate child whose other parent is still alive."

In one case the court granted an adoption order in favour of grandparents subject to the undertaking of the natural father to pay a weekly sum into the hands of the children's officer for disbursement to the child in the event of need.[22]

4.03 Other private adoptions prohibited

Before 15 February 1982 it was competent for an individual—including non-relatives of the child—to assist in the placing of the child: such persons might be doctors, nurses or merely friends. The number of such placements was tiny. The advantages were probably only greater speed and simplicity as compared with the more sophisticated apparatus which is available when an adoption agency is involved. The disadvantages were that the advice and support which can arise from the professionalism and experience of the trained staff of an adoption agency was not available to the parties. From 1982 the law has prohibited such private adoptions except where the proposed adopter is a relative of the child.[23] From 1985, there is no doubt that where a children's hearing makes a supervision requirement, which, in respect that it provides where the child is to reside, and thereby facilitates his being placed for adoption by an adoption agency, that requirement does not constitute an arrangement which is struck at by sections 11 and 65 (3) of the 1978 Act.[24]

4.04 Adoption societies and adoption agencies

An adoption agency is either a local authority, that is, a regional or islands council,[25] or an approved adoption society[26] (replacing the former registered adoption society[27]). The corresponding bodies in England and Wales may be included in these definitions if the 1976 Act is to be regarded as being in force for these purposes.[28]

Adoptions within the family are usually arranged privately by an

---

[22] *G. D., Petitioners*, 1950 S.L.T.(Sh.Ct.) 34.

[23] 1958 Act, s. 29 (1) (*a*) as amended by 1975 Act, s. 28 (1978 Act, s. 11(1); Children Act 1975 (Scotland) (Commencement No. 3) Order 1982 (S.I. No. 33), para. 3) The current provision is 1978 Act, s. 11 (1).

[24] Law Reform (Miscellaneous Provisions) (Scotland) Act 1985, ss. 27 and 60 (3) (*a*) reversing the opinion expressed in *R.* v. *Children's Hearing for Borders Region*, 1984 S.L.T. 65. That was a decision on the former provision contained in 1958 Act, s. 29 (1): see n. 23, above.

[25] 1978 Act, s. 65 (1).

[26] 1978 Act, s. 1 (4).

[27] 1958 Act, s. 57 (1) before amendment by 1975 Act, Sched. 3, para. 21 (3) and S.I. 1982 No. 33.

[28] 1978 Act, s. 65 (1) which refers to 1976 Act, s. 12; but that Act is not yet in force in England and Wales; nor are the corresponding provisions of the 1975 Act. Until these provisions come into force, the adoption services in England and Wales are referred to not as adoption agencies but approved adoption societies or local authorities. It is submitted that any reference in the Scottish legislation to an adoption agency under the 1976 Act would be taken as a reference to an approved adoption society or a local authority in England, on the ground that the provisions of the 1976 Act will repeal those of the 1975 Act. A list of adoption agencies in England and Scotland—with their addresses and telephone numbers—is contained in the booklet *Adopting a Child* which is noted in the preface.

individual such as the natural mother without the intervention of an adoption society. An adoption society is defined as a body of persons whose functions consist of or include the making of arrangements for the adoption of children and the body of persons may be incorporated or unincorporated.[29] Since 1984 there have been provisions for the setting up of local authority adoption services[30]; and in this scheme the local authority and the approved adoption societies may be referred to as adoption agencies.[31] Since 1982 it has been unlawful for a person other than an adoption agency to make arrangements for the adoption of a child or place a child for adoption unless the proposed adopter is a parent, step-parent or relative of the child,[32] or the child has been placed with him by a children's hearing.[33] In one case in which applicants for an adoption order had obtained the child not from an adoption society but from a foster-mother who was registered with the local authority as such, it was held that the application should be granted, but the sheriff-substitute observed that such an arrangement was irregular and would normally lead to the refusal of the application.[34] But non-compliance with the statutory provisions in this respect would provide no ground for reducing the adoption orders.[35] While it is unlawful for a person other than an adoption agency to place a child for adoption or to make arrangements for the adoption of a child, it is lawful to adopt a child who has been placed with the petitioners for a purpose other than adoption, for example, for fostering; but in such cases the period of care and possession must be 12 months.[36] In the case of placements by adoption agencies, the number of potential adopters greatly outweighs the number of available children: yet a substantial number of children usually because they are much older or because they are handicapped do not find adoptive homes. In one case, adopters with four boys of their own adopted a girl with Down's syndrome when the girl's parents could not face bringing her up themselves.[37] There is no objection to an adoption agency advertising for adopters and describing the child, subject to the strict requirements of confidentiality.[38]

---

[29] 1978 Act, s. 65 (1).
[30] 1978 Act, s. 1 (1).
[31] 1978 Act, s. 1 (4).
[32] 1978 Act, s. 11.
[33] See above, para. 4.03.
[34] *S. S.*, *Petitioners*, 1953 S.L.T.(Sh.Ct.) 29.
[35] *J. & J.* v. *C.'s Tutor*, 1948 S.C. 636 at p. 644.
[36] 1978 Act, s. 13 (2).
[37] *K. & K.*, *Petitioners*, Edinburgh Sheriff Court, E63/85, 21 September 1983 (unreported).
[38] See below, para. 5.02.

CHAPTER 5

Petition for Adoption; Petition to Free a Child for Adoption

5.01 A judicial process

Adoption in Scotland, as in England, is effected not by an administrative process but by a judicial process. That process is *sui generis*.[1] The process is effected by a petition—not an initial writ or summons. In relation to the Court of Session,

> "while procedure by summons is based on the idea that there is some person, whether an individual, body corporate or unincorporate, of the lieges, against whom the pursuer desires to establish a right or seek a remedy, a petition is an *ex parte* application craving the authority of the Court for the petitioner, or seeking the Court to ordain another person, to do an act or acts which otherwise the petitioner would be unable to do, or cause to be done."[2]

Since almost all petitions for adoption and other associated procedures at first instance are disposed of in the sheriff court, and since it is anticipated that petitions to free a child for adoption will also be presented almost exclusively in the sheriff court, reference has been made to the sheriff court procedure which is contained in the Act of Sederunt (Adoption of Children) 1984[3] as the leading provisions, with corresponding references to Court of Session procedure (which is contained in the Rules of Court 219–230L). The legislation envisages that there may be different statutory provisions for different circumstances[4]; and just as there are different rules in England and Wales for the High Court and the county court on the one hand and the magistrates' court on the other hand,[5] so in Scotland there are different rules in the Court of Session and the sheriff court. Within the limits of that legislation the court has considerable freedom to adopt the procedure which is most appropriate to the circumstances of the case.[6] But such flexibility would not permit an incompetent procedure, such as allowing a person who was not a party (such as the father of an illegitimate child in a freeing petition in respect of that child) into the proceedings, or allowing parties to be represented by unqualified persons.[7] " Where a new and special jurisdiction

---

[1] *J. & J.* v. *C.'s Tutor*, 1948 S.C. 636 at 642, *per* Lord President Cooper; approved in the House of Lords in Scottish and English appeals: *A.* v. *B. & C.*, 1971 S.C.(H.L.) 129 at 141; *Re D.* [1977] A.C. 602 at 626.

[2] Maclaren, *Practice*, p. 825, referred to in *J. & J.* v. *C.'s Tutor, supra* at 642.

[3] S.I. 1984 No. 1013.

[4] 1978 Act, s. 60 (5).

[5] Adoption Rules 1984 (S.I. 1984 No. 265) and Magistrates' Courts (Adoption) Rules 1984 (S.I. 1984 No. 611).

[6] *Cf. A.* v. *B. & C.*, 1971 S.C.(H.L.) 129 at 135, *per* Lord President Clyde in the Inner House.

[7] See below, para. 5.05.

is given to any Court the exercise of it must be regulated entirely by the conditions of the statute under which it is conferred, and that in the general case remedies which might have been competent in an ordinary civil process are not to be presumed or inferred to be given by the particular statute . . . . But, on the other hand, I imagine that where a well-known and recognised jurisdiction is invoked by the Legislature for the purpose of carrying out a series of provisions which are important for the public without any specific form of process being prescribed, the presumption is that the ordinary forms of that Court are to be observed in carrying out the provisions, and, indeed, generally that the Court has been adopted and chosen and selected because it is seen to be advisable that the ordinary rules of such Court and the forms of its procedure shall be applied to give effect to the provisions of the legislative Act."[8] The various modes of inquiry are discussed later.[9]

5.02 Confidentiality

Unlike most other judicial proceedings, which have for centuries been open to the public, adoption proceedings are strictly confidential. Briefly, this confidentiality has at least three aspects:

(a) The petitioners may keep their identity from any person who has to agree to the granting of an adoption order.[10]

(b) All proceedings are in general conducted *in camera*[11] unless the court otherwise directs, and all documents lodged in process may only be open to the court, the curator *ad litem*, the reporting officer, the parties (and presumably their solicitors or counsel) and the clerk of court unless the court otherwise directs.[12] Employees of petitioners' solicitors would be entitled to see the papers in so far as their duties required them to. The authors of reports made in terms of sections 22 and 23 are not entitled to see the process. In reports, opinions of the court, law reports and other documents, the circumstances of a case should only be referred to in a way that does not identify the parties.[13] It would be a breach of that confidentiality for solicitors to mention the names of the petitioners or the child in an adoption petition in newspaper advertisement which sought the whereabouts of the natural father.

(c) After the adoption order has been granted and communicated to the Registrar General for Scotland, the process must be sealed up and not made accessible to any person for 100 years except in certain circumstances, including the attainment by the adopted child of the age of 17 years.[14] The clerk of court will require to have a secure place to keep the processes while they are pending and after they have been sealed up. In England it has been held under the

---

[8] *Magistrates of Portobello* v. *Magistrates of Edinburgh* (1882) 10 R. 130, *per* Lord Justice-Clerk Moncrieff; *Central Regional Council* v. *B.*, 1985 S.L.T. 413.
[9] See para. 6.01.
[10] A.S. 19 (R.C. 222); see para. 5.05.
[11] 1978 Act, s. 57.
[12] A.S. 24 (R.C. 230 (6)).
[13] A party in prison should be designed by reference to his home address: see below, para. 8.02; *C. & C., Petitioners*, Glasgow Sheriff Court, 18 February 1982; Practice Note, 23 July 1952 (*PHB* C501).
[14] A.S. 28 (R.C. 230 (C)); see para. 11.04.

Adoption Agencies Regulations 1976[15] that where the social services committee of a local authority were dealing with reports prepared in connection with making arrangements for a child's adoption before any petition had been presented in court, the information in the reports might in very limited circumstances be divulged to all members of the local authority including elected members: the utmost care must be taken to prevent the unnecessary dissemination within the council of details relating to the child, to its natural parents, to any foster or adoptive parents and of sources of information.[16] The corresponding Scottish provision would appear to have the same effect.[17] That decision has no direct bearing on adoption proceedings in court; thus the curator *ad litem* and reporting officer who are appointed personally may not reveal any matters—even to other servants of the adoption agency with whom they happen to be employed.[18] In one case the court refused the request of the guardian *ad litem* in English access proceedings by a natural father of the child which was the subject of adoption proceedings in Scotland to have a sight of the report of the curator *ad litem* in the adoption proceedings.[19]

5.03 Avoidance of delay

There are consistent dicta about the dangers of delay in dealing with adoption petitions.[20] Delay may act as a circumstance in itself so as to make it virtually impossible to alter the *status quo*, or it may frustrate the adoption itself if the child is approaching the age of 18.[21] Delays can creep in at almost every stage in the proceedings—with the solicitor, between receiving instructions and presenting the petition or before presentation when the matter is with the adoption agency; in court, in the provision of a report by the local authority under section 22, between the remit to the curator *ad litem* and reporting officer and the return of the reports, between receipt of the reports and consideration of them by the court, in finding a diet for interview or proof; and in appeals, especially where a sist has been granted to allow a party to apply for legal aid. No doubt the need for expedition would be a consideration in refusing to grant a sist. In one case the court declined to sist the adoption proceedings which were before it to await the outcome of the investigations of the Ombudsman into the care of the child while the child was with the local authority in England.[22] In most cases the court would not sist adoption proceedings to await the outcome of proceedings in other courts, particularly if the adoption proceedings would supersede the other proceedings such as an action for custody[23] or proceedings for the assumption of parental rights. Even after an appeal has

---

[15] S.I. 1976 No. 1796.

[16] *Birmingham City District Council* v. *O. and Another* [1983] A.C. 578.

[17] Adoption Agencies (Scotland) Regulations 1984 (S.I. 1984 No. 988), paras. 24 and 25.

[18] See below, para. 7.02.

[19] *P. & P.*, *Petitioners*, Edinburgh Sheriff Court, E46/84, 13 September 1984 (unreported).

[20] *e.g. A.* v. *B. & C.*, 1971 S.C.(H.L.) 129 at 144, *per* Lord Guest.

[21] *J.*, *Petitioner*, Edinburgh Sheriff Court, 22 March 1985; *F. & F.*, *Petitioners*, Edinburgh Sheriff Court E59/85 and E60/85 (unreported).

[22] *P. & P.*, *Petitioners*, Edinburgh Sheriff Court, E46/84, 13 September 1984 (unreported).

[23] *Borders Regional Council* v. *M.*, 1986 S.L.T. 222.

been heard and advised, the appeal court may remit the case back to the lower court for a proof or a re-hearing.[24] In three recent cases the period between the decision of the sheriff and that of the appeal court has been two years.[25]

5.04 Procedure by petition; jurisdiction

All applications for an adoption order, or to free a child for adoption or to adopt a child abroad, are in the form prescribed in the rules of court,[26] with such variations as the circumstances require. If the petition is commenced by one spouse and it is desired that the other spouse should also be a party to the action, he can, no doubt, be sisted as an additional petitioner. In the overwhelming number of cases, only one child is being adopted at a time; in cases where several children are being adopted simultaneously a question arises whether there should be one petition for each child, or on the analogy of actions for custody of more than one child there should be a single petition comprehending all the children. As to competency, there is nothing in the legislation which prohibits an omnibus petition,[27] but there is no case in which the point has been argued and decided. In each of three cases where more than one child was being adopted at the one time, the law report referred to the petition in the singular[27a]; but the processes in the Scottish cases and a letter from the solicitors in the English case indicated in fact that there was one petition for each child. The matter is not free from difficulty; and there are arguments in favour of each of the inconsistent objectives—to preserve the confidentiality of the process, and to avoid the expense of a multiplicity of actions, which might bear heavily on petitioners who do not qualify for legal aid or who are faced with a substantial contribution as a condition of legal aid, especially if a proof or an appeal took place. And if the processes were to be self-contained strictly there would be no room for conjunction of actions for the purposes of a proof or other inquiry. In practice, almost all such cases involve brothers and sisters of the same family being adopted by their own parent on marriage or remarriage to the other petitioner; and accordingly, the maintenance of confidentiality may be rather artificial, especially where the children are rather older. In such cases, therefore, the children will already know all that they could find out when at the age of 17 they may have access to the process. Further, in law the child must be seised of certain information and has access to other information. Thus, by statute, if the children are of an appropriate age and understanding, the court must so far as practicable ascertain the wishes and feelings of the child and give due consideration to them[28]; the court must have a report on the wishes and feelings of the child regarding the proposed adoption[29]; and if the children are minors they must give their

---

[24] *A.B.* v. *C.D.*, 1970 S.C. 268; *Re F.* (*R*) [1970] 1 Q.B. 385.
[25] *A.* v. *W. & W.*, Glasgow Sheriff Court, 29 November 1978 (unreported); *A.* v. *A. & A.*, Glasgow Sheriff Court, 4 November 1980 (unreported).
[26] A.S. 1 (5) (R.C. 219).
[27] *Cf.* Interpretation Act 1978, s. 6 (*c*).
[27a] *I. & I.*, 1947 S.C. 485; *Z.* v. *Z.*, 1954 S.L.T.(Sh.Ct.) 47; and *Re H.* [1977] 1 W.L.R. 471.
[28] 1978 Act, s. 6.
[29] A.S. 21 (2) (*s*) (R.C. 224 (2) (*l*)).

consent in writing.[30] It would seem somewhat artificial to take the consents of each child while hiding the fact that they were brothers and sisters who were being adopted into the same family. In one case where the petitioner was unwilling that the child should be told of his illegitimacy, the court required that the child should be made aware of the whole circumstances set forth in the petition.[31] In any event, all documents lodged in process, including the report of the curator *ad litem*, must be open to " the parties," and if a child about to be adopted is to be regarded as a party—as he would appear to be in the event of an appeal by him—then all documents lodged in process, including the report of the curator *ad litem*, must be open to him[32]; and even if there were separate petitions in respect of each child, when any of the children reaches the age of 17[33] he is entitled to have access to the process as of right and to the report of the curator *ad litem* which is a step in the process and which contains a report on " particulars of all members of the petitioner's household and their relationship to the petitioner."[34]

In the Court of Session the petition should be presented in the Outer House.[35] In respect of an application for an order relating to a child, generally, jurisdiction is determined by reference to an "authorised court "[36]: where the child is in Scotland, the authorised court is either the Court of Session, or the sheriff court of the sheriffdom (not merely sheriff court district[37]) in which the child is; but the Court of Session has privative jurisdiction

(a) in a petition for adoption, or a petition to free a child, where the child is not in Great Britain when the application is made[38], and

(b) in a petition for a Convention adoption order[39];

and where there is an application to return a child taken away in cases where its removal is restricted and there is pending a petition for adoption or a petition to free a child, the authorised court is the one before which the petition is pending.[40] A petition for a Convention adoption order is presented in the Inner House.[41] However, the overwhelming number of petitions are for adoption or to free a child for adoption where the child is in Scotland; and all but a tiny number are raised in the sheriff court—no doubt, for reasons of economy. Since 1980 in the case of any action in the sheriff court in relation to the custody or adoption of a child the sheriff may, of his own accord, at any stage of the action remit the action to the Court of Session,[42] and the Court of Session may in relation to any action before it which could competently have been brought before a sheriff, remit that action (at its own instance or on the application of any of the parties to the

---

[30] 1978 Act, s. 12 (8) and A.S. 16 (3) (*f*) (R.C. 222 (9) (*b*)).
[31] *A., Petitioner*, 1936 S.C. 255.
[32] A.S. 24 (1) (R.C. 230 (6) (*a*)).
[33] See para. 11.05.
[34] A.S. 21 (2) (*d*) (R.C. 222 (7) (*h*)).
[35] R.C. 189 (*a*) (xxiv).
[36] 1978 Act, s. 56.
[37] See also Dobie, *Sheriff Court Practice*, pp. 52–53; see above, para. 2.05.
[38] 1978 Act, s. 56 (3).
[39] 1978 Act, s. 56 (4).
[40] 1978 Act, s. 56 (5)
[41] R.C. 230C.
[42] Law Reform (Miscellaneous Provisions) (Scotland) Act 1980, s. 16 (*b*) amending Sheriff Court (Scotland) Act 1971, s. 37.

action) to the sheriff within whose jurisdiction the action could have been brought, where, in the opinion of the court, the nature of the action makes it appropriate to do so.[43]

5.05 Serial number; legal aid; solicitors; fee of curator *ad litem* and reporting officer

If the petitioner in an adoption petition or a petition to adopt a child abroad, does not want his identity disclosed to any person whose agreement to the order is required, he may before presenting the petition apply to the clerk of court for a serial number to be assigned to him; and the record of the serial number is treated as confidential and is open only to the court[44]; this provision affects the document signifying the agreement of that person.[45] There is no provision as there is in England that this information should be withheld from the respondent: on the contrary, all documents must be available to the parties.[46] If legal aid has been granted the words " assisted person " should follow the name of the assisted person in every step of process in the proceeding to which he is a party.[46a]

It is trite law that the only persons who can appear in an action in court are the parties and their legal representatives, *i.e.* solicitor or counsel. If the party is a juristic person such as a local authority or an adoption agency they cannot appear by themselves but can only be represented by solicitor or counsel, not by one of their servants.[47] This rule includes all the procedural aspects of the case, including the presentation of papers to the court offices.[48] In certain circumstances it may also constitute a criminal offence for a person who is not a solicitor or advocate to prepare documents.[49] Only those solicitors who have a place of business in Edinburgh may borrow a Court of Session process, and only those solicitors having a place of business within the jurisdiction of a sheriff court can borrow a sheriff court process.[50] The general provisions relating to borrowing a process in the Court of Session[51] refer to all processes whereas those relating to the sheriff court[52] relate only to ordinary actions. In adoption petitions it is provided that unless the court otherwise directs " all documents lodged in process, including the reports of the curator *ad litem* and the reporting officer, shall be open only to the Court, the curator *ad litem* and the reporting officer and the parties."[53] In terms of that provision or at common law, the process is usually borrowed by the curator *ad litem* to enable him to furnish his report;

---

[43] Law Reform (Miscellaneous Provisions) (Scotland) Act 1985, s. 14, which section shall come into force on such day as the Lord Advocate may by order appoint: s. 60 (2) (*b*).
[44] A.S. 19 (R.C. 222 (3)).
[45] A.S. 19 (4) (R.C. 222 (3) (*b*)).
[46] A.S. 9, 24 (R.C. 230 (6)); Magistrates' Courts (Adoption) Rules 1984 (S.I. 1984 No. 611), r. 27 (4); *Re M.* [1973] 1 Q.B. 108 at p. 125; *cf.* Adoption Rules 1984 (S.I. 1984 No. 265), rr. 14 and 53.
[46a] Act of Sederunt (Legal Aid Rules) 1958 (S.I. 1958 No. 1872), para. 3 (1).
[47] *Equity and Law Life Assurance Society* v. *Tritonia*, 1943 S.C.(H.L.) 88; *Scottish Gas Board* v. *Alexander*, 1963 S.L.T.(Sh.Ct.) 27; *B. & B., Petitioners*, Edinburgh Sheriff Court, E92/83, February 1984, (unreported).
[48] *Rush* v. *Fife Regional Council*, 1985 S.L.T. 391.
[49] Solicitors (Scotland) Act 1980, ss. 31 and 32.
[50] Solicitors (Scotland) Act 1933, s. 46 as amended by Solicitors (Scotland) Act 1958, Sched. 2 and Sheriff Courts (Scotland) Act 1907, Sched. 1, r. 16.
[51] R.C. 31.
[52] Sheriff Courts (Scotland) Act 1907, Sched. 1, r. 39.
[53] A.S. 9 and 24 (R.C. 230 (6)).

and it is difficult to see how parties could properly conduct the case unless they were able to borrow the process. This is especially true at certain stages of the case, as where a party wishes to consider the terms of the petition of which he has only received notice,[54] or the terms of the report of the curator *ad litem* or other document, or the terms of any interlocutor, especially an interlocutor making or refusing an adoption order. The need to borrow would also be essential where copies of the process would be necessary as where there are correspondents or where counsel has been instructed. If a potential respondent is not to be regarded as a party, he may have access to the documents by direction of the court. The clerk of court would, no doubt, be particularly vigilant to see that only these persons have access to the process, and if he is in doubt he can consult the court. If the adopters have a legal aid certificate or if they put their solicitor in funds—at least to the extent of the fee of the curator *ad litem* and the reporting officer— considerable delays can be avoided in waiting for settlement of that fee. By practice notes of 13 November 1969, and 9 July 1974, governing " Remits to Reporter in Consistorial Causes " even where the remit is by the court *ex proprio motu* the pursuer or minuter " shall in the first instance be responsible for the Reporter's fees and outlays." There is no reason in principle why the same rule should not also apply to expenses of the report of a curator *ad litem* and reporting officer in an adoption process in the Court of Session or the sheriff court.[55]

5.06 Effect of petition or notice to local authority on care and possession of the child

The right of the adopters or the prospective adopters to maintain their care and possession of a child awaiting adoption can arise in three ways:

(a) where a petition is pending in a case in which a parent or guardian has agreed to the making of the adoption order, then he is not entitled against the will of the person with whom the child has his home, to remove the child from the care and possession of that person without the leave of the court[56];

(b) where a petition is pending in respect of a child made by the person with whom the child has had his home for the five years preceding the petition, then no person is entitled, against the will of the petitioner to remove the child from his custody, except with leave of the court, or under the authority conferred by any enactment, or on the arrest of the child[57];

(c) where a prospective adopter gives notice in writing to the local authority within whose area he has his home of his intention to adopt a child who has had his home with him for the preceding five years, then no person is entitled, against his will to remove the child from his care and possession except with leave of the court, or under authority conferred by any enactment, or on the arrest of the child.[58]

---

54 A.S. 8 and 22 (R.C. 222 (13)).
55 See para. 14.01.
56 1978 Act, s. 27.
57 1978 Act, s. 28.
58 1978 Act, s. 28.

It is a criminal offence to contravene these provisions. And the rights of the local authority to recover a child from the care and possession of an adopter or a prospective adopter are enforced with leave of the court.[59] Where the leave of the court is required in these situations, the application is made by minute (or note) lodged in the adoption petition process.[60] Further, the legislation makes provision for the class of "protected child." The position with regard to notice to the local authority has since 1984 been reversed. Now where the petitioner is a parent, step-parent or relative of the child he must give notice to the local authority within whose area he has his home of his intention to apply for an adoption order in respect of the child.[61] The child then becomes a protected child while he has his home with that person.[62] A local authority for these purposes includes not merely a regional or island council in Scotland but also the council of a county (other than a metropolitan county), a metropolitan district, a London borough or the Common Council of the City of London, in England and Wales.[63] The local authority has a duty to secure the well-being of protected children, and the court may order the removal of a child from unsuitable surroundings, subject to an appeal to the sheriff.[64]

5.07 Probable cost

It is not possible to say precisely what the probable cost of an adoption petition would be to the adopters; but generally, there are three elements in that cost:

(a) The dues of court are laid down in the Acts of Sederunt. These are of the order of £20 and are exigible when the petition is lodged.

(b) The solicitor is entitled to charge his fees and outlays in respect of the work which he carries out. Where the petition is straightforward and is unopposed—as is the case in most petitions—the solicitor's standard rate would be relatively modest. Where there is opposition involving hearings or an appeal, especially an appeal to the Court of Session, it would be considerably more.[65]

(c) The fee of the curator *ad litem* and reporting officer, unless these officers are appointed from the local authority panel of curators *ad litem* and reporting officers, in which case the local authority are obliged to pay.[66] The standard fee in respect of a joint appointment is presently £65, with extra fees in case of difficulty; but if the charges of the curator *ad litem* and reporting officer were to be made according to professional levels the fee would be very much more than that figure.[67] The petitioners should ascertain in advance, what

---

[59] 1978 Act, ss. 28 (3) and 30 (2).
[60] A.S. 30 (1) R.C. 227 (1); procedure is by petition in relation to s. 28 (3), see App. II, 23–26.
[61] 1978 Act, s. 22 (1).
[62] 1978 Act, s. 32.
[63] 1978 Act, s. 65 (1).
[64] 1978 Act, ss. 32, 33 and 34.
[65] See below, para. 14.01.
[66] Curators *ad litem* and Reporting Officers (Panels) (Scotland) Regulations 1984 (S.I. 1984 No. 566); Curators *ad litem* and Reporting Officers (Panels) (Scotland) Amendment Regulations 1985 (S.I. 1985 No. 1556). There is no liability on the local authority to pay these amounts if the adoption order is not made: rule 10 (c). The amendment came into force on 1 April 1986: but see below, paras. 7.02 and 14.01.
[67] *e.g.* Guide to fees for advocates preparing reports in cases involving children.

the fee is and who is liable to pay it. (Similarly, the curator *ad litem* and reporting officer should make the same inquiries in advance.)

A party is always entitled to conduct his own case, including an adoption case. However, there are serious qualifications to that general rule, partly legal and partly practical. In a petition to free a child for adoption, the petition can only be presented by an adoption agency and both local authorities and adoption societies are corporate bodies who can only appear and even lodge papers by a solicitor or advocate: any other form of representation is incompetent.[68] In a petition for adoption or in a minute (or note) to revoke a freeing order, the petitioner is a natural person who may sign writs, lodge papers and appear by himself, or who may do these things by solicitor or advocate: again, any other form of representation is incompetent. If there is any question of fee, gain or reward, such actings by unqualified persons may amount to a criminal offence.[69] It is most inadvisable for petitioners to act without a solicitor and attempt to do the work themselves. Any savings will almost inevitably be outweighed by the difficulties, delays and extra expense which may arise, often unexpectedly, even in the apparently most straightforward cases. One example will suffice: in several cases the application of the maxim *pater est quem nuptiae demonstrant* arises; a lawyer will appreciate at once that the question has arisen and he has the skill to deal with it; the layman may not even appreciate that it exists. If the petitioners are of reasonable means, the legal expenses of an adoption would normally be regarded as a small price to pay to ensure the expeditious and successful conclusion of a procedure whose end is the security of the child in a new home for the remainder of his childhood. If the petitioners are of limited means, they may be entitled to legal aid with or without a contribution by them towards the cost of the proceedings. Generally, where there is a legal aid certificate, the whole of their expenses is borne by the legal aid fund; but in the event of a party being found liable in the expenses of the proceedings, he may be liable to pay the expenses of his opponent, unless his liability for these expenses is assessed by the court at some lesser figure or at nil. His liability will not exceed the amount (if any) which in the opinion of the court is a reasonable one for him to pay, having regard to all the circumstances, including the means and conduct in connection with the dispute of all the parties.[70] In an opposed petition, where the solicitor's fee will be greater (because of the larger amount of work to be done) the question of legal aid becomes more important.[71]

5.08 Form of petition

There are separate styles or modifications of styles of petition for each kind of adoption order[72]:

(a) petition for adoption,[73] which is by far the most common;

---

[68] *Equity and Law Assurance Society* v. *Tritonia Ltd*, 1943 S.C.(H.L.) 88, *Scottish Gas Board* v. *Alexander*, 1963 S.L.T.(Sh.Ct.) 27; *Rush* v. *Fife Regional Council*, 1984 S.L.T. 391.
[69] Solicitors (Scotland) Act 1980, s. 32.
[70] Legal Aid (Scotland) Act 1967, s. 2 (6) (*e*).
[71] See C. N. Stoddart, *The Law and Practice of Legal Aid in Scotland* (2nd ed., 1985), Chap. 9.
[72] A.S. 3 (1), 11 (1) and 16 (1) (R.C. 220 (1), 221 (1), 222 (1) and Form 36).
[73] A.S. Form 7 (R.C. Form 36).

   (b) petition for adoption abroad[74];

   (c) petition for a Convention adoption order[75]; and

   (d) petition to free a child for adoption[76]: in this case in the Court of Session, no style is prescribed, but the rules provide that the petition in these cases shall include averments about, or refer to a report or other documents produced which deal with them, the 14 matters enumerated in the rules.[77]

   (e) minute (or, in the Court of Session, note) to revoke an order freeing a child for adoption in the process of the original petition[78]: again in the Court of Session no special style is prescribed but the general rules relating to petitions are applied to notes with the exception that the note is not intimated on the walls or in the minute book or advertised.[79] The general rules prescribe that a narrative or statement of facts in articulate numbered paragraphs setting forth the grounds of the note shall precede the prayer.[80]

   In all cases the matters which are set forth in numbered paragraphs should present little difficulty. These matters, averments, facts or circumstances—as they are variously called—are what the court has to be satisfied upon, either by reference to the reports before it, or by proof. These matters are dealt with later.[81] After the averments follows the prayer of the petition in which the petitioner craves the court to do certain things such as to dispense with the intimations (where that is appropriate), to grant an adoption order, or an order to adopt abroad or a Convention adoption order as the case may be, and to direct the Registrar General for Scotland to make the appropriate entries in the registers. The prayer is the appropriate place to state the name by which the child will be known after the adoption order has been granted. The part of the prayer which craves the court " to pronounce such other or further orders or directions upon such matters, including the expenses of this petition as the court may think fit," would entitle the court to grant an interim order, or to appoint a particular form of inquiry but not, it is thought, " to direct that the application is to be treated as if it had been made for custody of the child."[81a] The petition is signed by counsel or solicitor or by the parties.[82] Even where the child has been placed by an adoption agency, only the parties or their legal representatives can sign.[83] There is no place in adoption procedure for lodging a caveat[84]—that is, a document lodged in court by a party who is apprehensive that legal proceedings will be taken against him. A writ or warrant may not be issued

---

[74] A.S. Form 8 (R.C. Form 36).
[75] R.C. 230C (1) and (2) and Form 36.
[76] A.S. Form 1.
[77] R.C. 220 (3).
[78] A.S. Form 4.
[79] R.C. 191–196, 221 (1) and (2). However, it may be that *per incuriam* the exclusion of the general rule 191 was not extended to revocation procedure: *cf.* R.C. 220 (1) (freeing) and 222 (1) (adoption).
[80] R.C. 191 (*a*).
[81] See below, Chap. 6.
[81a] 1975 Act, s. 53.
[82] A.S. Forms 7, 8 (R.C. 193).
[83] See above, para. 5.05.
[84] *Cf. Wards* v. *Kelvin Tank Services Ltd.*, 1984 S.L.T.(Sh.Ct.) 39.

until he has had an opportunity to be heard: the persons entitled to notice of a hearing are those who are specified in the rules.[85]

5.09 Productions

The petition should be lodged along with the appropriate fee for the sheriff clerk; the sheriff clerk is "not required to do any act (including the acceptance of any writ)" before the fee is paid.[86] The productions to be lodged include:

(a) extract of the entry in the Register of Births (but not an abbreviated certificate of birth which only discloses the name of the child, the place and date of birth) relating to the child[87]; or in the case of a subsequent petition, an extract from the Adopted Children Register; and in the case where the adoption order in the former petition had been refused the process in that former case; if there is no birth certificate, as is sometimes the case in India or Pakistan, the birth will require to be proved by other evidence[88];

(b) in the case of a joint petition by spouses, the extract in the Register of Marriages relating to the petitioners[89]; and presumably also, in the case of a petition by one of two spouses[90];

(c) a medical certificate as to the health of the petitioner or each of the joint petitioners, except where the petitioner or one of the petitioners is a parent of the child: the legislation no longer provides the form of certificate[91]; in the Court of Session the medical *report* is to be on the health of the *child*, and only when the child was not placed by an adoption agency; but in the sheriff court, the former style of medical report is generally used, whereas in the Court of Session slightly different matters are specified.[92] The report should be reasonably up-to-date: but the health of the petitioners is not the *de quo* of the proceedings, as it is in a petition for the appointment of a *curator bonis* where the certificates should not be more than one month old.[93] In any event in adoption procedure the curator *ad litem* would on the visit to the home no doubt notice and report on any obvious ill-health of the petitioners;

(d) a report on the suitability of the petitioners and on any other matters relevant to the operation of section 6 (which deals with the duty to promote the welfare of the child) made by the local authority where the child was not placed by an adoption agency,[94] and by the adoption agency in other cases[95]; any other document founded upon by the petitioner in support of the petition,[96] as, for example, where the natural parent has died the death certificate should be produced,

---

[85] See below, para. 8.13.
[86] Act of Sederunt (Fees for Sheriff Clerks) 1977, para. 2 (2).
[87] 1978 Act, s. 45 and Sched. 1, para. 1 (4); A.S. 1 (R.C. 16 (3) (*a*), 222 (4) (*a*)).
[88] *C. & C., Petitioners*, Edinburgh Sheriff Court, E77/85, July 1985 (unreported).
[89] A.S. 16 (3) (*b*) (R.C. 222 (4) (*b*)).
[90] 1978 Act, s. 15 (1) (*b*).
[91] A.S. 16 (3) (*c*) (R.C. 222 (4) (*d*)).
[92] R.C. 222 (4) (*d*).
[93] *Encyclopaedia of Styles* (Green's) v. 387, n. 1.
[94] 1978 Act, s. 22.
[95] 1978 Act, s. 23.
[96] A.S. 16 (3) (*f*).

or where a petitioner has been divorced the extract decree of divorce should be produced;

(e)   if available, the consent of the minor child, and the agreement of the natural parents,[96a] or where the child has been freed for adoption, the order of the court which freed the child;

(f)   if the child has not been placed by an adoption agency, the acknowledgment by the local authority of the notice by the petitioners to that authority of their intention to apply for an adoption order; in sheriff court practice such notice is normally given before the petition has been presented, but in the Court of Session on presentation of the petition the court must make an order requiring the petitioners to give notice to the adoption agency or the local authority as the case may be; but the statute envisages the notice being given before the petition has been presented.[97] The notice must be in writing[98] and may be given by post[99];

(g)   in the case of a petition for an order to adopt a child abroad, in addition to the requirements already mentioned, the petitioner must adduce evidence of the law of adoption in the country in which he is domiciled; and the court may accept as evidence of that law an affidavit sworn by a person who is

   (i)   conversant with it and practises or has practised as a barrister or advocate in that country, or

   (ii)   a duly accredited representative of the government of that country in the United Kingdom[99a];

(h)   in the case of a petition for a Convention adoption order, the petitioners must lodge documentary evidence relative to *inter alia* the nationality of the petitioners or of the child and of consents[1];

(i)   where a litigant is an assisted person, the legal aid certificate or emergency certificate issued to him should be lodged by him when he enters the process.[2]

5.10 Evidential value of documents

The evidential value of the documents which are used in evidence in an adoption process varies depending on the character of the document and the statutory provisions regulating the matter.

(a) United Kingdom judicial and vital records are generally accepted without proof, not only as to the truth of the facts contained in them but also as to the identity of the persons mentioned in them.[3]

(b) Certain foreign vital records have at least an equal privilege in terms of the Evidence (Foreign and Colonial Documents) Act 1933, s. 1, and the Oaths and Evidence (Overseas Authorities and Countries) Act 1963, s. 5;

[96a] A.S. 16 (3) (*f*) (R.C. 222 (4) (*e*)).
[97] R.C. 222 (5) (*a*); 1978 Act, s. 22.
[98] 1978 Act, s. 62.
[99] 1978 Act, s. 65 (1). Intimation of a diet of hearing, however, would appear to be a judicial intimation to which the Citation Amendment (Scotland) Act 1882 applies: s. 3.
[99a] A.S. 17 (R.C. 224 (3) (*b*)).
[1] R.C. 230D–230F.
[2] Act of Sederunt (Legal Aid Rules) 1958 (S.I. 1958 No. 1872), para. 3 (2).
[3] See Walker & Walker, *Evidence*, pp. 232–233.

and orders in council have been made under this legislation covering about 50 countries, an up-to-date list of which can be found in the latest edition of *Index to Government Orders* (H.M.S.O.) under the title " Evidence."[4]

(c) Where the documents which have to be lodged are in a foreign language, the principals should be accompanied by translated copies which can be spoken to and identified by the person translating them and stating the name of the foreign language and the qualification of the translator.[5]

(d) The legislation envisages that the consent of a child or the agreement of a parent may be given in writing, and if the document signifying consent or agreement is witnessed in accordance with rules it shall be sufficient evidence of the consent without further proof of the signature of the person by whom it is executed.[6] The style of document is provided.[7] Where a serial number has been assigned to an applicant any form of agreement must not contain the name and designation of the petitioner but must refer to him by means of the serial number assigned to him and must specify the year in which and by which court such serial number has been assigned.[8] The statutory mode of attestation varies depending on the place of execution and the court in which the petition is presented: it is sufficiently attested in the following ways:

 (i) if in the United Kingdom

   (1) if a sheriff court petition, by the reporting officer;

   (2) if a Court of Session petition, by the reporting officer if within Scotland, but by a justice of the peace if in England and Wales or Northern Ireland. Formerly, the prescribed mode of authentication of consent or agreement was execution before two witnesses. Later that form was replaced by execution before a justice of the peace. From time to time, documents signifying consent or agreement are tendered in these old forms and also in other informal documents. The present statutory provisions do not exclude forms other than those specified in the Act: the Act merely gives a special privilege to documents which are executed in conformity with the statutory rules. It seems that any clear acknowledgment of agreement or consent may be proved by the general laws of evidence. Similarly, if a child or a parent who had formerly refused to give consent or agreement, did so in court, that consent or agreement, if recorded in an interlocutor of the court, would be sufficient evidence of that consent or agreement. In such a case, the court would deal with the other matters which in the normal case the reporting officer would have dealt with, namely, whether the parent understands the effect of the freeing order or the adoption order, as the case might be, would deprive him permanently

---

[4] See below, App. IV.
[5] *cf.* R.C. 230L.
[6] 1978 Act, s. 55 and A.S. 18 (R.C. 222 (9)).
[7] Forms 9, 10 (R.C., Forms 37A, 37B).
[8] A.S. 19 (4) (R.C. 222 (3) (*b*)).

of his parental rights, whether he has considered alternatives to adoption; and if the order is not actually being granted at that hearing, remind him that he may withdraw his agreement at any time before the order is made;

   (ii) if outside the United Kingdom

      (1) if the person by whom the document is executed is serving in Her Majesty's Forces by an officer holding a commission in any of those forces; or

      (2) in other cases, by a British consular official, or any person for the time being authorised by the law of the country in which the form is executed to administer an oath for any judicial or legal purpose.[9]

5.11 Interlocutors

Normally each stage in the course of an adoption process is effected by an interlocutor of the court which is partly an executive order and partly a minute of the proceedings. Thus, for example, it will be necessary to pronounce an interlocutor

   (a) to appoint a curator *ad litem* and a reporting officer[10];

   (b) on receipt by the court of the reports of the curator *ad litem* and reporting officer, to order a diet of hearing to be fixed and if appropriate to ordain the petitioners to serve a notice in terms of Form 11 (Form 39) on any of the persons mentioned in the Act of Sederunt, para. 22 (R.C. 222 (12)) (these are enumerated below)[11];

   (c) subsequently, as the situation demands, as for example, after a hearing, to record who was present, what documents were produced, what concessions were made, what facts were found to be proved, or to appoint further inquiry, or to make avizandum, or to grant the prayer of the petition.

In *A. v. B. & C.*[12] the absence of any reference by the sheriff to the date of a step in procedure became apparent in the House of Lords and had to be cleared up by means of a certificate by the sheriff clerk: " If the judge interviews any party, it is desirable that this should be recorded in his judgment."[13] In the case of a petition by one natural parent alone, the statute provides explicitly that the reason for excluding the other natural parent must be recorded by the court.[14] If a particular fact is contested or in doubt it may be desirable to make a finding in fact after such inquiry as may appear necessary; where the area of dispute is wide or where issues of credibility are important, the court may wish to proceed by way of proof as in an ordinary civil action and make findings in fact and findings in law with a

---

[9] A.S. 18 (3) (R.C. 230 (1)).
[10] A.S. 20 (R.C. 222 (5)).
[11] See para. 5.17.
[12] 1971 S.C.(H.L.) 129.
[13] *Per* Lord Guest at 142.
[14] 1978 Act, s. 15 (3).

note setting forth the grounds of the court's decision.[15] Proof by witnesses is discussed later.[16]

5.12 Freeing for adoption

From 1984 it has been open to an adoption agency (but not a private person) to proceed not by way of a petition for adoption in which all aspects of the matter are disposed of at the one time, but to seek an order merely disposing of the agreement of the natural parents in advance without there being any adoption of the child before the court. This new procedure is called freeing a child for adoption.[17] Generally, the provisions relating to the freeing of a child are identical to those parts of an adoption petition which deal with the agreement of the natural parents: two exceptions are the status of the father of an illegitimate child,[18] and, where it is sought to dispense with the agreement of the natural parent. In the latter case the child must be in the care of the adoption agency[19] otherwise both processes are effected by a petition; the conditions precedent—such as jurisdiction—are the same[20]; the court remits the question of the parental agreement and the welfare of the child to a curator *ad litem* and a reporting officer[21]; on receipt of the reports the court must appoint a hearing[22]; the specification of the grounds for dispensing with the agreement of the parent[23] and the consent of the child are the same as in a petition for adoption.[24] A reporting officer may be appointed in advance of the lodging of the petition, but only on cause shown,[25] *e.g.* that the natural parent is about to go abroad. The attitude of any person " claiming to be " the father of an illegitimate child[26] which is presumably different from " any person reputed to be the father " or " any reputed father "[27] has to be considered: before making an order: the court must satisfy itself that

(a) he has no intention of applying for custody of the child under section 2 of the Illegitimate Children (Scotland) Act 1930, or

(b) if he did apply for custody under that section the application would be likely to be refused.[28]

From past experience of petitions for adoption it would appear that this situation would arise only on very rare occasions. The court must also satisfy itself in relation to each parent or guardian of the child who can be found that he has been given an opportunity of making, if he so wishes, a declaration that he prefers not to be involved in future questions concerning the

---

[15] *Cf.* A.S. 23 (R.C. 230 (5)) and in the sheriff court, Sheriff Courts (Scotland) Act 1907, Sched. 1, r. 89.

[16] See para. 6.05.

[17] 1978 Act, s. 18; 1985 S.L.T. (News) 1.

[18] 1978 Act, s. 18 (7).

[19] 1978 Act 18 (2) (*b*); *cf.* Social work (Scotland) Act 1968, s. 44 (5); see below, para 10.09 (*b*).

[20] 1978 Act, ss. 12 (1) and 18 (1).

[21] A.S. 5 and 20 (R.C. 220 (6) and 222 (5)).

[22] A.S. 8 and 22 (R.C. 220 (12) and 222 (13)).

[23] 1978 Act, ss. 16 (2) and 18 (1) (*b*).

[24] 1978 Act, ss. 12 (8) and 18 (8).

[25] 1978 Act, s. 58 (3); A.S. 5 (3); there is no corresponding provision in the sheriff court for appointing a reporting officer before the lodging of a petition for *adoption*. (R.C. 225 (1)).

[26] 1978 Act, s. 18 (7).

[27] A.S. 6 (1) (*j*) (R.C. 220 (3) (1)).

[28] 1978 Act, s. 18 (7).

adoption of the child. Any such declaration must be recorded by the court.[29] Where freeing application is made with the consent of the natural parent, there need not be an actual adoption in prospect[30]; but if the adoption agency seeking the order applies for the agreement of the natural parent to be dispensed with, then the court must be satisfied that the child has already been placed for adoption or that it is likely that the child will be placed for adoption.[31] Also, if dispensation is sought the child must be in the care of the adoption agency.[32]

Against the possible advantages of proceeding first by way of a petition to free a child for adoption, should be considered the duplication of expense in having two petitions with the consequent delay, as well as in cases where the ground of dispensing with the agreement of a natural parent is that it is unreasonably withheld, it would be more difficult to hold that where there was no actual adoptive family in being the natural parent was withholding agreement unreasonably.

5.13 Effect of freeing for adoption

Where the order freeing a child for adoption has been made, the parental rights and duties relating to the child vest in the adoption agency[33] and the parental rights and duties of the natural parents are extinguished " as if the order were an adoption order and the agency were the adopters." Quite separately, it is still competent for a local authority to use their existing statutory powers and resolve that the relevant parental rights and duties with respect to any child shall vest in them or in a voluntary organisation.[34] Although the effect of an order freeing a child for adoption and a resolution assuming parental rights is similar, the order has as its avowed purpose the subsequent adoption of the child whereas the resolution has not.[35] Further, where an order under section 18 has been made, and the subsequent adoption proceedings are begun it is unnecessary to consider afresh the question of parental agreement.[36] On the other hand, where the parental rights are assumed under the 1968 Act, the parent retains the right to consent or refuse to consent to an application to free a child for adoption, and the right to agree or to refuse to agree to the making of an adoption order.[37]

The application to free a child for adoption is made by a petition in the sheriff court or in the Outer House of the Court of Session; and the petition must be in the form appearing in the rules or in " a form substantially to the like effect . . . as circumstances may require."[38]

---

[29] 1978 Act, s. 18 (6) and Health and Social Services and Social Security Adjudications Act 1983, s. 9 and Sched. 2, para. 40.
[30] 1978 Act, s. 18 (2) (*a*).
[31] 1978 Act, s. 18 (3).
[32] 1978 Act, s. 18 (2) (*b*).
[33] 1978 Act, s. 18 (5).
[34] 1968 Act, s. 16.
[35] *Cf. Lothian Regional Council* v. *H.*, 1982 S.L.T.(Sh.Ct.) 65.
[36] 1978 Act, s. 16 (1) (*a*).
[37] 1968 Act, s. 16 (3).
[38] A.S. 1 (5), 3 (1) Form 1 (R.C. 219 (3), 220 (3)).

5.14 Revocation of freeing order

Further procedure at the instance of the parent may be initiated to revoke an order under section 18.[39] This is begun by a minute (or note) in the original process granting the order under section 18.[40] Presumably, one or both parents can seek the revocation.[41]

If an application to revoke an order under section 18 is dismissed, the parent may in certain limited circumstances make a further application.

The application to revoke an order under section 18 may be made: (a) where the parent has agreed to the order under section 18[42] or (b) where the agreement of the parent has been dispensed with[43]. The application must be made after 12 months of the making of the order under section 18,[44] and an adoption order must not have been made in respect of the child and the child must not have his home with a person with whom he has been placed for adoption.[45] The parent craves the court to revoke the order under section 18 " on the ground that he wishes to resume parental rights and duties."[46] The effect of a pending application to revoke an order under section 18 is to prevent the adoption agency which has the parental rights and duties from placing the child for adoption without the leave of the court.[47] The effect of a revocation of an order under section 18 is that the parental rights and duties relating to the child are vested in " the individual or, as the case may be, the individuals " in whom they vested immediately before that order was made.[48] In addition, where the parental rights and duties, or any of them, were vested in a local authority[49] or a voluntary organisation,[50] these rights and duties will vest in the individual or as the case may be the individuals " in whom they vested immediately before they were vested in the local authority or voluntary organisation."[51]

Revocation of an order under section 18 also revives forthwith (a) any duty arising by virtue of an agreement or the order of a court to make payments, so far as the payments are in respect of the child's maintenance for any period after the making of the order in terms of the Adoption Act 1976, section 12 (3) (*b*), and (b) any duty owed to or by the child to pay or to provide aliment in respect of any period after the making of the order, and to make any payment arising out of parental rights and duties in respect of such a period in terms of section 12 (3) (*b*)[52]; but it does not affect any right or duty so far as it relates to any period before the revocation.[53]

5.15 Further applications to revoke freeing order

If an application to revoke an order under section 18 is dismissed, the

---

[39] 1978 Act, s. 20.
[40] A.S. 11 (1) and Form 4 (R.C. 221 (1)).
[41] *Cf.* 1978 Act, s. 20 (3); Interpretation Act 1978, s. 6.
[42] 1978 Act, s. 18 (1) (*a*).
[43] 1978 Act, s. 18 (1) (*b*).
[44] 1978 Act, s. 20.
[45] 1978 Act, s. 20 (1).
[46] A.S. Form 4.
[47] 1978 Act, s. 20 (2).
[48] 1978 Act, s. 20 (3) (*a*).
[49] *e.g.* under 1968 Act, s. 16 (1).
[50] *e.g.* under 1968 Act, s. 16 (1) (*b*).
[51] 1978 Act, s. 20 (3) (*b*).
[52] 1978 Act, s. 20 (3) (*c*).
[53] 1978 Act, s. 20 (3).

scope for further applications is restricted. An application can be made by " the former parent " who is defined as a person who has declared that he prefers not to be involved in future questions concerning the adoption of the child.[54] The former parent cannot make a further application to revoke an order under section 18 if the original application was " dismissed on the ground that to allow it would contravene the principle embodied in section 6."[55] This reference to section 6 is presumably to the whole of section 6, that is to say, that in reaching a decision on the application to revoke an order under section 18 the court " shall have regard to all the circumstances, first consideration being given to the need to safeguard and promote the welfare of the child throughout his childhood; and shall so far as practicable ascertain the wishes and feelings of the child regarding the decision and give due consideration to them, having regard to his age and understanding."

In the same circumstances the adoption agency is released from the duty of complying with the duty of giving the former parent notice of the making of an adoption order (if and when made), and meanwhile giving the former parent notice whenever the child is placed for adoption, or ceases to have his home with a person with whom he had been placed for adoption.[56]

However, there is a relaxation of these severe limitations on the right of a former parent to make a further application to revoke an order under section 18: namely, in the provisions of section 20 (4), where the court which dismisses the application gives leave to make a further application. However, such leave must not be given unless it appears to the court that because of a change of circumstances, or for any other reason, it is proper to allow the further application to be made.[57] These words echo the provisions of section 24 in relation to a further application for an adoption order where the earlier one had been refused.

5.16 Procedure where freeing order is in force

As has been noted, the freeing process deals with that part of the adoption process which relates to the agreement of the natural parent. Where the order freeing the child has been made in respect of every person whose agreement or consent to the making of the order is required to be given and remains unrevoked, and later a petition for adoption is presented in respect of the same child, there is no need to deal with these agreements again. The later petition for adoption need only deal with the merits, and there is no need to have a hearing.[58] Apart from these matters there is, in general, no difference in the procedural requirements in dealing with the merits.

5.17 Intimation

In a petition to free a child for adoption, a petition for adoption and a petition for adoption abroad there is no intimation of the *petition* on potential respondents. In the Court of Session there is an express provision

---

[54] 1978 Act, ss. 18 (6) and 19 (1).
[55] 1978 Act, s. 20 (4) (*a*).
[56] 1978 Act, s. 20 (4) (*b*).
[57] 1978 Act, s. 20 (5).
[58] 1978 Act, s. 59 (2), A.S. 8 and 22 (R.C. 220 (10), (11) and (12) and 222 (11), (12) and (13)).

which excludes from adoption petitions the normal rules appointing intimation of other classes of petitions.[59] Although the prayer set forth in the style of petition does crave the court " to dispense with intimation and order notice of this petition to be served on such persons as the court may think fit,"[60] in practice neither intimation nor service is in use. However, at a later stage, after the sundry reports have been lodged, the court must fix a hearing and then appoint the petitioners to intimate *the diet of hearing*[61] on the classes of persons specified in the rules. In a petition for adoption,[62] a petition to adopt a child abroad[63] and, presumably, a petition for a Convention adoption,[64] intimation of the hearing must be made to

- (a) every person who can be found and whose agreement (in the case of a parent or guardian) or consent (in the case of a child who is a minor) to the making of the adoption order is required to be given or dispensed with;
- (b) any person or body
  - (1) having the rights and powers of a parent of the child, or
  - (2) having the custody or care of the child, or
  - (3) a local authority having the child committed to their care
  by virtue of
  - (i) Guardianship of Infants Act 1886, s. 5,
  - (ii) Matrimonial Proceedings (Children) Act 1958, s. 10,
  - (iii) Social Work (Scotland) Act 1968, ss. 16 and 17,
  - (iv) Guardianship of Minors Act 1971, s. 9,
  - (v) Matrimonial Causes Act 1973, s. 43, or
  - (vi) Guardianship Act 1973, ss. 2 (2) (*b*) and 11 (1) (*a*);
- (c) any person liable by virtue of any order or agreement to contribute to the maintenance of the child;
- (d) the local authority to whom the petitioner has given notice of his intention to apply for an adoption order; or
- (e) any other person or body who in the opinion of the court ought to be served with notice of the hearing.[65]

In a petition to free a child for adoption, intimation must be made to every person who can be found and whose agreement or consent to the making of the order freeing the child for adoption is required to be given or dispensed with.[66] Where a serial number has been assigned to the petitioner by the clerk of court, in order to prevent disclosure of the identity of the petitioner, the intimation of the diet of hearing should be identified by reference to the serial number and the year.[67]

Nor are answers to the petition required: in the Court of Session the requirement for answers has been expressly excluded in petitions for adoption, for adoption abroad, and to free a child[68]; and are impliedly

---

[59] R.C. 220 (2) where the figure 191 appears to have been omitted, and 222 (2).
[60] A.S. Form 7 (R.C. Form 37).
[61] A.S. 8 and 22 (R.C. 220 (12) and 222 (13)).
[62] A.S. 22 (2) (*a*) (R.C. 222 (13)).
[63] A.S. 22 (2) (*b*) (R.C. 223 (2)).
[64] R.C. 230 B.
[65] A.S. 22 (3) (R.C. 220 (13).
[66] A.S. 8 (2) (R.C. 220 (12).
[67] "For all purposes connected with the petition": A.S. 19 (1) (R.C. 222 (3)).
[68] R.C. 220 (2) and 222 (2).

excluded in sheriff court procedure.[69] However, in a minute (or note) to revoke a freeing order, intimation of the process on the petitioners in the original petition to free the child and on other persons is required; and the sheriff court rules provide for answers.[70] Subsidiary procedures governing the whereabouts of the child during the adoption process and procedure dealing with amendment and revocation of adoption orders are dealt with later.[71] The statutory hearing only deals with the agreements and consents: other aspects of the case require to be proved, and that proof may take several forms.

---

[69] See below, para. 10.02.
[70] A.S. 11 (3) (R.C. 221 (3)).
[71] See below, para. 12.02.

CHAPTER 6

Proof

6.01 Statutory provisions

The legislation refers to " the facts stated in the petition,"[1] and to " the facts and circumstances averred in the petition. "[2] The court has to be satisfied that the matters averred in the petition have been established. The provisions envisage that many of these matters may be established by the production of documents—as has already been indicated[3]; and generally these facts are vouched by reports of the curator *ad litem*, the reporting officer and of the local authority or the adoption agency. Apart from proof by means of documents and these reports, proof may be by interview before the judge[4]; by oral evidence at the statutory hearing[5] or at a proof[6]; or by the report of a reporter which would take the place of a proof: in *A. v. B. & C.*[7] such a procedure was adopted by consent of parties and with approval of the appeal court.

6.02 Reports

The normal and most comprehensive mode of verification of the averments in the petition is the report or reports made to the court. One of the two main innovations in the 1978 Act was the increase in the number of reports. Formerly, there was a single report from the curator *ad litem*: now there are nine varieties of report. These reports may be classified according to the type of procedure:

    (a) in a petition to free a child

                (i) report of the adoption agency on the proposed adoption proceedings and the prospects for adoption,[8]

                (ii) report of the reporting officer,[9]

                (iii) report of the curator *ad litem*[10];

    (b) in a minute (or note) to revoke an order freeing a child

                (iv) report of the curator *ad litem*[11];

    (c) in a petition for adoption, or a petition to adopt a child abroad

                (v) report of the reporting officer,[12]

---

[1] A.S. 21 (2) (*b*) and 23.
[2] R.C. 224 (1) (*a*).
[3] See para. 5.10.
[4] See below, para. 6.03.
[5] A.S. 8, 13 and 22 (R.C. 220 (12), 221 (8) and 222 (13)).
[6] A.S. 23 (R.C. 230 (5)).
[7] 1971 S.C. (H.L.) 129.
[8] A.S. 3 (2) (*b*) (R.C. 224 (1) (*o*) and (*p*) where these matters are dealt with by the reporting officer): Adoption Agencies (Scotland) Regulations 1984 (S.I. 1984 No. 988), r. 23.
[9] A.S. 6 (1) (R.C. 224 (1)).
[10] A.S. 6 (2) (R.C. 224 (4)).
[11] A.S. 12 (R.C. 221).
[12] A.S. 29 (1) (R.C. 224 (2)).

(vi) report of the curator *ad litem*,[13]
(vii) report of the local authority where the child had not been placed by an adoption agency,[14]
(viii) report of the adoption agency where the child had been placed by the adoption agency,[15] or
(ix) report under regulation 23.[15a]

In the new legislation there is a significant difference of emphasis between the sheriff court and the Court of Session, in respect that the matters to be reported upon are distributed differently among those whose duty it is to report to the court; but in both jurisdictions the primacy of the curator *ad litem* as the officer on whom the duty of safeguarding the welfare of the child is placed has been maintained.[16]

It may be that in the case of an interim order or where an additional petitioner is sisted, the court would require a supplementary report dealing with the up-to-date circumstances. The curator *ad litem* and the reports to the court are discussed in greater detail later[17]; at this stage it is sufficient to note that the court may if it is not satisfied by the verification of the statements provided by the documents lodged or by the reports cause further investigation.[18] A common step would be to interview the petitioners or the curator *ad litem* in chambers. Where there are important matters in doubt or in dispute it would be appropriate to seek evidence beyond the report of the curator *ad litem*.[19]

6.03 Interview by the court; statutory hearing

In the straightforward case the petition is normally granted without an interview. It is quite common for the court to interview the curator *ad litem* alone to supplement the report or to discuss some difficulty; and such interview may be at the instance of the court or the curator *ad litem*. Similarly the court may wish to interview the author of any of the reports. Also, if the court feels that the gravity of the matter should be further brought home to the petitioners—especially where the child is not related to the petitioners—it may be desirable to speak to the petitioners. In other cases the circumstances may indicate the necessity of an interview where, for example, the court feels that it may refuse the petition, and that the parties should be given an opportunity to be heard.[20] The necessity for an interview will normally become apparent after consideration of the report of the curator *ad litem*; but in some cases an earlier interview may be appropriate as where questions of competency or jurisdiction arise. The court would normally appoint an interview by interlocutor; and the diet would be

---

[13] A.S. 21 (2) (R.C. 224 (6)). In a petition for a Convention adoption order, the report of the curator *ad litem* is expressly provided for; the report of a reporting officer is impliedly provided for: R.C. 230 C (3) and 230 B.
[14] 1978 Act, s. 22.
[15] 1978 Act, s. 23.
[15a] Adoption Agencies (Scotland) Regulations 1984 (S.I. 1984 No. 988), r. 23.
[16] 1978 Act, s. 58 (1) (*a*); A.S. 6 (2) (*a*) (freeing), 12 (*b*) (revoking) and 21 (2) (*a*) (adoption) (R.C. 220 (6) (*c*), 221 (3) (*b*) and 224 (5) (*d*)).
[17] See paras. 7.01 and 8.01.
[18] A.S. 23 (R.C. 230 (5)).
[19] *Cf. C.* v. *D.*, 1968 S.L.T.(Sh.Ct.) 39; *A. B. & C. B.* v. *X.'s Curator*, 1963 S.C. 124; *A. B.* v. *C. D.*, 1970 S.C. 268.
[20] Dobie, *Sheriff Court Practice*, p. 547.

intimated to the parties and their solicitors by the clerk of court. Depending on the circumstances of the case or the matters in dispute, the court would probably wish to interview, usually with their solicitor being present, the petitioners, the child and the natural parent. All the interviews are held privately; but as parties the petitioners may wish to be present throughout, and if any information is acquired outwith the presence of the petitioners they should, where appropriate, be given an opportunity to challenge it—as where, for example, in a petition for the adoption of a female child the male petitioner had a recent conviction for assault with intent to ravish. At an interview, the judge will normally ask the parties being interviewed about the matters which he has in mind, but there is no reason why the parties' solicitor or counsel should not examine them before or after the court. Generally, although the interview may be conducted informally round a table, the parties and witnesses should be put on oath and the sheriff should take notes to enable him to formulate findings in fact, and also for the use of the appellate courts.[21]

Since 1984 the statutory provisions relating to the agreement of the natural parents to the making of an adoption order have become more elaborate.[22] In a petition to free a child for adoption or a petition for adoption where the child has not been freed for adoption in an earlier freeing petition, the natural parent who wishes to agree to the making of the adoption order will normally do so in the prescribed form in the presence of the reporting officer.[23] When the report of the reporting officer on these matters has been lodged in court, along with the report of the curator *ad litem*, the court must, in cases where the child is not free for adoption,[23a] appoint a hearing of which the natural parent—and other persons entitled to appear—shall receive intimation. The purpose of the hearing is to deal with agreements and consents, not with the merits of the adoption. At the hearing a compearing natural parent may be heard; but at that hearing only in about one or two cases in 100 does the natural parent appear or is represented by a solicitor in order to continue to refuse to agree to the making of the adoption order. Accordingly, in all but a tiny number of cases the petitioners or their solicitor require to be present at the hearing in the absence of any contradictor merely to move the court to grant the adoption order. In the few cases where the natural parent (or other person entitled to be heard) does appear and wishes to be heard, the court may hear him, or order a further diet to be fixed at which he may be heard; and at such diets evidence given shall be given in the presence of the petitioner or his solicitor.[24] In practice, where the agreement of a natural parent is in issue, it would normally not be practicable to hear evidence at this statutory hearing, because at that stage the parties would have no certain knowledge of what matters were still in dispute and they would have had no time to instruct a shorthand-writer, to prepare a case or to apply for legal aid. Further, the court would still have to decide what form of inquiry was to take place.

---

[21] *Cf. A.* v. *B. & C.*, 1971 S.C.(H.L.) 129 at p. 144, *per* Lord Wilberforce.
[22] 1978 Act, ss. 58 (1) (*b*) and 59; A.S. 6, 8, 21 and 22 (R.C. 220 (12), 222 (12), 224 (1) and (2)).
[23] A.S. 18 (R.C. 224 (1) (2) and (3)).
[23a] 1978 Act, s. 59 (2); A.S. 22 (R.C. 222 (12) (*b*)) see above, para. 5.17.
[24] A.S. 8 (4), 22 (5) (*cf.* R.C. 220 (11), (12) and (13), 222 (12), (13) and (14)).

At the hearing—or before—the petitioner *must* lodge the execution of service. If the agreement of the natural parent has been given and has not been withdrawn and if the sheriff is satisfied on the merits, he would normally grant the order. If the natural parent does not agree, and does not appear at the hearing, the court may on the information contained in the reports dispense with the agreement of the natural parent. This might be more readily done when the ground for dispensing with the agreement is that the natural parent cannot be found or is incapable of giving his agreement. In other cases, *e.g.* where the ground relied upon by the petitioner is that the agreement is unreasonably withheld, the court may wish to make further inquiry, perhaps from the petitioners there and then, or by calling for further reports or by having a proof.[25] If the natural parent compears and does not agree to the making of the adoption order, it will almost always be necessary to appoint a proof to resolve the differences between the parties.

6.04 Report of a reporter

Where, after the statutory reports have been lodged, there are matters still unresolved, resort has been had to the report of a reporter. In *A. v. B.*[26] there was before the Court of Session a petition for the custody of a child in respect of which there was also a petition for adoption in Falkirk sheriff court. The Court of Session had the process in the sheriff court action transmitted to the Court of Session. After hearing argument in the petition for *custody*, on the question of further procedure, Lord President Clyde said[27] with the agreement of the other members of the court:

"The sole question for us at this stage is the form which the inquiry should take, since both sides recognise that an inquiry is essential for the determination of the question in the case. We have heard a full argument on the matter and have reached the conclusion that the proper course in the circumstances is to remit to a member of the Bar to report to this Court. The alternative would have been a proof, either before a member of this Court or before some other tribunal. A proof, even held *in camera*, might not have preserved that anonymity of the adopting parents which it is one of the prime objects of the Adoption Act to preserve, since at a proof the parties are entitled to be present and among the parties the adopting parents are included. Moreover, as I have indicated, adoption proceedings have already been commenced in the Sheriff Court at Falkirk. The sheriff-substitute has meantime of consent continued consideration of this petition as the present proceedings were being commenced in the Court of Session, but we have had the process transmitted here, and included in it is a report of a curator *ad litem* appointed in this sheriff court process. It seems to me that it would be most unsatisfactory to have the issues raised between the parties determined partly by a proof and partly by a report by a curator, which is confidential but which might well have a bearing on the ultimate decision in the petition before us."

---

[25] *Cf.,* A.S. 23 (R.C. 230 (5)).
[26] 1955 S.C. 378.
[27] 1955 S.C. 378 at 379.

In *X.* v. *Y.*[28] the sheriff-substitute quoted that passage and used the procedure in an adoption petition: "I have remitted the present issues to a reporter. The reporter will have available to him the report of the curator *ad litem*, and of course, the parties will be entitled to be heard on the report when it is available." The same sheriff-substitute (A. M. Prain) adopted the same course in a later petition for adoption but of consent. On appeal[29] the procedure of a report by a reporter was expressly approved by the Inner House and in the House of Lords. In the Inner House Lord President Clyde said[30]:

> "It is indeed in applications of this sort a perfectly proper way of ascertaining the situation, and where, as here, the petitioners exercised their right to remain anonymous, no doubt in the interest of the child himself, ascertainment of the situation almost necessarily can only be achieved by remit to a reporter. In any event, the anonymity of the parties is a well-recognised feature of applications such as the present, where the court is required to take such care to avoid publicity regarding the circumstances of an adoption."

In the Lords, Lord Reid said[31]:

> "In this case there were reports by a curator *ad litem* and a reporter. That appears to me to be a proper procedure. I agree with Lord President Cooper when he said in *J. & J.* v. *C.'s Tutor* (at p. 642) that 'adoption proceedings are *sui generis*, uniquely devised to effectuate a new statutory institution, and incapable of being forcibly compressed into any of our pre-existing categories of forms of action.' These reports were carefully and skilfully prepared. A reporter who sees the parties in an informal way has perhaps a better opportunity to form a correct impression than a judge who sees them for a short time in the unaccustomed atmosphere of a court. So I would attach great weight to their conclusions."

The reasoning of Lord Reid does no violence to the right of a party to see the process.[32] Wherever possible all reports and documents should not refer to the child or the parties by name, but should refer to them as "the child," "the male petitioner," "the natural father" and the like.

6.05 Proof by witnesses

Where there is a fundamental and substantial challenge of the averments in the petition or of the statements in the reports or where the interviews with the parties disclose irreconcilable differences on matters of substance, the court may *ex proprio motu* or on the motion of parties allow a proof which proceeds in the manner of an ordinary action and thereafter make findings in fact and in law. This course was adopted in *A. B. & C. B.* v. *X.'s*

---

[28] 1967 S.L.T.(Sh.Ct.) 87 at 88.
[29] *A.* v. *B. & C.*, 1971 S.C.(H.L.) 129.
[30] 1971 S.C.(H.L.) 129 at 135.
[31] 1971 S.C.(H.L.) 129 at 141.
[32] A.S. 24 (R.C. 230 (6)).

Curator.[33] In *A.* v. *B.* & *C.*[34] Lord Guest[35] referred to such a procedure without criticism: " It may be that, if a formal proof takes place and findings in fact are made by the Sheriff-substitute, these findings, unless altered by the Inner House, would be sacrosanct in this House: see the Court of Session Act 1825, section 40." In *A. B.* & *C. B.* v. *X's Curator*[36] the sheriff-substitute heard the evidence of the respective parties and their witnesses on separate days. This course may result in a sense of injustice in that one of the purposes of proceeding by way of proof is to resolve questions of credibility and that would be more difficult if the parties were not present throughout each other's case. This would be all the more so if the parties already knew each other's identity so that there was no confidentiality to preserve; further, in terms of the legislation all documents must be open to *inter alia* " the parties."[37] No doubt the circumstances of the case would determine the form which the proof took. In *A. B.* v. *C. D.*[38] where the sheriff-substitute did not hold a proof but interviewed the parties separately and decided that the natural mother was not withholding her consent unreasonably, it was held on appeal that the sheriff-substitute ought to have taken into consideration the welfare of the child, and the case was remitted to him to hold a proof. Lord Cameron was of the opinion that in such a situation a proof was not inevitable.[39] In *C.* v. *D.*[40] the sheriff-principal had adopted a similar course. In England, in *Re B.*[41] one of the judges expressed concern that " though there were disputes of primary fact, the justices had made no specific findings in fact." Presumably, in such cases the court would apply the civil standard of proof, namely, a balance of probabilities.

The petitioners are entitled to be present at the proof, but need not attend if, for example, they have no knowledge of the matters which are the subject of the proof, such as whether the natural parent is withholding his agreement unreasonably. Where three children, brothers and sisters, were being adopted by different petitioners, but where the petitioners were represented by the same solicitor and both natural parents were opposing all the petitions, parties agreed by joint minute in each process that the evidence in one proof would be the evidence in the two succeeding proofs, with separate interlocutors in each case[42]; the sheriff should hear parties on each of the petitions separately and then issue the appropriate interlocutor in each case.[43] The parties would be entitled to call the authors of the reports.

---

[33] 1963 S.C. 124 at 125. A similar view was expressed in relation to a question of access: it was held that a court should not depart from the recognised procedure of determining disputed questions of access by proof in open court, even with the consent of the parties: *Macdonald* v. *Macdonald*, 1985 S.L.T. 194.

[34] 1971 S.C.(H.L.) 129.

[35] *Ibid.* at 142.

[36] 1963 S.C. 124.

[37] A.S. 24 (R.C. 230 (6)).

[38] 1970 S.C. 268.

[39] *Cf. Re C.* [1981] C.L.Y. 1752.

[40] 1968 S.L.T.(Sh.Ct.) 39.

[41] [1975] Fam. 127 at 144.

[42] *R.* v. *O.*, *G.* v. *O.* and *S.* v. *O.*; Edinburgh Sheriff Court, E49/85, E50/85 and E51/85 (unreported). English decisions about separate hearings do not assist, because they turn on special rules: *C (A minor)* [1985] 7 C.L. 505b; *cf.* Magistrates' Courts (Adoption) Rules 1984 (S.I. 1984 No. 611), r. 27 (4) (*b*).

[43] *A. B.* v. *C. B.*, 1985 S.L.T. 514 at p. 516, *per* Lord Justice Clerk Wheatley.

CHAPTER 7

Curator *ad Litem* and Reporting Officer

7.01 Appointment by the court

Formerly in an adoption petition the curator *ad litem* had a twofold function, namely, to safeguard the interests of the child and to investigate the facts stated in the petition including the attitude of the natural parents to the adoption[1]; and the agreement of the natural parents was in terms of the regulations witnessed by a justice of the peace.[2] Since 1984 there has been the introduction of the new reporting officer and the rearrangement of the duties of the curator *ad litem* and the reporting officer. The curator *ad litem* retains his primary duty of safeguarding the interests of the child,[3] and he still reports on the circumstances of the adoption,[4] other than the giving of the agreement and consents; the reporting officer has the duty of witnessing the agreement of a natural parent and the consent of the child.[5] (Where a child has been freed for adoption and the agreement and consents have been disposed of there is no person whose agreement to the making of the adoption order is required to be given or dispensed with but the court will require to appoint a reporting officer: the court in the adoption process will have a copy of the order made in the freeing process.) Thus for the purposes of any application in Scotland for

(a) an adoption order,
(b) an order freeing a child for adoption,
(c) an order revoking a freeing order,
(d) an order for adoption of a child abroad, and
(e) a Convention adoption order,

the court appoints some person to act as curator *ad litem* of the child upon the hearing of the application with the duty of safeguarding the interests of the child.[6] It is difficult to see how the interests of the child—especially a young child—could be safeguarded without the appointment of a curator *ad litem* and this has been the law and practice for the 50 or more years that adoption has been part of our law. The interjection of an independent officer of the court is necessary because the child cannot look to his natural parents or to the petitioners to safeguard his welfare because they may have an interest which is contrary to his. The curator *ad litem* in that situation can report to the court with complete independence on the circumstances which persuade him that the interests of the child have been safeguarded. The

---

[1] 1958 Act, s. 10 (4).
[2] 1958 Act, s. 6 (1); A.S. 1 (*a*) (R.C. 219 (*b*)), under former provisions.
[3] 1978 Act, s. 58 (1) (*a*).
[4] A.S. 6 (2) and 21 (2).
[5] 1978 Act, s. 58 (1) (*b*).
[6] 1978 Act, s. 58. In this regard the subordinate legislation appears to give a discretionary power in the Court of Session (but not in the sheriff court): R.C. 222 (6), 221 (3) (*b*) and 222 (5) (*d*).

appointment of the curator *ad litem* and a person to act as reporting officer for the purpose of witnessing agreements to adoption and performing such other duties as the Rules of Court may prescribe,[7] is made by the court after the lodging of the petition. The appointment is effected by an interlocutor or interlocutors of the court; and at the same time the court instructs these officers to investigate and report to the court in terms of the legislation.[8] The interlocutor should specify a date on or before which the reports should be returned to court: otherwise there is a real danger of delay—which has been judicially deprecated.[9] If the curator *ad litem* or reporting officer requires an extension of the time—which is usually set at four weeks or thereby—he can come back to the court and state his reasons for the extension; and it may be that the additional information which the curator *ad litem* or reporting officer seeks time to collect is in the view of the court not necessary. It is desirable to bring to the attention of the curator *ad litem* by a note appended to the interlocutor appointing him, or otherwise warning him, that he should not take up the appointment if his employment by an adoption agency is incompatible with his acting, and reminding him that his report should only refer to the parties in the report in such a way that they cannot be identified.

It may be that the natural mother whose agreement is in question is a minor: in *A. B. & C. B.* v. *X's Curator*,[10] Lord President Clyde observed[11]:

> "The Sheriff-substitute has raised a subsidiary point as to whether in all applications for adoption where the mother of the child is a minor, a curator *ad litem* should be appointed to the mother. I see no necessity for any general rule to this effect, and there may well be cases in which such a step would be quite unnecessary. It is obviously unnecessary where the mother is legitimate and her father or mother is alive. But, even in other cases, it would rarely be necessary to make such an appointment. Where such an appointment seems necessary, the special need for it would be disclosed in the circumstances described by the curator *ad litem* to the child who is appointed under section 11 (4) of the Act."

It would appear that the curator *ad litem* in the execution of his duty of safeguarding the interests of the child before the court may regard it as necessary to be present or represented at the hearing of any proof; but there is no reported Scottish case of this, and it would be necessary for the court as a matter of course to intimate such hearings to the curator *ad litem* but this has not generally been done. Now there is provision for appearance or representation of the curator *ad litem* at the hearing, if required by the court.[12]

7.02 Who may be a curator *ad litem* or reporting officer; statutory panel

In practice the curator *ad litem* is usually a solicitor (or in the Court of Session, an advocate) or a person with social work training. It is usual in the

---

[7] A.S. 5, 12 and 20 (R.C. 224).
[8] See App. II. 2.
[9] *e.g. A.* v. *B. & C.*, 1971 S.C.(H.L.) 129, *per* Lord Simon at 147–148.
[10] 1963 S.C. 124.
[11] *Ibid.* at p. 137.
[12] R.C. 220 (13) (*a*) and 222 (14) (*a*).

smaller sheriff courts to have one or two curators *ad litem*, whereas in the larger courts a panel of curators *ad litem* is necessary. Some sheriffs take the view that since as soon as an adoption petition comes into court, the problem ceases to be a social one and becomes a legal one, it is more appropriate to have a curator *ad litem* with a legal background rather than a social work background because the court has to ensure that the legal requirements have been complied with. Where there is a panel of curators *ad litem* it is common to swear each in at the time of his appointment to perform faithfully the duties of the office in all petitions in which he may be appointed by the sheriff.[13] The curator *ad litem* will be appointed by interlocutor in the cases in which he is to act.[14] Since 1984, in addition to any informal list of curators *ad litem* that existed in the sheriff courts, there have been set up in the area of each regional and island council panels of curators *ad litem* and reporting officers,[15] for the purposes of petitions for adoption, to free a child for adoption, to adopt a child abroad and to revoke a freeing order.[16] The members of the panels are appointed by the local authority after consultation with the sheriff principal[17]; and the local authority may determine the standard of qualification or experience which should be attained by persons who may be appointed and such determination must be made after consultation with the sheriff principal.[18] One exceptional circumstance which may arise in a significant number of cases is that there may be a potential conflict between the independence of the curator *ad litem* and reporting officer—who are independent officers of the court—and the status of a member of the panel who may be an actual or recent employee of the local authority or adoption society. Thus by statute, a person who is employed

    (a) by the adoption agency which placed the child;

    (b) by the adoption agency which presented the petition to free the child; and

    (c) by the adoption agency which has parental rights and duties in relation to the child in an application to revoke a freeing order,

must not be appointed to act as curator *ad litem* or reporting officer for the purposes of the application[19]; and the court may feel that to ensure complete independence of these officers, the prohibition should extend also to those employed

    (d) in the case of an application where the child was not placed by an adoption agency, by the local authority which is required to furnish a report in terms of section 22.

The court may also feel that these restrictions should apply to persons who have been recently employed in these capacities. Since 1986 the local

---

[13] App. II. 1.

[14] App. II. 2.

[15] 1975 Act, s. 103; 1978 Act, s. 66 and Sched. 3, para. 17; Health and Social Services and Social Security Adjudications Act 1983, s. 9 and Sched. 2, para. 28; Curators *ad litem* and Reporting Officers (Panels) (Scotland) Regulations 1984 (S.I. 1984 No. 566) as amended by Curators *ad litem* and Reporting Officers (Panels) (Scotland) Amendment Regulations 1985 (S.I. 1985 No. 1556), para. 3.

[16] 1975 Act, s. 103 (*a*) (i).

[17] S.I. 1984 No. 566, para. 3 (2).

[18] S.I. 1984 No. 566, para. 6.

[19] 1978 Act, s. 58 (2).

authority must defray the expenses incurred by a member of a panel established for their area and must pay him such fees and allowances as they think fit in the case of an application

(a) to free a child for adoption,

(b) to revoke a freeing order,

(c) to adopt a child, and

(d) to adopt a child abroad.

There is an unusual qualification in cases (c) and (d) where the child was not placed by an adoption agency: the local authority will not be liable in these sums if the court does not grant the order—if that be the correct interpretation of the phrase, " which is made by a court."[20] This provision may have undesirable effects: a curator *ad litem* or reporting officer may be unwilling to act in such cases where there is a possibility that he will receive no remuneration from the local authority; if the adoption petition is refused (or overturned on appeal), the petitioners may be unexpectedly saddled with these fees; and the court may be unwilling to chose a curator *ad litem* or reporting officer from the local authority panel if his fee is to be in doubt. The court may always appoint as curator *ad litem* and reporting officer someone who is not a member of the local authority panel.[21] In that case, the party, not the local authority, is liable for the fee of the curator *ad litem* and reporting officer.[22] In no case does the area of a regional council or island council coincide with the area of a sheriff court district: accordingly, in practice the panels which have been set up may be subdivided according to the sheriff court districts in which the members of the panel are prepared to serve. Thus, in the area of Lothian Regional Council there are subdivisions of the panel for the sheriff court districts of Edinburgh, Linlithgow and Haddington. Although a curator *ad litem* or reporting officer may be a servant of an adoption agency, he is bound by the same strict duty of confidentiality as any other officer, and in relation to adoption proceedings in court he is not entitled to impart any information in his hands to any person, including any member of the local authority or adoption society unless the disclosure of such information is necessary for the proper discharge of his duties.[23] The position is different under the regulations governing the placement of children by adoption agencies where duties are placed not on an individual but on a corporate body such as a local authority or an adoption society.[24]

7.03 Personal appointment

The court can only appoint as a curator *ad litem* or reporting officer an individual person, not a body of persons[25]: and this is implied in the Act of Sederunt.[26] Further it is not open to the curator *ad litem* or reporting officer

---

[20] S.I. 1984 No. 566, para. 10 (*c*); see below, para. 14.01.

[21] 1975 Act, s. 103 (1); A.S. 5 (2), 12 and 20 (2) whereas in the Court of Sessions the court must appoint from the panel except in exceptional circumstances (R.C. 230 (8)) which appears to depart from the permissive power in the statute.

[22] The amount of and liability for fees are discussed later: para. 14.01.

[23] A.S. 24 (2) (R.C. 230 (6) (*b*)).

[24] Adoption Agencies (Scotland) Regulations 1984 (S.I. 1984 No. 988), r. 24.

[25] 1978 Act, s. 58.

[26] A.S. 5, 20 (R.C. 230 (8)).

to delegate his functions to another person, *delegatus non potest delegare*: his oath and appointment relate to him personally. The report of the curator *ad litem* or reporting officer must generally be made from his own investigations, not on the investigations of someone else. Apart from the principle, it would be impossible for the curator *ad litem* or reporting officer to be interviewed by the court on a matter in his report if he had not investigated it himself. If the curator *ad litem* or reporting officer is in any doubt he should indicate the state of his inquiries and the court can decide if further verification is necessary. The curator *ad litem* should always differentiate between facts observed by him and information obtained by him from other persons[27], such as doctors who have examined the child or petitioners, or social workers who have been visiting the family of the petitioners. The position is different in the case of reports which must be provided by an adoption agency or a local authority,[28] where there is no personal appointment and the duty of reporting is put on juristic persons. In these reports the person making the report should identify himself in the body of the report in case the court requires to interview that person.[29]

---

[27] Z. v. Z., 1954 S.L.T.(Sh.Ct.) 47.
[28] 1978 Act, ss. 22 and 23; see below, para. 8.09.
[29] See App. III, Nos. 7 and 8.

CHAPTER 8

Reports; statutory hearing

8.01 General observations

In the normal case the matters which have to be established before an order can be granted are verified by the reports which have been enumerated earlier.[1] Apart from the conditions precedent, two general matters must be dealt with:

    (a) the agreement of every parent, and

    (b) the merits, including the welfare of the child.

However, the procedure of the Court of Session differs from that of the sheriff court in that the matters in the petition which require to be verified in the reports are differently distributed between the reports[2]; and there are further procedural differences between the courts of Scotland and the courts of England and Wales, and between the High Court and County Court on the one hand and the Magistrates' Court on the other hand.[3] Notwithstanding these differences the sum of the matters which are reported upon to the court in each jurisdiction is substantially the same. For the present purpose, to avoid duplication, the commonest procedure—a petition for adoption—and the commonest forum—the sheriff court—have been taken as the leading exemplar, but with reference to the variations in the Court of Session and to variations in a petition to free a child, a petition to adopt a child abroad and a petition for a Convention order. In all cases the reports must be made according to the statutory requirements which are discussed below; but the person making the report must always have in mind the continuing need to proceed with expedition. He should not spend undue time trying to procure a particular piece of information or to resolve a problem: it is sufficient that he reports on " what steps he has found himself able to take " in dealing with the point; and the court can decide on what further inquiries (if any) should be made. He should not go beyond his duty to investigate and report: it is no part of his duty, for example, to seek to counsel the petitioners towards a particular course—such as encouraging them to drop the petition, or to seek some alternative remedy such as custody—but he should state the facts as he has found them and give his opinion as is required by the legislation. A report which is merely a copy of departmental files is of little value to the court. The report does require the application of the judgment of the reporter in the selection of the material which he uses and the opinion that he comes to. In most cases and with most topics all that will be necessary is a brief statement that the facts are in order: only if there is a difficulty will there need to be any elaboration. Obviously if

---

[1] See above, para. 6.02.

[2] *Cf.* 1978 Act, s. 60 (5).

[3] Adoption Rules 1984 (S.I. 1984 No. 265); Magistrates' Courts (Adoption) Rules 1984 (S.I. 1984 No. 611).

anything appears to be amiss, the report would draw the attention of the court to it and the court can decide on the appropriate action. If the report discloses a variance with the averments in the petition, no doubt the solicitor can deal with this by amendment or otherwise—such as seeking to challenge the statement in the report by other evidence. The court is not, of course, bound by the terms of the report: but the court must have regard to the advice of the curator *ad litem* as, for example, to the effect that the proposed adoption is consistent with the welfare of the child.[4] The court may wish to interview the curator *ad litem* or reporting officer on additional matters or to amplify some part of his report.

8.02 Statutory requirements

The form of the reports will obviously be determined by the list of matters on which he must report in terms of the legislation.[5] Some courts provide the curator *ad litem*, the reporting officer, the adoption agency and the local authority with a *pro forma* report which can be adapted to the circumstances of each case.[6] It would seem logical to have the report in numbered paragraphs which correspond with the numbered paragraphs in the legislation.[7] The report should be preceded by any interlocutor of the court which authorises it and be followed by the instance and the serial number (if any) and the register number, and the report proper should begin with a separate page headed with the number of the case and throughout only referring to the persons involved as " the child," " the natural parent," " the male petitioner " and the like rather than referring to them by name and not referring to any matter whereby the parties or the child may be identified. In this way, if the report requires to be seen by some other party the top sheet can be removed and complete confidentiality maintained. However, if a party—such as a compearing natural father—seeks to see the process it would seem difficult to resist a motion to that effect in view of the terms of the Act of Sederunt, para. 24.[8] The position in England is different.[9] The question whether there should be one report for each child or one report for each petition dealing with more than one child has been discussed already[10]: in the case of a report by a reporter, it may be that the court would ask for a separate report for each child.

8.03 Content of the reports

Briefly, in the sheriff court in most cases the same person will normally be appointed as both reporting officer and curator *ad litem*;[11] and
    (a) the reporting officer witnesses the agreement of each natural parent and reports on that aspect of the case.[12] Where a parent states to the reporting officer that he will not agree to the making of the order,

---

[4] *H. & H., Petitioners*, 1976 S.L.T. 80 at p. 83.
[5] 1978 Act, ss. 22 (3) and 23; A.S. 6, 12 and 21 (R.C. 224).
[6] A style of report appears in App. III.
[7] A.S. 6 (1); 21 (1); 6 (2), 12, 21 (2) (R.C. 224 (1)–(6)).
[8] A.S. 24 (1) (R.C. 230 (6) (a)); but see *A.* v. *B. & C.*, 1971 S.C.(H.L.) 129, *per* Lord President Clyde at pp. 135–136.
[9] *Re G.* [1963] 2 Q.B. 73 at 97, *per* Donovan L.J.; *Re P. A.* [1971] 1 W.L.R. 1530.
[10] See para. 5.04.
[11] 1978 Act, s. 58 (2); A.S. 5 (1), 20 (1).
[12] 1978 Act, s. 58 (1) (b); A.S. 6 (1), 21 (1) (R.C. 224).

the reporting officer should merely report that fact: he has no duty to consider the grounds for dispensing with agreement;

(b) the curator *ad litem*
> (i) reports on whether the interests of the child have been safeguarded,
> (ii) generally ascertains the truth of the averments in the petition, and
> (iii) deals *seriatim* with the particular matters specified in the rules[13];

(c) the local authority, where the placement was not made by an adoption agency,[14] and the adoption agency, where the placement was by an adoption agency,[15] must report on
> (i) the petitioners,
> (ii) the child, and
> (iii) in a placement not made by an adoption agency whether there was any contravention of section 11, which relates to illegal placements.

There is also an obligation on the adoption agency to produce to the court not only a report in terms of section 23 but also a report in terms of the regulations " giving such information . . . as it had been able to discover in accordance with the regulations."[16]

8.04 Report of curator *ad litem*: circumstances of the petitioner: criminal convictions

The character of the petitioner is a matter which often gives rise to difficulty when the curator *ad litem* is dealing with the circumstances of the petitioner under this general provision and also more particularly under the later provision relating to his personality.[17] This difficulty usually relates to the petitioner's bad, and especially criminal, character. There is no authority in the adoption legislation or in the appointment of a curator *ad litem* which would justify the curator *ad litem* as a matter of course seeking to know the contents of any criminal records kept by the police: those are for most purposes confidential. Nor is any greater right of inquiry into the criminal background of a petitioner conferred on a curator *ad litem* by the Rehabilitation of Offenders Act 1974: indeed, the purposes of that Act are quite the reverse; one of its purposes is " to penalise the unauthorised disclosure " of certain convictions of rehabilitated offenders. True, the Act provides for rehabilitation of certain persons but these provisions have limitations, and shall not " affect the determination of any issue, or prevent the admission or requirement of any evidence relating to a person's previous convictions or to circumstances ancillary thereto . . . in any proceedings relating to adoption."[18] However, it would seem that that provision would not authorise the routine inquiries which are undertaken long before " any

---

[13] 1978 Act, s. 58 (1) (*a*); A.S. 6 (2), 21 (2) (R.C. 224).
[14] 1978 Act, s. 22.
[15] 1978 Act, s. 23.
[16] Adoption Agencies (Scotland) Regulations 1984 (S.I. 1984 No. 983), reg. 23.
[17] A.S. 21 (2) (*r*) (*cf*. R.C. 222 (7) (*g*)).
[18] s. 7 (2) (*c*).

proceedings relating to adoption " by some local authorities into the criminal records of those applying to become adopters or other members of the applicant's household. But the Adoption Agencies (Scotland) Regulations 1984[19] provide that an adoption agency shall not place or secure the placement of a child in the care of any person until the agency has so far as is reasonably practicable ascertained whether the prospective adopter has been convicted of an offence against children. Where a child has not been placed by an adoption agency, there is no such requirement. However, if a curator *ad litem* does receive information that a petitioner has what the curator considers to be significant criminal convictions—especially if they involve children—he should include that information in his report to the court; and thereafter, the court can decide what other inquiry should be made: for example, the court can procure extract convictions from the appropriate court, or interview the petitioner. Most trivial convictions—such as minor road traffic matters—can have little bearing on the suitability of a petitioner to be a parent; but the situation may be very different if the convictions relate to more serious offences. In one unreported case, where the petitioners and the child lived in rather crowded conditions in the house of the mother of the female petitioner, the male petitioner had a conviction for assault with intent to ravish in respect of which he was sentenced to three years' imprisonment. The offence had occurred at about the time that the former marriage of the male petitioner was in difficulty. He continued to assert his innocence—which assertion was apparently accepted by his new wife who was the female petitioner and whose female child was the child whose adoption was sought. That petition was withdrawn for other reasons; but the existence of a conviction for an offence of this nature would be most relevant to the welfare of the child, even if, as was likely, the child would remain in the household of the petitioners whether or not an adoption order was granted. If the petition had proceeded and the adoption order had been granted in favour of both petitioners and if difficulties had arisen, then the male petitioner would have had rights of custody enabling him to have control of the child; whereas if the adoption order were not granted the natural mother would have the sole right of custody and could lawfully remove the child from the household at the first sign of danger. However, in a single judge decision in an appeal from the decision of the justices, it was held that, although the male petitioner's conviction for indecent assault on a six-year-old girl 15 years before was a grave matter, particularly when one was concerned with the adoption of a female infant, nevertheless, it would be wrong to hold that it must always and necessarily be detrimental to a child to be adopted by a man with this particular stain on his record and that, in the present case, the court ought not to interfere with the decision of the justices.[20] In a case where the petitioners were the grandparents of the child and where the male petitioner was also the father of a child by an incestuous relationship with the mother of the child, the order was granted. Again, a petitioner who is a persistent offender may be so often in custody that his ability to provide properly for the child is called in question; or that he may

---

[19] S.I. 1984 No. 988, regs. 16 and 17 and Sched. 3, Pt. IV, para. 13 (*g*).
[20] *Re G. (D. M.)* [1962] 1 W.L.R. 730.

lead the child into a life of crime. Each case must depend on its own circumstances: it may very well be, for example, that the child has been with the petitioner for such a long time that it appears that his ability to look after the child is well substantiated notwithstanding his way of life. In other cases, there may be room for considering that an interim order should be made to see if the petitioner's good behaviour is maintained. By statute, in any civil proceedings—which would include adoption proceedings—the fact that a person has been convicted of an offence by or before any court in the United Kingdom or by a court-martial there or elsewhere shall be admissible evidence for the purpose of proving, where to do so is relevant to an issue in those proceedings, that he committed that offence, whether he was so convicted upon a plea of guilty or otherwise and whether or not he is a party to the civil proceedings[21]; and if the conviction is proved the person shall be taken to have committed the offence unless the contrary is proved.[22]

8.05 Sundry paragraphs of the report of curator *ad litem*

The 19 numbered paragraphs in a petition for adoption in the sheriff court which are lettered (a) to (s) and which set forth the detailed questions and matters upon which the curator *ad litem* must report are not wholly systematic. The paragraphs are discussed *seriatim*. In some instances—for example, in the question of the welfare of the child in paragraph (k)—the commentary goes some way beyond the strict terms of the paragraph: this course has been adopted in order to draw together in one place any matters related to the subject-matter of the paragraph and to avoid the necessity of repeating it when considering the other reports.[23] Of course the person reporting should, if need be, report on relevant matters which go beyond the numbered paragraphs.

(a) *Generally safeguard the interests of the child whose adoption is the subject of the petition*

As has been noted, the primary function of the curator *ad litem* is to look after the interests of the child, because the child being under age has either no capacity or only a limited capacity; and because the child unlike children in family cannot rely on his natural parent nor the adoptive parents (the petitioners) to act as curators because potentially there is a conflict of interests between them and the child. No doubt if the whole circumstances as set out in the remaining paragraphs of the report so indicate, the curator *ad litem* would be able to report that in his opinion the interests of the child have been safeguarded. It is difficult to conceive of a situation where the curator was not of that opinion but was not also of the opinion that the adoption was likely to safeguard and promote the welfare of the child throughout his childhood as set forth in paragraph (k).

(b) *Whether the facts stated in the petition are correct and if they are not, establish the true facts*

If the statements are true the curator *ad litem* should say so: if they are

---

[21] Law Reform (Miscellaneous Provisions) (Scotland) Act 1968, s. 10 (1).
[22] s. 10 (2).
[23] See above, para. 6.02.

not, he should report what is not true and also state what the truth is. In that situation the petitioners or their representatives can deal with the contradiction by amending the petition or leading further evidence or lodging further productions. Similarly, if the curator *ad litem* is in doubt about a matter—such as whether the child was sufficiently mature to be able to express his wishes and feelings regarding the proposed adoption—he should report his doubt to the court which can make such other inquiry as seems appropriate including an interview with the curator *ad litem*. In one case an error appearing in the birth certificate of the child was corrected before the sheriff granted the petition.[24] Obviously this paragraph will be qualified by circumstances. Some matters cannot be established, or cannot be established without undue expense or delay. In that situation the curator *ad litem* should report to the court on what steps he has been able to take.

(c) *Accommodation*

Particulars of the accommodation in the petitioner's home and the condition of the home.

(d) *Members of the petitioner's household*

Particulars of all members of the petitioner's household and their relationship (if any) to the petitioner.

Paragraphs (c) and (d) are self-explanatory.

(e) *Exclusion of one spouse*

Why in the case of a petition by one of two spouses the other spouse does not join in the petition. An adoption order may be made by one spouse if the court is satisfied that:
 (i) the other spouse cannot be found, or
 (ii) the spouses have separated and are living apart and the separation is likely to be permanent, or
 (iii) the other spouse is by reason of ill-health, whether physical or mental, incapable of making an application for an adoption order.[25]
 There have been no reported cases of this situation arising.

Although this paragraph of the report does not deal with the case of a petition by a natural mother or father alone, it would appear to be an appropriate place in such a case to report on whether:
 (i) the other natural parent is dead or cannot be found, or
 (ii) there is some reason justifying the exclusion of the other natural parent.[26]

(f) *Means and status of the petitioners*

Whether the means and status of the petitioners are such as to enable them to maintain and bring up the child suitably. The circumstances of the petitioners may not be ideal: the curator *ad litem* should merely report the facts and give his opinion on them but in the knowledge that the choice is not between the adoption applied for and some other better adoption, but

---

[24] *A. & A., Petitioners*, 1949 S.L.T.(Sh.Ct.) 77.
[25] 1978 Act, s. 15 (1) (*b*).
[26] 1978 Act, s. 15 (3).

between the current adoption and no adoption, and that in many households which do not come under the scrutiny of the court in an adoption process, the parents are able (perforce) to bring up their children suitably on very limited means and that in unprepossessing houses and districts. In most cases it is sufficient to note the nature of the petitioner's employment—if he is employed—the income of the household which is available for bringing up the child, and the major outgoings, such as rent and rates or repayments of bond or mortgage interest. If any question arises the court can call for further information. There is less of a problem where the child—as in the case of a mother adopting her own child—has in fact been maintained suitably by the adopters for some time; and in such cases even if the order were not granted the child would in all probability remain with the petitioners. Where there is a competition between two households—such as that of the petitioners and that of the natural parent, the welfare of the child (including the material welfare) is a relevant consideration in a question whether the natural parent is withholding his or her agreement unreasonably.[27]

(g) *Property of the child*

The purpose of this information is not so much to establish how well provided the child is, but to guard against the adoption being used to acquire control or possession of the property of the child, or to balance the material welfare of the child in the event of the adoption order being granted: thus, for example, substantial aliment payable by a natural parent might come to an end after adoption. Generally, in the absence of special provisions, when an adoption order is granted the adoptive parents become the tutors and curators of the child's estate and on the child's death become his heirs. In the overwhelming bulk of cases the child has no estate of any significance. Such as there is, should be referred to—heritable property, shareholding or, more commonly, the amount at credit of any bank account. Insurances over the life of the child are dealt with below.[28]

(h) *Petitioners' understanding of adoption*

Whether the petitioners understand the nature and effect of an adoption order and, in particular, that the order, if made, will render them responsible for the maintenance and upbringing of the child. In most cases the petitioners will have a reasonable understanding of the effect of an adoption order on themselves and the child; but the curator *ad litem* should ascertain that their understanding is correct, and explain to them that they will become—as far as is possible—the natural parents of the child to the exclusion of the real parents, and that the adoptive child will be equal with any natural children of theirs; and that they will require to do all the things that any natural parent would do by feeding, clothing, educating and advising the child. If the petitioners have any reservations or lack of understanding of these matters the curator *ad litem* should report that fact to the court.

---

[27] *A. B. & C. B.* v. *X.'s Curator*, 1963 S.C. 124.
[28] See para. 8.05(1).

(i) *Period of care and possession*

When the mother of the child ceased to have care and possession of the child and to whom care and possession was transferred. The whole history of the child should be narrated detailing the circumstances of the child leaving the natural mother including her reasons for giving up the child and any period in care or in hospital or in a foster home. It should also be said whether the adoption arrangements were undertaken privately or by the intervention of an adoption agency, whose name and address should be included. The statutory requirements as to the duration of the period of care and possession have already been discussed.[29]

(j) *Payments and rewards*

Whether any payment or other reward in consideration of the adoption has been received or agreed upon. Generally, it is not lawful to make or give to any person any payment or reward for or in consideration of:

(a) the adoption by that person of a child;
(b) the grant by that person of any agreement or consent required:
(c) the transfer by that person of the care and possession of a child with a view to the adoption of the child;
(d) the making by that person of any arrangements for the adoption of a child.[30]

Any person who makes or gives or agrees or offers to make or give, any such payment or reward, or who receives or agrees to receive or attempts to obtain any such payment or reward is liable to a fine not exceeding £400 or imprisonment not exceeding three months or both. In addition the court may order any child in respect of whom the offence was committed to be removed to a place of safety until he can be restored to his parents or guardians or until other arrangements can be made for him.[31] There are exceptions in the case of certain payments made to an adoption society or a local authority or those made by the authority of the court.[32] Since 1977, the court must be satisfied in relation to a child that the petitioners have not contravened these provisions.[33] It is almost unheard of for such an offence to take place. Sometimes a natural mother who is about to adopt her own child along with her new husband will forgo her claim to arrears of aliment under her decree of divorce; but in most cases she does so because she realises that the prospect of payment is remote and because she wishes to wash her hands of her former marriage, not in consideration of him giving his agreement to the adoption order. The curator *ad litem* should report on these matters as his investigations indicate. The section does not strike at payments made in accordance with a scheme approved by the Secretary of State whereby an adoption agency makes payment to persons who have adopted or intend to adopt a child where the arrangements for the adoption were made or are to be made by that agency.[34] In Scotland all the adoption agencies which are

---

[29] See para. 3.02.
[30] 1978 Act, s. 51 (1).
[31] 1978 Act, s. 51 (2) and (4).
[32] 1978 Act, s. 51 (3).
[33] 1978 Act, s. 24 (2).
[34] 1978 Act, s. 51 (5).

the Regional and Island Councils have had their schemes approved by the Secretary of State; but none of the voluntary adoption societies has submitted such schemes for approval.[35] The curator *ad litem* should report on whether any such payments have been made and if so he should report on:

   (a) whether the scheme under which the payments purport to have been made have been approved by the Secretary of State;
   (b) what the payments amount to;
   (c) how long the payments will continue;
   (d) why the payments have been made; and
   (e) whether the payments were known to the petitioners and the child before the decision to adopt was made.

However, the report should note not only whether the payments are lawful, but also whether or not they militate against the adoption; in relation to the petitioners in that the petitioners may have been more motivated by the prospect of gain than by genuine feelings for the child; and in relation to the child in that he may on learning of the situation doubt the motives of his adoptive parents in adopting him.[36] The curator *ad litem* should say, for example, whether he thinks the petitioners would have adopted the child even if there had been no payment made or in prospect, or whether the petitioners could not proceed to adoption because the fostering allowance would come to an end.[37]

(k) *The welfare of the child*

   Whether the adoption of the child is likely to safeguard and promote the welfare of the child throughout his childhood. Formerly the requirement was that the adoption should be "consistent with the welfare of the child." This was altered to the present form of words on the passing of the 1975 Act; and the present form echoes the words of the statute.[38] The change effected by the passing of the 1975 Act has been referred to in *Re D.*[39] as no more than elucidatory and confirmatory of the previous law (Lord Simon of Glaisdale[40] and Lord Edmund-Davies[41]) whereas Lord Wilberforce[42] was of the opinion that if section 3 did alter the law it did so by increasing the importance to be attached to the long-term interests of the child. In Scotland it has been held that the section did not innovate upon the tests of the settled laws relating to the considerations which should be given by the natural parent to the welfare of the child when deciding whether to withhold agreement.[43] The curator *ad litem* should deal with the welfare of the child, and the court in reaching its decision shall have regard to all the circumstances including the welfare of the child. In most cases the facts found by the curator *ad litem* in his report will make it self-evident that the

---

[35] Information supplied to author by Social Work Services Group, 17 Oct. 1985.
[36] Kilmarnock Sheriff Court, D12/85, 13 Dec. 1985 (unreported).
[37] *H., Petitioner*, Edinburgh Sheriff Court, E68/85, 3 Oct. 1985 (unreported).
[38] 1975 Act, s. 3; 1978 Act, s. 6.
[39] [1977] A.C. 602, see also *A.* v. *B. & C.*, 1977 S.C. 27.
[40] *Ibid.* at p. 638.
[41] *Ibid.* at p. 645.
[42] *Ibid.* at p. 629.
[43] *A. & B.* v. *C.*, 1977 S.C. 27 at p. 31.

welfare of the child is likely to be safeguarded; but if the matter is in balance or if there is some special item of doubt the curator *ad litem* should narrate these matters and give his opinion as to the welfare of the child. Welfare can be defined as " benefit,"[44] and includes material and non-material benefit.[45] Clearly if the child were to be integrated into a materially better household or were to become financially better off as a result of an adoption order these would be benefits for the child. In *A. B. & C. B.* v. *X's Curator*,[46] it was held that in determining whether consent (now agreement) had been unreasonably withheld the sheriff-substitute ought to have taken into account all the circumstances of the case, including *inter alia* the welfare of the child.[47] Benefit could also arise as a result of an adoption order if it would bring to an end fostering whereby the petitioners would be exposed to the changes of view of the local authority and the applications of the natural parents or bring the child into a normal family,[48] or add another brother or sister to the household,[49] or even in some cases would maintain the status quo and avoid uprooting the child,[50] or give the child at the beginning of a school life a name which is the same as that of the persons who to all in the locality would apear to be the child's mother and father,[51] or remove the stigma of illegitimacy[52] (it is doubtful if any general rule to the contrary can be drawn from an earlier sheriff court case[53]) or to avoid having in the same family some natural children and some stepchildren or give the child British nationality if that were to promote the welfare of the child throughout his childhood,[54] but in a single judge decision " an accommodation adoption " was refused where the purpose was to acquire British nationality.[55] Sometimes it is not possible for all brothers and sisters to be adopted by the same petitioners, as where the children of the one family had been brought up in different foster homes and the separate petitioners met the particular needs of each child. An order was made where the petitioners were the mother and stepfather of the child which had been in their care for eight years, but where all three were of low intelligence. The family was happy but the house was not clean. The curator *ad litem* and the local authority reported that the granting of the order would be for the welfare of the child[56]. In an unreported case where the male petitioner who was a British subject and the female petitioner who was a Venezuelan national were seeking to adopt a Venezuelan child who was liable to be deported and the parties had another child of their own who was a British subject, the court

---

[44] *Cf. Re D.* [1959] 1 Q.B. 229; *Re A.* [1963] 1 W.L.R. 231.

[45] *Re Adoption Application 41/61 (No. 2)* [1964] Ch. 48 at 53, *per* Wilberforce J. and approved in the House of Lords in *J.* v *C.* [1970] A.C. 668 at 713; *A.* v. *B. & C.*, 1977 S.C. 27.

[46] 1963 S.C. 124.

[47] *Cf. A. B.* v. *C. D.*, 1970 S.C. 268.

[48] *H. & H., Petitioners* 1976 S.L.T. 80 at 83; *Re R.* [1967] 1 W.L.R. 34.

[49] *Re Adoption Application 41/61 (No. 2)* [1964] Ch. 48; *Re P. (E.)* [1968] 1 W.L.R. 1913.

[50] *A. B. & C. B.* v. *X's Curator*, 1963 S.C. 124 at p. 136, *per* Lord President Clyde, but *cf A.* v. *B. & C.*, 1971 S.C.(H.L.) 129 at p. 142, *per* Lord Reid.

[51] *H. & H., Petitioners*, 1976 S.L.T. 80 at p. 83.

[52] *Re P. (E.)* [1968] 1 W.L.R. 1913; *W., Petitioners*, (1945) 61 Sh.Ct.Rep. 130.

[53] *C.D., Petitioners*, 1963 S.L.T.(Sh.Ct.) 7.

[54] *W. (A. Minor) (Adoption: Non-Patrial)* [1985] 8 C.L. 396; *Re A. (An Infant)* [1963] 1 W.L.R. 231.

[55] *Cf. Re A.* [1963] 1 W.L.R. 231; *Re R.* [1967] 1 W.L.R. 34; *Re H.* [1982] Fam, L. 121; *Re W.* [1985] 8 C.L. 396; *Re. H.* [1981] *Adoption and Fostering* 62.

[56] *L. & L., Petitioners*, Edinburgh Sheriff Court, E98/84 (unreported).

took the view that an adoption order would keep the family together in Britain. On the other hand, in *Re D.*[57] Sir George Baker said that all too often adoption was sought "by the mother to disguise from her new neighbours on remarriage that she had been involved in a failed marriage; it cannot by itself be a ground for adoption or generally in the interests of the children": the criterion is the welfare of the child not the welfare of the parent. The payment by an adoption agency of an allowance before and after adoption which if made in terms of the statute is lawful may on the one hand be to the material benefit of the child, but on the other hand may call in question the motives of the petitioners in seeking to adopt the child, and may then or later colour the view which the child may have of the motives of the petitioners.[58] It was unreasonable of a father to withhold his agreement merely to maintain his right of custody or access.[59]

While a petition by a single parent is clearly competent[60] it may present difficulties. Thus, for example, in one case, an adoptive father was charged with having sexual intercourse with his adopted daughter then aged about 14.[61] Clearly the court cannot guard against every wrongdoing by an adoptive parent towards an adoptive child, but the likelihood of such wrongdoing is less where there are two adoptive parents. Some circumstances may favour a single-parent adoption, as where a couple intended to adopt a child but one of them died before the petition was presented or in the course of the proceedings.[62] Similarly, where the single petitioner is a relative or friend who has for some time before presenting the petition taken over the child on the death or default of the natural parents. In cases like that, the child has usually been with the petitioner for a considerable time without any problems arising; and in most cases the child is likely to remain with the petitioner whether the petition is granted or not, as with an unmarried woman of 38 adopting a boy of 14 who had been in her care for over a year.[63] On the other hand, where the single petitioner has had custody of the unrelated child for a short period, the welfare of the child would be less easy to demonstrate. But, as always, the whole circumstances of each particular case must be taken into account.

From 1986 the court must consider the question of custody as an alternative to adoption.[64]

(1) *Insurance on the life of the child*

What insurance (if any) has been effected on the life of the child. This provision is not designed to ensure that the child is adequately covered by insurance because generally a life policy apart from questions of collateral does not benefit the person whose life is covered but the beneficiary who may be the petitioner. The paragraph is designed rather to enable the court

---

[57] 1973 Fam. 209 at p. 216.
[58] 1978 Act, s. 51 (5); see also para. 8.05 (j).
[59] *A. B., Petitioners*, Second Division 12 June 1985 (unreported); *A. v. B. & C.* Second Division, 26 Nov. 1980 (unreported).
[60] 1978 Act, s. 15 (1); see above, para. 3.01 (d).
[61] *H. M. A. v. R. M.*, 1969 J.C. 52.
[62] *H., Petitioner*, 1960 S.L.T.(Sh.Ct.) 3; *J., Petitioner*, Edinburgh Sheriff Court, 22 March 1985 (unreported); *cf.* para. 4.02.
[63] *M., Petitioner*, Edinburgh Sheriff Court (unreported) 21 Jan. 1985.
[64] See above, para. 1.03 (e).

to assess the probable effect of a substantial sum assured on the life of the child on the motives of the petitioner who may be the beneficiary under the policy or the heir of the child in the event of the adoption order being granted. Statute has dealt with one situation where such a case might arise: a person who maintains a protected child[65] is deemed for the purposes of the Life Assurance Act 1774 to have no interest in the life of the child.[66] Policies of insurance other than life policies if they are of a significant amount or value may be regarded as assets; if so they would no doubt be dealt with as part of the right or interests in property which the child has in terms of paragraph 21 (2)(g). The rights and liabilities under a policy in respect of funeral expenses effected by the natural parent are by virtue of an adoption order transferred to the adoptive parents.[67]

(m) (i) *Interim orders*

Whether it is desirable for the welfare of the child that the court should be asked to make an interim order. The court has power in an application for an adoption order where the requirements of an adoption order are satisfied:

(a) to postpone the determination of the application; and
(b) to make an interim order giving custody of the child to the petitioners for a period not exceeding two years by way of a probationary period on such terms as regards the provision for the maintenance and education and supervision of the welfare of the child and otherwise as the court may think fit.[68]

If the court were, in the opinion of the curator *ad litem* or on information acquired otherwise, of a mind to grant an interim order, it would no doubt indicate to the petitioners that such a disposal was in issue, and give the parties an opportunity to be heard on the matter at interview or otherwise. An interim order would be appropriate where, for example, the petitioners appeared to be rather immature; or where for some similar reason the passage of time might resolve a difficulty other than testing the suitability of the applicants as adopters, for example, to see whether the child's best interests would be best served by a transfer to the natural father.[69] In *S.* v. *Huddersfield Borough Council* Buckley L.J. was of the opinion[70] that "probationary" imports a process of investigation and experiment in relation to all the circumstances relevant to the proposed adoption and not merely to the suitability of the applicants. The probationary period may be up to two years, or for less than two years with extensions up to two years in all. An interim order is not an adoption order, and does not affect the status of the child nor nationality nor succession. The interlocutor granting the interim order requires to award custody to the petitioners and if appropriate directs that they aliment the child or ensure that he attends a particular school.[71] Towards the end of the probationary period there should be a

---

[65] See para. 5.06.
[66] 1978 Act, s. 37 (2).
[67] 1978 Act, s. 43.
[68] 1978 Act, s. 25.
[69] *S.* v. *Huddersfield Borough Council* [1975] Fam. 113.
[70] *Ibid.* at p. 124.
[71] See App. II. 5.

supplementary report from the curator *ad litem* which should indicate whether there has been a change in the circumstances of the petitioners in general and whether the matter which occasioned the interim order has been resolved. If there is to be supervision by another body such as the local authority there should be a report from that body also. Since there is a maximum time limit for the duration of an interim order, the interlocutor which makes the order should specify the date before which the supplementary reports are to be available—in any event in good time before the termination of the order. As has been indicated, there are separate provisions for England and Scotland whereby the court in an adoption process may in lieu of granting an adoption order direct that the application be treated as if it had been made for the custody of the child.[72]

(ii) *Particular terms and conditions*

Whether it is desirable for the welfare of the child that the court should be asked to impose in making an adoption order particular terms or conditions or to require the petitioner to make any particular order for the child and (if so) what provision. It is clear that the imposition of conditions in making an adoption order would tend to qualify the normal free relationship between the new parents and child which the institution of adoption is designed to create. Thus, for example, it would appear, one would have thought, that it was inconsistent with the creation of the new relationship between adoptive parents and an adoptive child which has been created by an adoption order if a condition were attached to the adoption order whereby the natural father retained access to the child. Nevertheless, in England it has been held in a case where an adoption order was made that although the tenor of the Adoption Act 1958 emphasised by section 13 (1) was that, from the time of the adoption, the adoptive parents took over the role of parents of the child completely, the court had jurisdiction to impose a condition relating to access under section 7 (3) of the 1958 Act if special circumstances made it desirable to do so and an undertaking, clearly drafted, was entered into by the parties.[73] That decision approved an earlier single judge decision which had also made access a condition of the adoption order.[74] The matter has been considered recently in three Scottish cases. In one case Lord Hunter was at one with the other judges when he said:

" I do not consider it necessary to decide in the present case whether it is competent to adject to an adoption order a condition governing access. I wish distinctly to reserve my opinion on this point since I am not at present satisfied that the English cases cited to us justify such a course, particularly in view of what appear to be differing procedures in the two jurisdictions and the legal nature and consequences of an adoption order."[75]

However, in *G. & G., Petitioners*,[76] it was held to be competent, but in very special circumstances. In a sheriff court case there was an agreement for

---

[72] 1975 Act, ss. 37 and 53.
[73] *Re S.* [1976] Fam. 1.
[74] *Re J.* [1973] Fam. 106.
[75] *A. B.* v. *C. B.*, 1985 S.L.T. 514 at p. 516. Lord Wheatley at p. 516.
[76] First Division, 19 July 1985, (unreported).

access between the petitioners and the natural parent in the form of a joint minute. The court took the view that it was not necessarily bound by the agreement and requested the curator *ad litem* to consider the new situation and report on the welfare of the child.[77] Thereafter the court decided to interpone authority to the joint minute. Further, not only would the enforcement of any conditions be difficult—whether by proceedings for breach of an undertaking given by the petitioners in court, or by breach of caution—but the imposition of such sanctions could very well be detrimental to the family in which the child is. There is nothing in the legislation providing for any sanction for the enforcement of a condition attached to an adoption order.[78] Formerly, a parent could make the giving of his *consent* to the making of an adoption order conditional on the religious persuasion in which the child was to be brought up[79]: now all that is required is that an adoption agency shall in placing a child for adoption have regard (so far as reasonably practicable) to any wishes of the child's parents and guardians as to the religious upbringing of the child.[80] In view of the terms of the statute—*an adoption order* may contain such terms and conditions as the court thinks fit[81]—it would be competent to impose a condition on the petitioners that the child be brought up in a particular religious persuasion. Other conditions which might reasonably be imposed could include one that the child attend a particular school so that his education is not interrupted, or that he undergo necessary medical treatment. In a case where the petitioners were grandparents of the child whose inferior prospects of survival might prejudice the child financially, the sheriff granted the order subject to the undertaking of the natural father to pay a weekly sum into the hands of the children's officer for disbursement to the child in the event of need.[82] In cases where such conditions are imposed they require to be expressed in the order. A certified copy of the order is sent to the Registrar General for Scotland and the principal remaining with the process will be sealed up and as a result a party claiming a right to enforce a condition would have the difficulty of learning what the precise terms of the condition were and enforcing it.

(n) *Petitioners not ordinarily resident in the United Kingdom*

If the petitioner is not ordinarily resident in the United Kingdom, whether a report has been obtained on the applicant's home and living conditions from a suitable agency in the country in which he is ordinarily resident. The former express provisions allowing adoption by persons who are not ordinarily resident in Great Britain[83] have been repealed; and the requirements are now governed by the generality of section 13 whereby the child must have his home with the petitioners for one of three specified

---

[77] Glasgow Sheriff Court 15 April 1983, (unreported).
[78] *Re G. (T. J.)* [1963] 2 Q.B. 73, a decision of the Court of Appeal under the 1958 Act.
[79] 1958 Act, s. 4 (2); but this provision was repealed and has not been re-enacted in the 1975 Act.
[80] 1978 Act, s. 7, see para. 8.05 (p).
[81] 1978 Act, s. 12 (6).
[82] *G. D., Petitioners*, 1950 S.L.T.(Sh.Ct.) 34.
[83] 1958 Act, s. 12 (3); *Re W.* [1962] Ch. 918. *Cf.* J. F. Josling and Allan Levy, *Adoption of Children* (10th ed.), p. 36. *In re Adoption Application. AA*, 121/1984, [1985] 7 C.L. 505a.

periods.[84] The place of the home is restricted by the requirement that the local authority (which includes English local authorities[85]) in a placement not by an adoption agency and the adoption agency in a non-relative adoption must be afforded sufficient opportunity to see the child with the petitioners *together* in the home environment.[86] It is for the court to decide if the local authority has had sufficient opportunity to see the child with the petitioners together in the home environment. In one exceptional case the petitioners' family was resident in the area of the local authority. The male petitioner, who was on military service in Germany and about to be posted to the Falkland Islands, was due to be in residence for certain periods during the three months before the granting of the petition. The petitioners' solicitors wrote and telephoned repeatedly to the appropriate social work office of the local authority in whose area the family had its home, telling them of these dates. The local authority did not acknowledge the letters and did not approach the family or the court. The court was satisfied that sufficient opportunities had been afforded to the local authority.[87] It may be that in similar situations as, for example, where the petitioners had satisfied the requirements of domicile,[88] where the family has its home within a local authority area in Scotland, where the child is in the home environment with the petitioners, but the family is temporarily physically abroad in military, civil or commercial service or for pleasure, the requirements of the legislation can still be satisfied by the petitioners. Clearly, the domicile of the petitioners will not be affected by temporary absence abroad. The child would need to be in Scotland at the time of presenting the petition. The child must have his home with the petitioners or one of them for, in most cases, at least 13 weeks,[89] but there is no requirement in that section that the care and possession need be in Scotland. In cases where the petitioner is a relative of the child or the child has been with the petitioners for at least 12 months, intimation must be given by the petitioners to the local authority within whose area they have their home of their intention to apply for an adoption order[90]: but the petitioners do not need to be in Scotland to do that, and in many cases it is done by solicitors. In terms of the legislation the local authority or the adoption agency must investigate and report to the court on the adoption. Both these bodies are juristic persons who can only do such acts through their servants or agents. The court will no doubt be satisfied that these bodies have had sufficient opportunities to see the child with the petitioners in their home environment if they entrust that aspect of the case to an agent such as a consular official, local social worker, or solicitor or military welfare officer[91]; and any matters required to be reported upon in terms of sections 22 or 23 can also be dealt with by that agent; and in so far as the inquiry relates to the petitioners' home in Scotland, the local authority or adoption agency can investigate and report in the normal way. Similarly, the

---

[84] See above, paras. 3.02 and 8.05(i).
[85] 1978 Act, s. 65 (1).
[86] 1978 Act, s. 13 (3).
[87] *O. & O. Petitioners*, Edinburgh Sheriff Court, E90/84, January 1985 (unreported).
[88] 1978 Act, ss. 14 (2) and 15 (2); see above, para. 2.04.
[89] 1978 Act, s. 13 (1).
[90] 1978 Act, s. 22.
[91] 1978 Act, s. 13 (3).

report of the curator *ad litem* and, where appropriate, the reporting officer would reflect the absence abroad of the family. And if the court is not satisfied that the facts stated in the petition are supported by the documents or the reports of the curator *ad litem* and the reporting officer, it may make further inquiry by way of production of further documents or by hearing oral evidence.[92] If the child is not in the United Kingdom when the application is made, only the Court of Session has jurisdiction.[93]

If the petitioner is obviously ordinarily in the United Kingdom, the curator *ad litem* should merely state that fact: normally this will be self-evident and will be stated in the petition at paragraph 2. If the facts as seen by the curator *ad litem* appear to be otherwise, he will report that to the court which will decide on the question of residence. Where a foreign report is required, no doubt, it can be provided by someone who is in use to provide such reports in that country or in the case of service personnel, someone with legal training.

(o) *Petitioners' reasons for adopting*

Why the petitioner wishes to adopt the child. (The additional matters for investigation now contained in this paragraph and in paragraphs (p), (q) and (r) were introduced in 1966). The information gleaned under this head will enable the court to learn something of the character of the petitioners and judge how responsibly they are approaching the problem of coping with a new child in the household. The usual reasons why petitioners wish to adopt are that they are unable to have children of their own either at all or without danger to the health of the female petitioner, that they wish to give the child the security of a family home, that they wish to add to their existing family, or that in the case of a mother adopting her own child on marriage or remarriage to the male petitioner the petitioners wish to give legal authority to a *de facto* situation which may have subsisted for years and which often becomes pressing when the child is about to go to school with a surname which is different from that of the male petitioner.[94] The motives of the petitioners might be affected by the receipt or the prospect of an allowance from an adoption agency under the Act.[95]

(p) *Religious persuasion of the petitioners*

The petitioner's religious persuasion, if any. Religion emerges in at least three ways in adoption law.

(i) Until 1975 the consent of any person to the making of an adoption order could be given subject to conditions with respect to the religious persuasion in which the infant was proposed to be brought up[96]; but as has been noted, it would appear to be still competent for the court to impose a condition in the adoption order that the child be brought up in a particular persuasion under the general power to make such terms and conditions as it thinks fit.[97]

---

[92] A.S. 23 (R.C. 230 (5)).
[93] 1978 Act, s. 56 (3).
[94] *Cf. H. & H., Petitioners*, 1976 S.L.T. 80 at p. 83.
[95] See above, para. 8.05 (j).
[96] 1958 Act, s. 4 (2) repealed by 1975 Act, s. 108 (1) (*b*) and Sched. 4, Pt. IV.
[97] 1978 Act, s. 12 (6); see para. 8.05 (m) (ii).

(ii) There is a statutory obligation imposed on an adoption agency, but not on the court, to have regard (so far as practicable) to any wishes of the child's parents and guardians as to the religious upbringing of the child.[98] If the wishes of the parents or guardians were also before the court no doubt it would take them into account.

(iii) The present provision relates to the religious persuasion of the petitioners. This information will enable the court to know whether there is likely to be a difference between the spouses on the question of religion which might affect the welfare of the child. Most reports not only state the religious persuasion of the petitioners but also the faith in which the child is to be brought up. In *H. & H., Petitioners*,[99] the sheriff granted an adoption order where Jewish petitioners sought to adopt a Christian child and bring him up in the Jewish faith. In the 1970s at least two other similar unreported cases were decided in the same way: and with the greater population of non-Christian faiths now resident in Britain such adoptions have become more common.

(q) *Age difference between petitioners and child*

The considerations arising from the difference in age between the petitioner and the child if such difference is greater or less than the normal difference in age between parents and their children. As has been indicated a petitioner must have attained the age of 21.[1] The present paragraph is directed to the situation where the petitioner may be too close in age to the child, or is too old to be a parent. Under adoption legislation now repealed, the applicant had to be, generally, at least 21 years older than the child.[2] Accordingly, the curator should deal with the matter by stating the ages of the petitioners and the child and whether it appears that there are any circumstances in that regard which would qualify the ability of the petitioners to look after the child properly, such as the fact that the character of the petitioner belies his or her age. Clearly the court would be unlikely to consider granting an adoption order where the petitioners and the child were each anywhere near the statutory limits applying to them, namely, a 21-year-old petitioner and a 17-year-old child—a situation which could arise in the adoption of a stranger child. Where the petitioner is adopting her own child, it would be very difficult to envisage a situation where the court would regard the difference in ages between the petitioner and the child as being against the welfare of the child. If the suggestion is that the petitioner is too old, the court would wish to have the views of the curator *ad litem* on that aspect of the case and if he feels that it has a bearing on the welfare of the child, as where the petitioner is too old to cope with the child.

In one opposed sheriff court case the male petitioner was 63 and the child was four[3]; and in a recent English case the grandparents were in their middle sixties and the child was seven[4]: in both cases the adoption order was made.

---

[98] 1978 Act, s. 7.
[99] 1949 S.L.T.(Sh.Ct.) 68.
[1] See para. 2.03.
[2] 1930 Act, s. 2 (1) (*b*).
[3] *T. F. & H. F., Petitioners*, 1949 S.L.T.(Sh.Ct.) 48.
[4] *Re W.* [1980] Fam. 190; [1981] C.L.Y. 1751.

(r) *Suitability of the petitioners*

Such other matters, including an assessment of the petitioner's personality and, where appropriate, that of the child, as having a bearing on the mutual suitability of the petitioner and the child for the relationship created by adoption, and on the ability of the petitioner to bring up the child. These matters are largely self-explanatory and the content and detail of the report will be governed by the circumstances of the case; and accordingly little guidance can be given. The curator *ad litem* is in a particularly advantageous position in that he sees the family in its natural setting and is able to give an assessment of these matters which can seldom be achieved in the more anxious circumstances of a hearing or a proof before a judge.

(s) *Wishes of the child*

The ascertainment, as far as practicable, of the wishes and feelings of the child, regarding the proposed adoption. This is a new paragraph (although similar provisions have existed in previous legislation, such as the 1930 Act, s. 3 (*b*)). It follows upon the new formula in the 1978 Act that the court:

"shall have regard to all the circumstances, first consideration being given to the need to safeguard and promote the welfare of the child throughout his childhood; and so far as practicable ascertain the wishes and feelings of the child regarding the decision (relating to the adoption of the child) and give due consideration to them having regard to his age and understanding."[5]

There are three situations in which the child may be:

   (i) if he has no understanding of these matters, the curator *ad litem* need only report that fact and the reason for the lack of understanding, such as non-age or mental inadequacy;

  (ii) if the child has sufficient understanding, the report should state what his wishes and feelings are and this should be done whether or not he is a minor; and

 (iii) if the child is a minor—that is a girl who is over 12 and not yet 18, or a boy who is over 14 and not yet 18—he must consent in writing to the making of the adoption order, except that where the court is satisfied that the minor is incapable of giving his consent, it may dispense with that consent. Otherwise, the adoption order cannot be made.[6] In England and Wales the consent of the child is not required.[7]

These provisions may raise difficult questions if the child has not been informed that he is about to be adopted by persons whom he has taken to be his natural parents, and if the petitioners are unwilling to let the child know the true position. It is not impracticable to take the child's views merely because it is inconvenient or unwelcome to the petitioners.[8] In relation to the manner of dealing with the wishes of the child it was said in *Re G.(T. J.)*[9]:

"The child was aged 12 at the time; and in such a case I think that,

---

[5] 1978 Act, s. 6.
[6] 1978 Act, s. 12 (8).
[7] 1975 Act, s. 8 (6) (1976 Act, s. 12).
[8] *C. & C., Petitioners*, Edinburgh Sheriff Court, E5/85 9 March 1985 (unreported).
[9] [1963] 2 Q.B. 73 at 97, *per* Donovan L.J.

subject to what follows, the judge should satisfy himself about the child's understanding by speaking to the child himself. No doubt in most cases this would best be done in private. But where, as here, he has a very recent report by the child welfare officer of the local authority which tells him, *inter alia*, what the child's wishes are, I see no reason why the judge should not accept that report if he thinks it right to do so. If the report were some months old—as I gather it could be in some cases—he should, and I have no doubt would, verify for himself that the child's wishes remained the same, since the section does require, in my opinion, the ascertainment of those wishes as at the time of the hearing or near enough to that time to make no difference.''

The curator *ad litem* should in advance of visiting the home of the petitioners make inquiries of the petitioners or their solicitors about the state of knowledge of the child and the attitude of the petitioners about the best time and the most propitious circumstances for broaching the matter with the child. Petitioners who are anxious about this aspect of the investigations of the curator *ad litem* can be reminded that if the child is not told not only will it be impossible in the case of a child of sufficient understanding for the adoption to be granted, but that it is almost inevitable that the child will be told of his status by third parties perhaps in an undesirable way, and that the child will be entitled as of right to see the adoption process at the age of 17 and he will thereby see that he is adopted and learn the identity of his natural parents if they appear in the process. In *A., Petitioner*,[10] in the course of an adoption, the court directed that a 19-year-old child who was the subject of an adoption process should be told the circumstances of his birth, his consent only being valid if given in the full knowledge of his parentage. If a child is not of the required understanding this fact should be reported on; and the petitioners should be asked what their intentions are about informing the child later. If they are unwilling to agree to inform the child an attitude which sometimes arises out of a fear of hurting the child or, but less so nowadays, the unwillingness to reveal to the child that he was born out of wedlock it may be appropriate for the sheriff to interview the petitioners on this matter with a view to getting the petitioners to undertake that they will inform the child that he is adopted, as soon as a convenient opportunity presents itself. In most cases it is desirable to inform the child as early as possible, so that when the emotional maturity of the child grows the fact of the adoption will have little significance to him.

(t) *Report by adoption agency or local authority*

Since there is now a statutory obligation on the adoption agency[11] or the local authority[12] to report to the court on the suitability of the parents and the welfare of the child, it seems appropriate that the curator *ad litem* should go beyond the sundry paragraphs which are prescribed in the rules, and report on whether he has been able to see the appropriate report and to say whether he has any comments on it.

---

[10] 1936 S.C. 255.
[11] 1978 Act, s. 23.
[12] 1978 Act, s. 22.

8.06 Modification in report of curator *ad litem* in other applications

Modification of the report of the curator *ad litem* is necessary in petitions other than the usual petition for adoption.

(a) In a petition to adopt a child abroad, the report should, in addition, deal with the special averments in the petition relating to the foreign element, such as, the non-British domicile of the petitioners[13] and the law of the country in which it is intended to adopt the child.[14]

(b) In a petition for a Convention adoption order, the report should deal with the additional matters which relate principally to the foreign elements and which are specified in the rules.[15]

(c) In a petition for freeing a child for adoption, the report should deal with more limited matters. The report of the curator *ad litem* should deal with:
  (i) the welfare of the child in terms of section 6 of the 1978 Act,
  (ii) the truth of the facts stated in the petition,
  (iii) the consent of any minor child,
  (iv) whether the freeing would promote the well-being of the child, and
  (v) the current circumstances.
The report should also deal with the care of the child.[16]

(d) In a motion (or in the Court of Session, a note), to revoke an order freeing a child for adoption there need only be the report of the curator *ad litem* dealing with the very limited matters of:
  (i) the facts stated in the minute, and
  (ii) the circumstances and care of the child with regard to his welfare.[17]

8.07 Report of the reporting officer

The reporting officer may be appointed before the petition is presented in a petition to free a child for adoption in the sheriff court, and in a petition to free a child for adoption, or a petition for adoption in the Court of Session.[18]

In sheriff court petitions for adoption the reporter must carry out five duties and report thereon.[19] These proceed on the basis that there has been no earlier order freeing the child for adoption, and accordingly the agreement of the natural parents is still outstanding. (Even in petitions for adoption where the child is free for adoption, a reporting officer must be appointed[19a]; although there is no requirement in that case that there should be a hearing.[20]) The regulations provide that the reporting officer undertakes five duties and report thereon.

---

[13] 1978 Act, s. 49 (1).
[14] A.S. 17 and Form 8 (R.C. 224 (3) (*b*)).
[15] R.C. 230C (1) and (2).
[16] A.S. 6 (2) (*a*) to (*e*) (R.C. 224 (4), where the duties of the reporting officer are more limited).
[17] A.S. 12 (R.C. 224 (5), where the matters are set forth in greater detail, but are substantially to the same effect.)
[18] 1978 Act, s. 58 (3); A.S. 5 (3) (R.C. 225).
[19] A.S. 21 (1) (R.C. 224 (3)).
[19a] 1978 Act, s. 58 (1); A.S. 20 (1).
[20] 1978 Act, s. 59 (2), A.S. 22 (1) (R.C. 222 (12) (*b*)).

(a) To witness any agreement executed by a parent or guardian (but not the consent of a child) within the United Kingdom in a sheriff court case and in Scotland only in a Court of Session case.[21] The reporting officer should lodge the agreement in process. Clearly, if the person whose agreement is required refuses to execute the agreement, or refuses to agree in any circumstances or cannot be found, the reporting officer should report that fact and state what efforts he has been able to take to ascertain the whereabouts of the parent. The style of report envisages that the parent will agree: there is no style for a parent not agreeing. Where the parent is outwith the United Kingdom, the agreement may be executed according to the statutory provisions which have already been dealt with.[22]

(b) To ascertain that each parent or guardian whose agreement is required or may be dispensed with understands the effect of the adoption. The reporting officer should ascertain that that understanding is the correct one, namely that the effect of an adoption order would be to deprive the parent or guardian permanently of his parental rights.[23]

(c) To ascertain whether there is any person other than those mentioned in the petition upon whom notice of the petition should be served.[24] This paragraph corresponds to the phrase in the crave of the petition: " and to order notice of this petition to be served on such persons, if any, as the court may think proper."[25] The court must also deal with intimation of a *diet of hearing*.[26] It is rare that there are any such persons: where a parent who hitherto could not be found, or was thought to be dead or had been thought not to be a parent emerged as a person whose agreement is required that would be a case for taking his agreement but hardly a case for giving him notice of the petition.

(d) Where a parent or guardian whose agreement is required, or may be dispensed with, can be found, to ascertain whether alternatives to adoption have been discussed with him. The main obvious alternative to adoption is custody; but in most cases that alternative is not a realistic alternative because, for example, the parent has not kept up with the child while the child was with the adoption agency, or in the care of the local authority by virtue of an assumption of parental rights, or in the care of an adoption agency by virtue of an order freeing the child for adoption or in the care of the mother and her new husband who are the petitioners.[27]

(e) To confirm that each parent or guardian whose agreement is required understands that he may withdraw his agreement at any time before the order is granted.[28]

---

[21] A.S. 21 (1) (*a*) and Form 10 (R.C. 224 (1) (*c*), (2) (*c*) and (3), and Forms 37A and 37B).
[22] See above, para. 5.10.
[23] A.S. 21 (1) (*b*) (R.C. 222 (7) (*k*)).
[24] A.S. 21 (1) (*c*) (R.C. 224 (1) (*h*), 224 (2) (*h*) and 224 (3) (*a*)).
[25] Form 7 (R.C. Form 36).
[26] See below, para. 5.17.
[27] A.S. 21 (1) (*d*) (R.C. 222 (7) (*d*)).
[28] A.S. 21 (1) (*e*), 6 (1) (*g*).

8.08 Modifications in the report of reporting officer in other applications

In the case of a petition to free a child for adoption the report of the reporting officer should deal with the agreement of each natural parent and the consequences of a freeing order,[29] and also deal with the three additional matters which arise in a petition to free a child:

  (i) that the parent may seek revocation of any order,[30]
 (ii) that the parent may declare that he would prefer not to be involved in future questions concerning the adoption of the child,[31] and
(iii) the likelihood of any person " reputed to be the father of the child " successfully raising proceedings for custody of the child.[32]

That phrase is at variance with the words of the primary statute which refers merely to any person " claiming to be the father."[32a]

8.09 Reports under sections 22 and 23

In cases where there is no dispute, these reports would indicate whether from the point of view of the local authority or the adoption agency there was anything amiss. In adoption agency cases the adoption agency will already know all about the case; and in most of the other cases the petitioner will be a mother adopting her own child. The report should begin with the name and designation of the author of the report, and should state that the source of the information is a visit to the home of the petitioners, or as the case may be. By statute the matters which require to be reported upon are:

  (a) the suitability of the petitioners. The report should outline the occupations, the house and the members of the household, as well as the emotional and material ability of the petitioners to look after the child. As in the case of the report of the curator *ad litem*, there is no authority in the adoption legislation which would justify the author of the report seeking to know as a matter of course the contents of the criminal records of the petitioners;

  (b) any other matters relevant to the operation of section 6, which relates to the welfare of the child. The report should state that either the circumstances which have been noted make clear that the granting of the order is likely to safeguard and promote the welfare of the child throughout his childhood; or that it is not, for the reasons specified, e.g. the character of the petitioners or the wishes of the child;

  (c) in the case of a placement other than by an adoption agency, whether the child has been placed contrary to section 11, which relates to illegal placements. The report need only say that in the circumstances, for example, the petitioner is a relative of the child, or the child was placed by an adoption agency, and accordingly there has been no breach of section 11; or, there has or appears to have been a breach of section 11, in respect that someone other than an

---

[29] A.S. 6 (1) (*a*) to (*g*) (R.C. 224 (1) (*b*)).
[30] A.S. 6 (1) (*h*) (R.C. 224 (1) (*m*)).
[31] A.S. 6 (1) (*i*) (R.C. 224 (1) (*n*)).
[32] A.S. 6 (1) (*j*) (R.C. 224 (1) (*j*)).
[32a] 1978 Act, s. 18 (7).

adoption agency or a relative purported to make arrangements for the adoption of the child or to place the child for adoption.

In the Court of Session elaborate rules provide for detailed information of the kind which in the sheriff court is provided by the report of the curator *ad litem*.[33]

8.10 Adoption agency reports

Parallel legislation which governs the functions of adoption agencies[34] puts a duty on the adoption agency where an application is made to the court:

(a) to free the child for adoption, or

(b) to adopt the child which has been placed by an adoption agency under the 1978 Act and the regulations

to provide a report to the court. The matters to be reported on are:

(a) such information on the background and circumstances of the child, his family and (where appropriate) the petitioners, as the adoption agency has been able to discover in accordance with the regulations; and

(b) any other matters

(i) relative to the welfare of the child, or

(ii) by reiteration, as may be required by the court in accordance with section 23 of the 1978 Act.[35] Section 23 only applies to adoptions.

The information which the adoption agency has been able to discover in accordance with the regulations refers to the matters which the adoption agency must obtain, and these are set forth in the numbered particulars relating to the child, the natural parents, the guardian and the petitioners.[36]

8.11 Procedure up to the hearing

In most cases the reports under sections 22 and 23 will be in process, along with the reports from the adoption agency in terms of their regulations.[37] In some cases the report of the local authority under section 22 may not have been prepared, because the local authority will only have knowledge of the need for a report after the petitioners have given them notice of intention to adopt.[38] After the lodging of the petition the sheriff must appoint a curator *ad litem* and a reporting officer or reporting officers and, where reasonably practicable, appoint the same person as curator *ad litem* and reporting officer in the same petition.[39] As indicated,[40] the interlocutor appointing these officers should require the report to be made on or before a specified date, usually about four weeks ahead, but this may

---

[33] R.C. 222 (7).

[34] Adoption Agencies (Scotland) (Regulations) 1984 (S.I. 1984 No. 988), reg. 23.

[35] Reg. 23 refers to "section 21" of the 1978 Act, which is presumably a misprint for "section 23."

[36] Regs. 15, 16 and 17 and Sched. 3, Pts. 1 to 4.

[37] See above, para. 8.10.

[38] 1978 Act, s. 22(1).

[39] A.S. 20 (adoption), 5 (freeing) and 12 (revoking) (R.C. 222 (5), 220 (6), 221 (3)); see above, para. 5.12.

[40] See above, para. 7.01.

suffer exception where the natural parent is outwith Scotland and even more so if outwith the United Kingdom. When the reports of the curator *ad litem* and the reporting officer have been received, the sheriff will normally consider these reports and if the child is not free for adoption, instruct the clerk of court (usually by a scroll instruction written on the report) to fix the hearing and prepare an interlocutor appointing the petitioners to intimate the diet of hearing. In the case of a petition to free a child for adoption, intimation must be made on every person who can be found and whose agreement or consent to the making of the order is required to be given or dispensed with,[41] that is, the natural parent and the child who is a minor. The sheriff has no express power to order intimation on anyone else in a freeing application, whereas the Court of Session does.[42] In petitions for adoption, in addition to the natural parents and the minor children, as we have seen, a wider group of persons may also receive intimation.[43]

8.12 The hearing

In every application to free a child for adoption and in every petition for adoption where the child has not previously been freed, a hearing must take place even where all the parties are agreeable to the granting of the adoption order; and if no one entitled to appear at the hearing appears to be heard, the sheriff may grant the adoption order on the motion of the petitioner.[44] The motion is invariably oral and is moved by the petitioner in person or by his solicitor or advocate. Strictly, appearance on behalf of the petitioner is not specified, but it is virtually unavoidable if the petitioner is to learn whether there is to be an appearance by any person entitled to appear. If the agreement of a parent is to be dispensed with, and there is no appearance by that parent, the court can usually proceed on the information in the process; and if the natural parent compears and still declines to agree, matters would presumably be required to be resolved by proof. If a person entitled to appear does appear and wishes to be heard, the court may hear him. A hearing on any matter of significance does not in practice take place at this stage, because the petitioner and court have no prior knowledge of the stance of the person entitled to appear. Obviously, if that person is persisting in a refusal to agree to the making of the adoption order, the petitioners could not be expected to be ready to go to proof there and then, and the court could not reasonably be expected to provide an immediate diet for such procedure. In that case, the rules provide that the court may order a further diet to be fixed at which evidence may be given in the presence of the petitioner or his solicitor.[45] In most cases this later diet would take the form of a proof and thereafter the court would proceed to a decision.

---

[41] A.S. 8 (2) and Form 11 (R.C. 220 (12) and Form 38).
[42] R.C. 220 (12).
[43] See above, para. 5.17.
[44] A.S. 22 (4) (adoption), 8 (3) (freeing) and 13 (revoking). In the Court of Session the provisions are more elaborate: R.C. 222 (12) (13) and (14) (adoption), 220 (11) (12) and (13) (freeing) and 221 (7) (8) and (9) (revoking).
[45] See above, para. 6.03.

CHAPTER 9

Decision of the Court

9.01 Preliminary matters

In a petition for adoption where the child is not free for adoption, the court has to deal with the three aspects of the case—the preliminary matters, otherwise called "the conditions precedent," the agreements of the natural parents (along with the consent of the child) and the merits. In a petition for adoption where the child has been freed for adoption, the agreements are no longer in issue and the court need only deal with the conditions precedent and the merits. In a petition to free a child for adoption, the merits are generally not in issue, and the court need only deal with the conditions precedent and the agreements.

When the court has before it all the information by way of productions, reports, interview (if any), hearing or proof it will be able to deal with the averments in the petition and any other issues which have arisen. Some of the items (which are referred to as the conditions precedent) are straightforward, such as the status and circumstances of the petitioners and the child, questions of domicile, jurisdiction, care and possession. No doubt the court will confirm that the child mentioned in the extract of the entry in the Register of Births corresponds to the child mentioned in the petition and that the proposed new name for the child as set forth in the prayer of the petition corresponds with the name in the adoption order. There remain to be considered the merits of the proposed adoption and in some cases the question of dispensing with the agreement of a parent.

9.02 The merits

In reaching any decision relating to the adoption of a child—of which the decision whether to grant an adoption order is one—the court must have regard to all the circumstances, first consideration being given to the need to safeguard and promote the welfare of the child throughout his childhood. To regard as decisive one fact—such as that the petitioners are the grandparents of the child[1] or that it is a step-parent adoption—would be contrary to the law; by statute the court must have regard to "all the circumstances".[2] Obviously such a relationship is a circumstance among others to which the court must have regard, but in cases of these kinds the court must balance the advantages from the point of view of the welfare of the child.[3] In addition, the court must so far as practicable ascertain the wishes and feelings of the child regarding the decision and give due consideration to

---

[1] *e.g. Re D. X.* [1949] Ch. 602.
[2] 1978 Act, s. 6; *Re W.* [1971] A.C. 682 at p. 699, where Lord Hailsham referred to the "totality of the circumstances".
[3] *H. & H., Petitioners*, 1976 S.L.T. 80.

them, having regard to his age and understanding.[4] In every case, the court will have to consider the welfare of the child, but the feelings of the child will only arise if the child is of an age at which they can be ascertained; and of all the circumstances other than these, the chief is whether the agreement of a parent who does not concur in the adoption order should be dispensed with by the court. The same three elements—the agreement of the parent, the welfare of the child, and the wishes of the child—were set forth in the earlier legislation but in a slightly different arrangement.[5] The decisions in Scottish and English cases on the law before the 1975 Act appear to be more in conformity with the view that section 3 of that Act does not alter the law: "The issue must primarily depend upon how the welfare of the child is best secured."[6] "The true question in all such cases which is relevant to both the merits of an application and to the motion to dispense with consent is whether the making of the order or refusing to make it is more likely to enure to the welfare of the child."[7] "No doubt the child's interests come first, and in some cases they may be paramount."[8] This dictum of Lord Reid was taken up by the departmental committee which preceded the 1975 Act and section 3—now in Scotland, section 6 of the 1978 Act—was the statutory result.[9] If section 3 is to be regarded as no more than elucidatory and confirmatory of the previous law,[10] then any shift in the law must have come before the 1975 Act: in the same case Lord Wilberforce said[11] that the decision in *A. v. B. & C.*[12] "shows how far the erosion of the natural parent's rights had gone." A more satisfactory view may be that the law in this regard has remained quite consistent; that since there may be a "band of possible reasonable decisions,"[13] the decision in *A. v. B. & C.*[14] was a case decided on its own facts. Thus even the well and firmly expressed words of the judges in *Re B.*,[15] including the observation that "it is quite wrong to use the adoption law to extinguish the relationship between the protesting parent and the child, unless there is some really serious factor which justifies the use of the statutory guillotine," were regarded in the House of Lords as containing "no revolutionary or even new doctrine."[16] These words would only be relevant in the circumstances of cases of the same kind, that is, where there was not only a protesting father but also a father who continued to have a relationship with the child. The welfare of the child and the feelings of the child have been discussed in relation to the report of the curator *ad litem*.[17] When each parent has given his or her agreement to the making of the adoption order, the merits of the case can be disposed of; and in most of the cases where the court is asked to dispense with the agreement of a

---

[4] 1978 Act, s. 6.
[5] 1958 Act, ss. 5, 7 (1) (*b*) and 7 (2).
[6] *A. B.* v. *C. D.*, 1970 S.C. 268 at p. 269.
[7] *H. & H., Petitioners*, 1976 S.L.T. 80 at p. 83.
[8] *A.* v. *B. & C.*, 1971 S.C.(H.L.) 129 at p. 141, *per* Lord Reid.
[9] For a detailed analysis of the making of s. 3, see Professor E. M. Clive, annotation to Adoption (Scotland) Act 1978, s. 6, in *Scottish Current Law Statutes*.
[10] *Re D.* [1977] A.C. 602 at pp. 638 and 645.
[11] [1977] A.C. 602 at p. 626.
[12] 1971 S.C.(H.L.) 129.
[13] *Re W.* [1971] A.C. 682 at p. 700, *per* Lord Chancellor.
[14] 1971 S.C.(H.L.) 129.
[15] [1975] Fam. 127.
[16] *Re D.* [1977] A.C. 602 at p. 627, *per* Lord Wilberforce.
[17] See para. 8.05 (k) and (s).

parent—apart from the ground that the parent is withholding his agreement unreasonably where the welfare of the child is also relevant—the court can dispose of that aspect of the case without having to qualify its views on the merits.

9.03 Dispensing with the agreement of a parent

The authorities are—apart from the decision following on *Re D.*[18]—at one in regarding the welfare of the child as relevant to the decision whether to dispense with the agreement of a parent in relation to the grounds to which it could apply, particularly the ground that the parent is withholding his agreement unreasonably. The new legislation provides that in "any decision relating to the adoption of a child" the court must have regard to all the circumstances including the welfare of the child.[19] There are dicta of the Court of Appeal to the effect that "any decision" does not apply to a decision to dispense with the agreement of a parent,[20] but observations in the House of Lords to the contrary are more agreeable to the words of the Act:

> "As at present advised, I feel some reservation about accepting the construction put by the Court of Appeal (*obiter*, I think) on the Children Act. . . . Moreover, it is a strong thing in an Act of this sort to read 'any decision relating to the adoption of a child' in other than the ordinary and primary sense of these words."[21]

In the situation where there is a compearing and protesting parent who has kept up with the child, the court, which may have come to a provisional view on the merits in favour of granting the adoption order, would have to reconsider that view since there has been added to the totality of the circumstances the additional question whether it is in the interests of the child that his relationship with his parent should be cut off. It is trite law that unlike the situation in questions of custody where the interests of the child are paramount,[22] in a question of adoption the welfare of the child is only the first consideration.[23] In a custody matter the relationship of parent and child is not called in question; whereas in adoption proceedings it is; and that relationship may be extinguished for all time. Thus if the continuation of the child's relationship with his father is in the best interests of the child, the original provisional view of the court on the merits would have to be discarded. In practice, the court will often be faced with the report of the curator *ad litem* which indicates that all the requirements of the statute have been complied with, and that in terms of paragraph 21 (2) (*k*) the adoption is likely to safeguard and promote the welfare of the child throughout his childhood; but the reports may also show that the agreement of a parent is absent. The parent may not persist in this stance or he may agree at first and later withdraw his agreement. At a later proof the court may take the view that the parent's agreement is not unreasonably withheld. The

---

[18] [1977] Fam. 25.
[19] 1978 Act, s. 6.
[20] *Re. P.* [1977] Fam. 25.
[21] *Re D.* [1977] A.C. 602 at p. 641.
[22] Guardianship of Infants Act 1925, s. 1.
[23] 1978 Act, s. 6.

circumstances of the case will no doubt determine whether the court deals with the two questions—the merits and the issue of dispensing with the agreement of a parent—together or *seriatim*.[24] In England the justices have been criticised for dealing with a case " the wrong way round."[25] This aspect of the decision of the court is dealt with later.[26] In cases where the petition is opposed, the procedure becomes more complicated.

---

[24] *Cf. Re W.* (1976) 120 S.J. 857.
[25] *Re. B.* [1975] Fam. 127 at p. 137, *per* Sir George Baker P.
[26] See para. 10.08.

CHAPTER 10

Opposed Petitions and the Grounds of Opposition

10.01 Most petitions unopposed

The great majority of petitions for adoption proceed without opposition. The court may grant the adoption order with or without conditions or make an interim order on such terms as the court may think fit. The court may refuse to grant the order; or the court may dismiss the petition; or allow it to be withdrawn or direct that the application be treated as if it had been made for custody of the child.[1] If the court is satisfied that the necessary agreements and consents have been given or dispensed with, and if the other statutory requirements have been complied with—particularly that the court in reaching its decision has had regard to all the circumstances, first consideration being given to the need to safeguard the welfare of the child throughout its childhood[2]—there seems to be no reason why the adoption order or order freeing the child for adoption should not be granted: certainly there is no need for there to be a "compelling reason" for granting the order.[3] Normally the court will be satisfied with the verification of the statements in the petition provided by the documents and the reports; although some courts feel that in the case of adoption of a child who is not the child of either of the parties the welfare of the child cannot be properly assessed without the court's interviewing the petitioners as well. In England, attendance before the court by the petitioners is obligatory except in a few cases.[4] In Scotland the new requirement of compulsory hearings may not necessitate the personal presence of the petitioners[5] although the practice in some courts is to have them attend in every case.

10.02 Opposed petitions

"A petition is an *ex parte* application craving the authority of the Court for the petitioner, or seeking the Court to ordain another person, to do an act or acts which otherwise the petitioner would be unable to do or cause to be done."[6] Because of the nature of procedure by petition there is no necessary contradictor. In adoption petitions a contradiction or defence to the prayer of the petition may arise where the agreement of a parent, or rarely the consent of a child, has not been given and it is sought to dispense with that agreement or consent. A contradiction could also arise where one

---

[1] 1978 Act, s. 30 (3); see above, para. 1.03 (*f*).
[2] 1978 Act, s. 6.
[3] *H. & H., Petitioners*, 1976 S.L.T. 80.
[4] *e.g.* Adoption Rules 1984 (S.I. 1984 No. 265), para. 23 (4).
[5] A.S. 22 (R.C. 222 (14), 223 (4) (*c*)).
[6] Maclaren, *Practice*, p. 825, referred to in *J. & J.* v. *C.'s Tutor*, 1948 S.C. 636 at p. 642.

of the persons upon whom the court in its discretion has ordained the petitioner to serve a notice of date of hearing in Form 11 seeks[7] to enter the process. Such opposition is almost unheard of. The authority to dispense with the agreement of a parent is often craved in the prayer of the petition or if the issue only arises later by a separate motion. There is no place in adoption proceedings—other than a motion (or a note) to revoke a freeing order—for answers, even although in one case the court allowed fairly full answers for the respondent, and thereafter amendments for the parties.[8] Similarly, in *W. v. C.*[9] the natural mother who refused to consent to the making of the order lodged answers to the petition. However, in an unreported case dealing with the former analogous provisions decided by the Sheriff Principal of Lothian and Borders (Sir William Bryden) it was said: " The proper procedure was simply to ordain the Petitioners to serve on him a Notice in the form provided (Form C) informing him (1) of the date of the hearing, (2) of his right to ' appear and be heard,' and (3) that the court was being asked to dispense with his consent on the ground that he was withholding it unreasonably (See Act of Sederunt (Adoption of Children) 1959 as amended by Act of Sederunt (Adoption of Children Amendment) 1966)." As has been noted, in the sheriff court there is no provision for answers but only a notice in terms of Form 11 which is of similar import to the previous Form C; and in the Court of Session answers are expressly excluded,[10] whereas, in a minute (or note) to revoke a freeing order, answers are expressly provided for.[11] In addition, there seems to be no reason why a parent, for example, should not be heard on an allegation that the proposed adoption would be detrimental to the welfare of the child—and that whether or not he was agreeing to the making of the order: such objectors—as with anyone else who had information that the petitioners were unsuitable—might be treated as witnesses or just sources of information which would put the court upon its inquiry and perhaps cause the court to seek comment or rebuttal from the petitioners. Contradiction might also arise where a party such as a natural parent was seeking access[12]—which must be an exceptional qualification of the principle that an adoption order has the effect of depriving the natural parents permanently of their parental rights: but there are examples.[13] There have been cases where the respondent has challenged the relevancy of the petitioner's case; but in one case it was held that the particular averments were relevant since such a petition could not be dismissed unless the facts were patently insufficient in law.[14] If the petitioners do not pursue their action by keeping in touch with their solicitor, the respondents may seek to dismiss the petition. Since the welfare of the child is the first consideration, the court would be slow to grant such a motion until it was satisfied that the petitioners

---

[7] A.S. 22 (3) (R.C. 220 (13) (c), 222 (13) (c)).
[8] *A. v. B. & C.*, 1971 S.C.(H.L.) 129 and Session Papers.
[9] (1939) 55 Sh.Ct.Rep. 261.
[10] See above, para. 5.17.
[11] A.S. 11 (3) (R.C. 221 (2)).
[12] The question of access in relation to adoption has already been discussed: see above, para. 8.05 (m).
[13] *Re J.* [1973] Fam. 106; *Re S.* [1976] Fam. 1; see para. 8.05 (m).
[14] Z. v. Z., 1954 S.L.T.(Sh.Ct.) 57.

could not be found or that they had not answered an intimation to them to state whether they intended to proceed with the action. If the petition is dismissed, the petitioners can present a new petition.

10.03 Agreement of parent or guardian

Before an adoption order can be made the court must be satisfied that

    (a) the child is free for adoption by virtue of an order made in England and Wales under section 18 of the Adoption Act 1976 and not revoked, or made in Scotland under section 18 and not revoked, or

    (b) (i) each parent or guardian freely, and with full understanding of what is involved, agrees unconditionally to the making of the adoption order (whether or not he knows the identity of the applicants), or

       (ii) his agreement to the making of the adoption order should be dispensed with on certain grounds which are specified in the section.[15]

The form which the agreement should take has already been discussed.[16] Formerly, the consent was also required from the person or body with actual custody of the child, or who was liable to contribute to the support of the child[17]; now these categories of persons are ones upon whom the court may in its discretion ordain the petitioner to serve a notice in Form 11.[18] The natural parent's agreement must exist at the time of making the adoption order; accordingly, a parent can withdraw his agreement up to that time.[19] However, it was noted in the judgment of Ormrod L.J. in *Re H.*[20] with which the other judges agreed, that

    "it ought to be recognised by all concerned with adoption cases that once the formal consent has been given . . . or perhaps once the child has been placed with the adopters, time begins to run against the mother and, as time goes on, it gets progressively more and more difficult for her to show that the withdrawal of her consent is reasonable."

10.04 Parent defined

Parent is not defined in the legislation, but the term always includes the natural mother of the child, whether or not the child is legitimate. There is no statutory provision which excludes from the category of person whose agreement is required a parent merely because he or she is also a petitioner: the statute refers to "every parent or guardian of the child."[21] Similarly, the petitioners must intimate the diet of hearing to every person whose agreement is required, even although one of these persons is one of the petitioners. In the case of a natural mother adopting her own child along with the stepfather of the child, the effect of the adoption order would be to

---

[15] 1978 Act, s. 16 (1).
[16] See para. 5.10 (d).
[17] Adoption of Children (Scotland) Act 1930, s. 2 (3); 1950 Act, s. 2 (4) (a).
[18] A.S. 22 (3) (R.C. 222 (12)); see above, para. 5.17.
[19] e.g. *A.B., Petitioner*, 1976 S.L.T.(Sh.Ct.) 49.
[20] [1977] 1 W.L.R. 471 at 472.
[21] 1978 Act, s. 16 (1) (b).

deprive her permanently of her sole parental rights which would thereafter be shared with her husband. There is a relaxation of other provisions, such as the necessity to have medical certificates as to the health of the petitioners,[22] in cases where the petitioner or one of the petitioners is a parent of the child. On the other hand " parent " for this purpose does not include—apart from the case of the father of an illegitimate child who is a guardian of the child by virtue of a deed or will or certain statutes[23]—a natural father who was not married to the natural mother[24] even if he has an order for access to the child[25]; but such a father will become a parent whose agreement will be required if he subsequently marries the mother of the child and thereby legitimates the child. This development occurred in one case during the currency of the litigation.[26] If a father is not a parent because he was not married to the natural mother, he does not become a parent merely because his name appears on or because he has adhibited his signature to the birth certificate of the child. Some courts nevertheless did serve a notice in Form C on the unmarried father of the child. However, the father of a child who is not married to the mother is a " relative " for the purposes of the legislation.[27] The agreement of the husband of the natural mother, if he is not in fact or is not presumed to be the father of the child, is of no value. In legal aid applications for adoption therefore, it would appear to be pointless to require the applicant to do more than state that the child was illegitimate. The position of a father of an illegitimate child may be relevant in a petition to free the child for adoption: but that is of no moment, because in such cases only an adoption agency, not a natural parent, can be the petitioner.[28] (The father of an illegitimate child is, however, a relative who may properly be a petitioner and, as such, the child may be placed without the intervention of an adoption agency.)[29]

10.05 The natural mother

Where the natural mother is also a petitioner there is seldom any difficulty. However, where the natural mother is giving up her child for adoption, several problems may arise. In the case of a mother, but not in the case of a father, the agreement is ineffective if it is given by her less than six weeks after the birth of the child.[30] This provision takes into account the effect of childbirth on the mother's ability to make the best decision for herself and the child. In addition to the medical effects of the birth, a mother at any stage may be in emotional turmoil over the decision whether to deprive herself permanently of her parental rights over the child. In some cases, there may also be the personal reminder of illegitimacy or the fear of relatives learning of it. Although these considerations appear to bulk less large nowadays, care should be taken by the reporting officer and the

---

[22] A.S. 16 (3) (*c*) (R.C. 222 (3) (*d*)).
[23] Which are noted later: see para. 10.07; 1978 Act, s. 65 (1).
[24] *A*. v. *B.*, 1953 S.C. 378; *A*. v. *B. & C.*, 1971 S.C.(H.L.) 129.
[25] *G. & G. Petitioners*, First Division, 19 July 1985 (unreported).
[26] *A*. v. *B. & C.*, 1971 S.C.(H.L.) 129.
[27] 1978 Act, s. 65 (1).
[28] 1978 Act, ss. 13 (1) and 65 (1).
[29] 1978 Act, s. 18 (7).
[30] 1978 Act, s. 16 (4).

solicitor for the petitioners in dealing with the mother, particularly when she may feel that the question of agreeing to the adoption order has been raised several times over a period of several months—when she is first asked about giving up the child, when she signs the form of agreement, when she confirms to the reporting officer that the effect of the adoption order would be to deprive her permanently of her parental rights, when she receives intimation of the hearing and when she attends the hearing, if she attends. Solicitors, reporting officers and curators *ad litem* should avoid distress in such cases by sending letters—if so requested—to the address selected by the mother, or by using plain envelopes or the like. It has been suggested that where the child is averred to be illegitimate and it is reasonably clear that the natural mother's husband is not the father the practice is not to serve on him.[31]

10.06 *Pater est quem nuptiae demonstrant*

In relation to the natural father, the presumption of paternity is expressed in the Latin brocard *pater est quem nuptiae demonstrant*, that is, he is the father of the child as is indicated by the marriage. Children born in wedlock are presumed to be the legitimate children of the husband and wife.[32] Generally, as long as the marriage subsists until dissolved by death or divorce the presumption will apply and in the case of a petition for adoption of the child the agreement of the husband will be required because he is presumed to be the father of the child. It is, of course, possible to overcome the presumption with contrary evidence, such as non-access by the husband at the time of conception—as where the husband was abroad or in prison (which fact is sometimes vouched by a letter from the prison authorities or an extract conviction from the appropriate court)—or where the husband is not capable of procreation. If the presumption has been displaced, then the husband is not the father and accordingly his agreement is not required and he does not become a parent for the purpose of agreement, because his position has to be looked at in a freeing application,[33] or because he is a relative for the purposes of placing a child.[34] It is illogical and pointless for the husband of the natural mother who is not the father of the child to give his agreement to the making of the adoption order.[35] No doubt the circumstances of the case will determine whether the court is satisfied that the presumption has been overcome on the information contained in the reports, or whether additional evidence should be called for.[36] In one unreported case there was a suggestion that the former husband of the natural mother who was also a petitioner was impotent or sterile and that the child was conceived as a result of artificial insemination in a foreign country by an unknown donor or donors. Had this been proved, it would have made

---

[31] Dobie, *Sheriff Court Practice*, p. 547, citing *E., Petitioner*, (1944) 60 Sh.Ct.Rep. 127 where the decision of the court proceeded on the inquiries made of the Registrar of Births as to the procedure adopted by him before registering a married woman's child as illegitimate; Registration of Births, Deaths and Marriages (Scotland) Act 1965, s. 18.

[32] Trayner, *Latin Maxims and Phrases*, *s.v.*; Gloag and Henderson, *Introduction to the Law of Scotland* (8th ed.), p. 747, and the authorities there cited.

[33] 1978 Act, s. 18 (7).

[34] 1978 Act, ss. 11 and 65 (1).

[35] *E., Petitioner*, (1944) 60 Sh.Ct.Rep. 127.

[36] A.S. 23 (R.C. 230 (5)).

it unnecessary to have the agreement of the husband. However, the court was not satisfied that the husband was unable to procreate or that he did not have access at the time of conception.

10.07 Guardian defined

It is also necessary for the court to be satisfied that each guardian freely agrees unconditionally to the making of the adoption order.[37] Guardian means:

(a) a person appointed by deed or will in accordance with the provisions of the Guardianship of Infants Acts 1886 and 1925 or the Guardianship of Minors Act 1971 or by a court of competent jurisdiction to be the guardian of the child; and

(b) in relationship to the adoption of an illegitimate child, includes the father where he has custody of the child by virtue of an order under section 9 of the Guardianship of Minors Act 1971, or under section 2 of the Illegitimate Children (Scotland) Act 1930.[38]

Further the relevant parental rights and powers with respect to any child which may be vested in a local authority under a resolution made by them do not include the right to agree or refuse to agree to the making of an adoption order,[39] an order to adopt a child abroad or an order freeing a child for adoption.

10.08 Dispensing with agreement and consent

Once the identity of the parent or guardian has been established, the agreement of that person to the making of the order must be disposed of. If the parent or guardian has died—and that fact can be established by the production of the extract of an entry in the Register of Deaths or by other evidence—the difficulty has been overcome. If the person is not dead and does not agree to the making of the adoption order, or has withdrawn his agreement before the making of the order, the order cannot be made unless the court dispenses with the agreement on a ground specified in the Act. The grounds are now set out in a systematic manner.[40] If it be (contrary to the majority view of the judges in *Re P.*[41]) that "any decision relating to the adoption of a child" includes the decision by the court to dispense with the agreement of a parent, then the court in so doing "shall have regard to all the circumstances, first consideration being given to the need to safeguard and promote the welfare of the child throughout his childhood." However, it is difficult to envisage a situation where the welfare of the child would be relevant to any of the grounds other than where the parent "is withholding his agreement unreasonably."[42] In this regard Stamp L.J. said: "with the possible exception of a decision by subsection (2) (*b*) none of those decisions can possibly be regarded as a decision relating to an adoption within section

---

[37] 1978 Act, s. 16 (1) (*b*).
[38] 1978 Act, s. 65 (1).
[39] Social Work (Scotland) Act 1968, s. 16 (3).
[40] 1978 Act, s. 16 (2).
[41] [1977] Fam. 25.
[42] 1978 Act, s. 16 (2) (*b*).

3 because that section cannot possibly apply "[43]; and in the same case Sir John Pennycuick said[44]:

> " It seems to me that upon the natural construction of section 3 the words 'In reaching any decision relating to the adoption of a child,' wide as they are, are addressed to the exercise by a court of its discretion to make or withhold an adoption order and cannot sensibly be applied to a determination by a court of a question of fact, welfare is not itself the question."

There is a difference in the case of dispensing with the consent of a minor child who is the subject of the adoption petition in respect that there is only one ground on which the court could so find, that is, that the minor is incapable of giving his consent.[45] Whether the ground is made out is a question of fact[46]; but in Scotland in *A. B. & C. B.* v. *X.'s Curator*[47] although the sheriff-substitute found as a fact " (35) The consent of the mother of the child has not been unreasonably withheld," and said[48] " I have no difficulty in holding in fact that the parent of the child has not unreasonably withheld her consent "; and the appellants regarded it as a finding in law[49]; and the respondents as a mixed finding of fact and law[50]; the court did not decide this point but the better view is to regard it as a question of fact in Scotland also.

10.09 Grounds for dispensing with agreement or consent

The grounds for dispensing with agreement or consent are discussed *seriatim*. The grounds are not mutually exclusive: for example, the parent who has persistently failed without reasonable cause to discharge his parental duties in relation to the child is very often also the parent who cannot be found.

(a) (i) *Cannot be found*

This is one of the more common grounds; and is usually decided on the information contained in the reports and the productions. The reporting officer should state what steps he has been able to take in trying to trace the parent. Sometimes relatives of the natural parent are able to assist in providing an address or in forwarding communications to the parent. Failure to follow up such lines of inquiry have been commented upon and an appeal was allowed on the grounds that the petitioners had failed to take proper steps to serve notice of the proceedings on the natural mother.[51] In that case the petitioners

> " wrote, or instructed their solicitors to write, to her last address, and the letter was returned ' Gone away.' They caused advertisements to be inserted in the press, notifying her of the proposed proceedings. They caused enquiries to be made from the post office and other sources in an

---

[43] *Re P.* [1977] Fam. 25 at 30.
[44] *Ibid.*, at 38.
[45] 1978 Act, s. 12 (8).
[46] *Re P.* [1977] Fam. 25.
[47] 1963 S.C. 124.
[48] *Ibid.* at 131.
[49] *Ibid.* at 132.
[50] *Ibid.* at 133.
[51] *Re F. (R.)* [1970] 1 Q.B. 385.

attempt to trace her whereabouts, but all these steps proved to be fruitless";

however, it was contended that petitioners " knew that the mother's father was in touch with the mother and that they knew his address " and that there was " one reasonable step which they omitted to take, and that was to get in touch with her father and ask him to tell the mother what they proposed." The court allowed the appeal and ordered a rehearing to give the mother a chance of being heard. The addresses which appear on the extract of an entry in the Register of Births or Register of Marriages or other productions may be the addresses of the party whose agreement is being sought or of his or her relatives. Government departments or employers may be prepared to pass on a communication to someone whose address they have but are unwilling to disclose to the petitioners. If a registered or recorded delivery letter is posted at the address of the natural father and the letter is taken in and nothing more is heard, or if it is returned marked " not known," " gone away " or " refused," the returned letter would be evidence that the natural father could not be found—at least at that address. That fact may also be proved by other evidence. In a single judge decision in England the phrase " cannot be found " was applied to the situation where the natural parents had returned to a hostile totalitarian state and there was no practical means of communicating with them.[52] If intimation of the hearing on a natural parent has been effected and he does not compear, it cannot be said that he cannot be found: then some other ground would have to be established. It is for the petitioners to establish that the natural parent cannot be found.

(ii) *Is incapable of giving agreement*

This ground which is less common applies not only to the case of dispensing with the agreement of a parent or guardian but also to the case of dispensing with the consent of a minor child who is the subject of a petition for adoption.[53] Normally, the evidence of mental or physical incapacity would be that of a medical report on the condition of the person and the effect of that condition on his ability to understand what was required if he was asked to give his agreement or consent.[54] If the report is disputed, the matter would require to be resolved by proof. If the parent is of doubtful mental capacity, particularly if intimation of a hearing on the parent might be detrimental to the health of the parent, the court may *ex proprio motu* or on the motion of the solicitors for the parent, appoint a curator *ad litem* to the parent who can report to the court on his capacity. There may be cases where the petitioners know of the whereabouts of the natural parents and that they are in good health but because they are resident in a totalitarian country which is hostile to them to such an extent that they would not be capable of giving their agreement freely, the court will hold that they are incapable of giving their agreement.[55]

---

[52] *Re R.* [1966] 3 All E.R. 613; *cf. Re B.* [1958] 1 Q.B. 12.
[53] 1978 Act, s. 12 (8).
[54] *Lothian Regional Council, Petitioners*, Edinburgh Sheriff Court, E83/85, 3 Oct. 1985 (unreported).
[55] *Re R.* [1966] 3 All E.R. 613.

(b) *Is withholding his agreement unreasonably*

This ground is frequently relied upon and it has given rise to the greatest proportion of the adoption litigation in England and in Scotland, although the number of contested cases constitutes a very small part of the total number of adoption petitions. Whether the agreement is being withheld unreasonably is to be decided at the hearing[56] or proof. The test in deciding whether this ground exists is not the sincerity of the parent whose agreement is in question but the reasonableness of his withholding the agreement.[57] In *B. & B., Petitioners*,[58] it was regarded as reasonable for the natural mother to see her child and meet the female petitioner before giving her consent; but it has been held by a court of seven judges (with one dissent) that disclosure to the natural parent of the identity of the proposed adopters was not an indispensable prerequisite of a valid consent.[59] In an appeal from the Court of Appeal, Lord Wilberforce narrated that the judges " said that a direction to dispense with consent should be given sparingly, and only in rare and exceptional cases: this was all the more so in cases such as *Re B.* (as the present) where the adoption is desired by one natural parent and the other refuses consent " and said of these observations that " they contained and set forth no revolutionary or even new doctrine."[60] The effect of section 3 of the 1975 Act and the meaning of "welfare of the child" have been discussed.[61] The existence of this ground is a question of fact; and in such a situation no general rules can be laid down. Apart from the clear exception of *H. & H., Petitioners*,[62] where the parent although not consenting to the making of the adoption order did not appear in the process, almost all the reported cases have been ones in which there has been a live issue between the compearing parties—namely, whether the parental rights of the natural parent should yield to the welfare of the child which may result by the making of the adoption order: but a significant consideration in deciding this question is whether the parent whose agreement is in issue is in reality a protesting parent or even a compearing parent. If in an unopposed petition there is credible information such as would be contained in the reports and there is no challenge of it and no contrary information and that information supports the motion of the petitioners at the hearing that the agreement of the parent should be dispensed with, there is no reason why the court should not dispense with that agreement and proceed to deal with " the merits of the petition."[63] In that case the decision on dispensing with parental agreement was made much easier in that the parent was not only a non-protesting parent and a non-compearing parent but also a parent who had " washed his hands " of the child; " and that he had accordingly persistently failed without reasonable cause to discharge his obligations " as a parent of the child. The court did not deal with the other ground for dispensing with the agreement of the parent—that it was unreasonably withheld—although that had been in

---

[56] *Re D.* [1973] Fam. 209; *A. B., Petitioner*, 1976 S.L.T.(Sh.Ct.) 49.
[57] *Re W. (An Infant)* [1971] A.C. 682 at pp. 698 and 699.
[58] 1946 S.L.T.(Sh.Ct.) 36.
[59] *H. & H. Petitioners*, 1944 S.C. 347.
[60] *Re D.* [1977] A.C. 602 at p. 627.
[61] See paras. 9.02 and 8.05 (k).
[62] 1976 S.L.T. 80.
[63] *H. & H., Petitioners*, 1976 S.L.T. 80 at p. 83.

issue in the sheriff court; but it seems that the same information would have justified upholding that ground also. This and other cases can illustrate rather than define the meaning of the ground. Lord Wilberforce in *Re D.*[64] said that the decision in *A. v. B. & C.*[65] " shows how far the erosion of the natural parents' rights " had gone; and in *A. v. B. & C.* Lord Guest pointed out[66] that " No case was referred to in which the consent of the natural parents of a child to an adoption order was dispensed with when the parents had married "—but the marriage of the natural parents in that case took place during the currency of the litigation and after the natural father became free to marry. Nevertheless, " it has been said more than once that, other things being equal, it is in the best interests of a child to be with its natural parents."[67] It is almost trite law that what is to be considered in assessing the reasonableness of the natural parent in deciding whether he should give his agreement to the making of the order is " the totality of the circumstances."[68] The words of Lord Reid in the same case[69] provide a succinct statement of the position:

" The test is an objective test—would a reasonable parent have withheld consent? I think a reasonable parent, or indeed any other reasonable person, would have in mind the interests and claims of all three parties concerned—the child whose adoption is in question, the natural parents, and the adopting family. No doubt the child's interests come first, and in some cases they may be paramount. But I see no reason why the claims of the natural parents should be ignored. If the mother were deeply attached to the child and had only consented in the first place to adoption because of adverse circumstances, it would seem to me unjust that on a change of circumstances her affection for the child and her natural claim as a parent should be ignored. And the adopting family cannot be ignored either. If it was the mother's action which brought them in in the first place, they ought not to be displaced without good reason. So to balance these claims is no easy task. Often no ideal solution is possible. We are dealing largely with future probabilities, for the decision once made is irrevocable. So we cannot be certain what will be in the child's best interests in the long run. That seems to me to be an additional reason for giving considerable weight in proper cases to the claims of the natural parents and the adopting family."[70]

That case followed *Re W.*[71] in which the words of general import made by the Lord Chancellor were referred to with approval; for completeness the whole paragraph is noted:

" I only feel it necessary to add on this part of the case that I entirely agree with Russell L.J. when he said, in effect [1970] 2 Q.B. 589, 598, 599, that it does not follow from the fact that the test is reasonableness

---

[64] [1977] A.C. 602 at p. 626.
[65] 1971 S.C.(H.L.) 129 (also cited as *O'Connor* v. *A. & B.* [1971] 1 W.L.R. 1227).
[66] 1971 S.C.(H.L.) 129 at 143.
[67] *Ibid.*, *per* Lord Guest at p. 143.
[68] *Ibid.*, *per* Lord Simon at p. 147.
[69] *Ibid.*, at p. 141. *Re K.* [1952] 2 All E.R. 877.
[70] " There is a trinity of interests involved—those of the child, those of the mother and those of the respondents ": *A.* v. *B. & C.*, Second Division, 26 Nov. 1980 (unreported).
[71] [1971] A.C. 682 at p. 700.

that any court is entitled to substitute its own view for that of the parent. In my opinion, it should be extremely careful to guard against this error. Two reasonable parents can perfectly reasonably come to opposite conclusions on the same set of facts without forfeiting their right to be regarded as reasonable. The question in any given case is whether a parental veto comes within the band of possible reasonable decisions and not whether it is right or mistaken. Not every reasonable exercise of judgment is right, and not every mistaken exercise of judgment is unreasonable. There is a band of decisions within which no court should seek to replace the individual's judgment with his own."

The cases can do no more than emphasise the words of the statute that the test is reasonableness. There are cases which are examples of particular applications of that general rule, such as the case of adoption of the children of a marriage after divorce and remarriage. In this regard Cumming-Bruce J. said in *Re B.*[72]:

"I appreciate that in this case, as in many, it is strongly in the child's interest that he should be settled in the family life of the mother and her second husband; that he should form a close relationship with the father figure represented by that husband. I also appreciate that in this case, as in many, the fact that the child continues to have a relationship with his natural father is a source of practical inconvenience and irritation to the mother, who wishes to put her first husband out of her life as completely as possible. And, of course, the second husband may be expected to wish to keep the first husband completely out of their family life. Also it is common experience that the emotional effect on the child of an attempt to maintain dual and frequently conflicting loyalties to both parents, and to the stepfather, is deeply disturbing and sometimes gravely destructive to the stable development of his personality. But the appropriate court to regulate and control these difficult problems is usually the court seised of the family problems of the first marriage. It may, on the facts of the present case, be wise to restrict access on the part of the father. The High Court and the county court are there to grapple with these problems. It is quite wrong to use the adoption law to extinguish the relationship between the protesting father and the child, unless there is some really serious factor which justifies the use of the statutory guillotine. The courts should not encourage the idea that after divorce the children of the family can be reshuffled and dealt out like a pack of cards in a second rubber of bridge. Often a parent who has remarried and has custody of the children from the first family is eager to achieve just that result, but such parents, often faced with very grave practical problems, are frequently blind to the real long-term interests of their children."

The observations in that case "well and firmly though they were expressed . . . contained no revolutionary or even new doctrine."[73] *Re B.*[74] was followed in a sheriff court case[75]; and a similar approach had been

---

[72] [1975] Fam. 127 at p. 143.
[73] *Re D.* [1971] A.C. 602, *per* Lord Wilberforce at p. 627.
[74] [1975] Fam. 127.
[75] *A. & B.* v. *C.*, 1977 S.L.T.(Sh.Ct.) 55.

adopted earlier in *A. B., Petitioners.*[76] In cases in which this ground is relied upon the claim of the natural parent looms larger than in other cases. The strictures in *Re B.*[77] in favour of custody and against adoption as the proper method of securing the welfare of the child and the dicta to the effect that only where the welfare of the child " so overwhelmingly requires adoption " should a father be deprived of that status[78] can only have application where there is a protesting parent whose child is in the custody of the mother after divorce and is sought to be adopted by her and her new husband. In an unopposed case in Scotland the judgment of the court was that there was no need to show a " compelling reason " why adoption should be granted[79]; " The true question in all such cases which is relevant to both the merits of an application and to the motion to dispense with consent, is whether the making of the order or refusing to make it is more likely to enure to the welfare of the child (see *A. B.* v. *C. D.*, 1970 S.C. 268, the opinion of Lord President Clyde at p. 269)." The divergence in the law in relation to adoption by a parent and a step-parent has been discussed earlier.[80]

(c) *Has persistently failed without reasonable cause to discharge the parental duties in relation to the child*

A parent has by reason of the relationship of parent and child the duty to aliment the child and guide the child in his upbringing; and in England it has been said that parental duty also includes " the natural and moral duty of a parent to show affection, care and interest towards his child."[81] This would include adequate provision of housing, clothing and food, as well as ensuring that the needs of the child such as education and medical treatment were properly met. The commonest failure of a parent is in not providing aliment for the child; and the majority of those cases is where there is a decree for payment of aliment either in the decree of divorce or in a separate decree or agreement associated with the decree of divorce and the former husband has not paid anything or has paid very little. If the failure is without reasonable cause, as where the parent is able to pay or even is able to earn a livelihood, the court may dispense with agreement on this ground; but the whole circumstances should be considered, for example, whether the parent has kept up with the child by exercising any right of access, by writing letters or by sending cards or presents at Christmas or on birthdays. In *Re D.*[82] it was held that the existence of the ground was a question of fact and degree; and where a father has temporarily withdrawn from the family during the period of the breakdown of the marriage and subsequent divorce and ancillary proceedings there was not such a degree of permanence as would deprive a father of his parental rights. A different situation may arise if the petitioner has engineered the apparent indifference of the parent to the child by refusing him access or making its exercise virtually impossible or by rejecting

---

[76] 1959 S.L.T. (Sh.Ct.) 49.
[77] [1975] Fam. 127.
[78] *Ibid.* at 140 and 145; *cf. Re D.* [1973] Fam. 209.
[79] *H. & H., Petitioners*, 1976 S.L.T. 80 at 83
[80] See para. 1.02.
[81] *Re P.* [1962] 3 All E.R. 789 at 794.
[82] [1973] Fam. 209.

his tender of aliment or the like.[83] Normally, the evidence in support of this ground would be the decree in which the aliment was fixed and the evidence of those who could speak to the non-payment of the aliment or other circumstances. Although in proceedings by a local authority to assume parental rights of a child, a similar phrase, namely, "has so persistently failed without reasonable cause to discharge the obligations of a parent or guardian as to be unfit to have care of a child," is used, "the question of adoption, however, is not concerned with a parent's fitness to have care of the child sought to be adopted but of her right to refuse to agree to give up once and for all her parental rights and duties towards that child which is quite a different matter."[84]

(d) *Has abandoned or neglected the child*

The words of this ground echo part of other legislation such as the Children and Young Persons (Scotland) Act 1937, s. 12. Abandonment means leaving the child to its fate without intention of recovering it; in *Watson* v. *Nikolaisen*[85] it was held that the abandonment must be of the kind which would render the parent liable to criminal prosecution. Neglect includes temporary abandonment, such as leaving the child at home unattended, and failing to provide the child with necessary food, clothing, shelter or cleanliness. Evidence in support of this ground can take the form of an extract conviction under statutes such as the Children and Young Persons (Scotland) Act 1937, s. 12, or reports of the social work department or of the like or the evidence of the makers of the reports or anyone else having knowledge of the matters. It is suggested that this ground would be less likely to have been made out if the conduct of the parent was far in the past and had ceased.

(e) *Has persistently ill-treated the child*

This ground, unlike the next, envisages a course of conduct over a period which may not amount to serious ill-treatment. In respect of this there is no provision for excluding the ground because rehabilitation of the child within the household is likely.

(f) *Has seriously ill-treated the child*

This ground differs from the previous one in that conduct here may amount to only one incident as long as it is serious, such as one assault; and the ground does not apply unless (because of the ill-treatment or for other reasons) the rehabilitation of the child within the household of the parent or guardian is unlikely.[86] This is a new provision. Proof of this and the previous ground would depend on medical and lay evidence and if appropriate any extract conviction of an offence by the parent against the child or the reports on the child by the social work department or the like. If the ground is established and the court decides to make the order sought in the petition it will do so by an interlocutor.

---

[83] *A. & B.* v. *C.*, 1977 S.L.T.(Sh.Ct.) 55; *Re B.* [1975] Fam. 127.
[84] *A. & B. Petitioners*, Outer House, 7 July 1982 (unreported).
[85] [1955] 2 All E.R. 427.
[86] 1978 Act, s. 16 (5).

CHAPTER 11

Making the Order

11.01 Interlocutor

If the court is satisfied that all the statutory requirements such as agreements, domicile, care and possession and the like have been complied with, and the court is satisfied that the granting of the order will safeguard and promote the welfare of the child throughout his childhood, then it will make the adoption order with or without conditions. The interlocutor may be in the form "Grants the prayer of the petition."[1] At the same time the court will make a certified copy of the adoption order for transmission to the Registrar General for Scotland,[2] the principal of which will remain with the process.[3] In almost every case intimation of the adoption order to the Registrar General for Scotland is all that the petitioners require and, indeed, all that they have sought in the prayer of the petition. No extract of an adoption order may be issued except with the authority of the court which made the order. This procedure is extremely rare. An extract may be sought by lodging a petition setting forth the reasons for which an extract is required. If an extract is sought after the process has been sealed up, the petition should also crave authority to open up the process.[4] This rule only applies to adoption orders. An extract may be sought in the normal way in the case of other orders, such as an interim order which the petitioners would require to have for their purposes.[5] Presumably, for the same reasons, an extract of an order for adoption of a child abroad and an order freeing a child can be issued as in an ordinary action in court. In the case of a freeing order, an extract would be asked for by the solicitor for the adoption agency. Where in a petition to free a child for adoption, a natural parent makes a declaration that he prefers not to be involved in future questions concerning the adoption of the child, such declaration must be recorded by the court.[6] Where some particular matter has been in issue and has been resolved, usually by proof or some other form of inquiry beyond the verification contained in the reports, the court should make findings in fact on these matters, such as,

"(1) that the father of the child was married to the natural mother; (2) that the letters (Nos. of process) have been returned by the Post Office marked 'Gone away'; Therefore dispenses with the agreement of the natural father on the ground that he cannot be found in terms of the Adoption (Scotland) Act 1978, s. 16 (2) (a)"

---

[1] *H. & H., Petitioners*, 1976 S.L.T. 80 at p. 82.
[2] A.S. 26 (R.C. 229).
[3] See App. II.6.
[4] A.S. 27 (R.C. 230 (3); App. II.18.
[5] See above, para. 1.03 (c).
[6] 1978 Act, s. 18 (6); A.S. 7 (1) and 10 (3) (R.C. 230 (2)).

and if appropriate the sheriff should write a note setting forth the grounds on which he has proceeded.[7] Apart from the situations in which the court would as a matter of course insert in the interlocutor and order any particular terms or conditions, the court must in the case of an adoption by one person where one of the parents is excluded record the reason justifying that exclusion.[8] In the case of an interim order the interlocutor should echo the words of the statute and postpone the determination of the adoption order until a specified date, appoint the curator *ad litem* to furnish a supplementary report on or before a date which is well before the date of postponement, make an interim order of custody of the child in favour of the petitioners for that period, ordain them to aliment the child[9] generally or at a particular amount per week. The former provisions allowed the court to add such other conditions as to education and supervision of the welfare of the child and otherwise as the court thought fit.[10] These powers are implied in the order vesting custody of the child in the petitioners. Similarly, in the case of an order to adopt a child abroad the interlocutor should authorise the petitioners to remove the child from Great Britain immediately (or after a certain period) for the purpose of adopting the child under the law of the state of a particular country and vesting in them the parental rights and duties relating to the child pending his adoption.[11]

11.02 Order not granted

The court may refuse to pronounce an adoption order, or an interim order

(a) if the court is not satisfied that the facts stated in the petition are supported by the documents lodged with the petition or by the reports of the curator *ad litem* and reporting officer, or

(b) if for any other reason the court considers it appropriate without production of further documents or hearing oral evidence.[12]

One would expect that unless there was some fundamental and incurable impediment to the granting of the order, the party would be given an opportunity to amend his case or lead additional evidence; and that in most unopposed cases the court would not require the personal attendance of the petitioners or the child—apart from the petitioner or his representatives being present at the hearing to move that the adoption order be granted.[13] In the case of refusal—with or without additional evidence—the interlocutor of the court would refuse the prayer of the petition and add a note setting forth the grounds of the refusal; and if appropriate the court may set forth findings in fact including negative findings.[14] The legislation envisages that a petition can "lapse" or be withdrawn,[15] for example, where in the face of supervening opposition of a natural parent, the petitioners do not wish to

---

[7] Sheriff Courts (Scotland) Act 1907, Sched. 1, r. 89.
[8] 1978 Act, s. 15 (3); see App. II.12.
[9] 1978 Act, s. 25, App. II.5.
[10] 1958 Act, s. 8 (1); see App. II.5.
[11] 1978 Act, s. 49; see App. II.7.
[12] A.S. 23 (R.C. 230 (5)).
[13] A.S. 8 (3) and 22 (4). There is no obligation on a petitioner to be present: 1978 Act, s. 59 (2) and R.C. 222 (14).
[14] Lees, *Interlocutors*, p. 17; *cf. Brown & Lynn* v. *Western S.M.T.*, 1945 S.C. 31 at 46.
[15] *e.g.* 1978 Act, s. 32 (4) (*a*).

proceed, or the petitioners realise that the petition is incompetent, as where one of the petitioners is under 21. But it is a question whether standing those powers relative to refusal, there is any statutory power in the court to dismiss the petition: there is in England a reference to the power to dismiss[16]: and in Scotland an inherent power to do so. Where the order is not granted certain results may follow. Where a previous application for a British adoption order has been refused, the court "shall not proceed to determine" an application by the same petitioners in relation to the same child unless

  (a) in refusing the previous application the court directed that this provision should not apply, or
  (b) it appears to the court that
      (i) because of the change in circumstances, or
      (ii) for any other reason
it is proper to proceed with the application.[17] A British adoption order means an adoption order granted in

  (a) Scotland under the 1978 Act, s. 12,
  (b) England under the 1975 Act, s. 8 (1) (or prospectively 1976 Act, s. 12 (1)),
  (c) Northern Ireland,
  (d) the Channel Islands,
  (e) the Isle of Man,
  (f) a British colony, being a country designated for the purposes of that provision by an order of the Secretary of State or, if no country is so designated, any of those countries.[18]

Where the second adoption is by different persons, this section does not apply; but in most cases the court would want to know the history of the child. Also refusal by the court or withdrawal of the application or expiry of the period of an interim order without an adoption order having been made brings into operation the provisions whereby the child is returned to the adoption society or local authority which placed the child[19]; or the court may put the child under supervision or commit the child to the care of a specified local authority[20]; and there is provision for intimation to the local authority who may make representations by minute (or note) which must be intimated to the petitioners before the diet of hearing thereon and the petitioners may lodge answers thereto.[21]

11.03 Registrar General for Scotland

The communication to the Registrar General for Scotland of

  (a) any adoption order,[22]
  (b) amendment or revocation to an adoption order,[23] or
  (c) cancellation of an adoption order on legitimation of the child[24]

to be made by the clerk of court, is effected by sending to the Registrar a

---

[16] 1975 Act, s. 10 (3) (1976 Act, s. 14 (3)).
[17] 1978 Act, s. 24.
[18] 1978 Act, s. 65 (1).
[19] 1978 Act, s. 30.
[20] 1978 Act, s. 26.
[21] A.S. 30 (R.C. 227).
[22] 1978 Act, s. 45, Sched. 1, para. 1 (7).
[23] 1978 Act, s. 45, Sched. 1, para. 4 (2).
[24] 1978 Act, s. 45, Sched. 1, para. 6.

certified copy of the order by recorded delivery post in an envelope marked "confidential," or by personal delivery by the clerk to the Registrar.[25] These provisions do not apply to an interim order nor to an order of custody granted in lieu of an adoption order,[26] nor where the order is refused, dismissed or withdrawn, nor to a freeing order, nor an order revoking a freeing order. The principal order will remain with the process to be sealed up with it. It is usual for the clerk of court to delay sealing up the process until he has received acknowledgment from the Registrar that he has received the order. Further, since the parties are entitled to have open to them all documents lodged in process they should be entitled to have a sight of the process before it is sealed up, if only to check the interlocutor " at once " and in order to see if it correctly represents what the parties intended,[27] particularly that the proposed new names of the child as they appear in the prayer of the petition have been correctly transcribed in the order; or to decide what further action, such as an appeal, should be taken.

The adoption order contains a direction to the Registrar to make an entry regarding the adoption in the Adopted Children Register with the proposed forenames and surname of the child and to mark the original entry in the Register of Births with the word " Adopted ".[28] Similarly, where an adopted child is adopted again the Registrar must mark the Adopted Children Register with the word " Re-adopted ".[29] Where the child has been adopted or re-adopted in England, the Registrar must on notification from the English Registrar mark the entry with the words " Adopted (England) " or " Re-adopted (England) " as the case may be, and similarly with adoptions granted in Northern Ireland, the Isle of Man or any of the Channel Islands. In the case of an adoption abroad, the Registrar must make an entry in the Register of Births consisting of the words " Proposed Foreign Adoption " or " Proposed Foreign Re-adoption " with the name of the country in which the order was made.[30] Clearly, where the birth of the child was registered outwith Scotland or where the child was never registered in any country (as was the case of a child found abandoned in Delhi), the Registrar's duty is limited to making an entry in the Adopted Children Register. For the sake of complete identification of a child born outwith the United Kingdom, the adoption order should, where possible, contain the date and place of birth of the child and details of the register in which the birth of the child was noted. Once the entry is made in the Adopted Children Register, an extract can be obtained as in the case of any of the other registers.

11.04 Sealing the process

In the case of an application to any court the process must immediately after

    (a) the communication to the Registrar General for Scotland of an

---

[25] A.S. 28 (1) (R.C. 229, personal delivery only).
[26] 1975 Act, s. 53.
[27] Lees, *Interlocutors*, pp. 1, 33.
[28] 1978 Act, s. 45 and Sched. 1, para. 1 (5).
[29] 1978 Act, s. 45 and Sched. 1, para. 1 (6).
[30] 1978 Act, s. 45 (3) and Sched. 1 para. 2 (4).

adoption order, an amendment to an adoption order or a revocation
of an adoption order being made, or

(b) the issue of an extract (if any)[31]

be enclosed by the clerk of court in a sealed envelope; and the sealed
envelope shall not be opened by the clerk of court, nor by any person having
the control of the records of any court.[32] Generally, the more recent records
are in the custody of the clerk of court, whereas the older records are
transmitted from time to time to the Scottish Record Office and the custody
of the Keeper of the Records of Scotland.[33] In terms of these provisions only
the officers mentioned have custody of the process: and on a strict
construction of the powers the sheriff or Lord Ordinary would have no *locus*
to permit or refuse to open up the process; however, in practice, the clerk
would discuss any doubtful application with the court. After the process has
been transmitted from the court, in law, the court has no control over this
aspect of the case, and in practice the Keeper of the Records of Scotland
deals with transmitted Court of Session processes.[34] The process in a
petition which was not granted does not require to be sealed up; and there is
no provision to the effect that rules about confidentiality still apply in such a
case. Certainly, where a second petition was presented, it would be very
necessary to have the earlier process before the court in order to determine
whether there had been " a change in circumstances."[35] Where an earlier
petition has been withdrawn, it would be desirable to reveal the
circumstances of that earlier petition in the later proceedings.

11.05 Access to the process

After the process has been sealed in a sealed envelope, not only may it
not be opened by the person having control of the records of the court, but
the process must not be made accessible to any person for 100 years after the
date of the adoption order except in certain situations.[36] The process may be
made available before the end of the 100-year period as follows:

(a) To an adopted child who has attained the age of 17 years, and to
whom the adoption order refers. Once the child has been satisfactorily
identified by the person having custody of the records of the court, he has an
indefeasible right to have access to the process. No formal application is
required. In replying to a written request, the sheriff clerk would no doubt
keep in mind that the applicant may not wish other members of his
household to know that he is writing, and may be under some stress; and in
these circumstances he may wish to use a plain envelope. It is desirable to
ask the applicant to telephone and arrange a time to see the process and to
tell the applicant to bring some means of identification. Most inquiries are
done personally: but it is submitted that the custodier of the records might
with propriety act on a request of an agent if he is satisfied that the identity of

---

[31] A.S. 27 (2) and (3) (R.C. 230 (3)).
[32] A.S. 28 (2) (R.C. 230 (4) where the extractor is substituted).
[33] Preservation of Sheriff Court Records Regulations 1969 (S.I. 1969 No. 1756), para. 5;
Public Records (Scotland) Act 1937, s. 2 (1); Public Registers and Records (Scotland) Act
1948.
[34] *Cf.* R.C. 32A.
[35] See para. 3.05.
[36] A.S. 28 (R.C. 230 (4)).

the child and that the authority of the agent are sufficiently vouched, particularly if the child lives at a distance, and all the more so if the child lives abroad: once the child knows the information he can tell whomsoever he likes; accordingly, there seems to be little objection to the child authorising an agent to seek out the information on his behalf. And in any event, bodies outwith the United Kingdom can petition the court for access to a process.[37] It may be desirable to have the agent give a written undertaking that he will only communicate the information to the child. The child should give ample notice in writing of his request so that the clerk of court can search out the process or discover whether it has been transmitted to Register House.[38] In some cases the information which the child may glean from the process may be unexpected and upsetting to the child; for example, the child may learn for the first time that he or she is an illegitimate child. Accordingly, especially in the case of a teenage child it may be prudent for the custodier of the records to suggest that the child be accompanied by a relative or friend on the visit to the court or Register House. There are provisions for counselling of those children who seek access to the records of the Registrar General for Scotland. If the process has been transmitted to the Register House from the court which granted the adoption order, and if the application is made to the court, no doubt the Keeper of the Records can re-transmit the process to the sheriff clerk there for the inspection of it by the child. There can be no objection to the child taking notes from the process or even having a copy made: no doubt the clerk of court would charge the appropriate fee for copying. The motives of the child in having access to the process do not matter; and there would appear to be no *locus* for the court to seek to counsel the child not to exercise his right. In addition, the child can at the age of 17 have access to the Adopted Children Register, the index thereto and such other necessary registers and books which are kept by the Register General for Scotland[39]; and when the Registrar General for Scotland gives the child such information he must advise the child that counselling services are available.[40] This counselling is optional. Further, the child and anyone else having reasons therefor can petition the court by whom the adoption order was pronounced to issue an extract,[41] but such a course is not common.

    (b) By or to the clerk of the court (or extractor) on the written application to him by
        (i) a local authority, or
        (ii) an adoption agency

with the consent of the adopted person for the purpose of ascertaining the name of the agency, if any, responsible for the placement of that person, and informing the applicant of that name.[42]

---

[37] See below, para. 11.05 (c).
[38] Transmissions of processes are authorised by orders of the Lord President made under Public Records (Scotland) Act 1937, Public Registers and Records (Scotland) Act 1948 and Preservation of Sheriff Court Records Regulations 1969 (S.I. 1969 No. 1756).
[39] 1978 Act, s. 45 (5).
[40] 1978 Act, s. 45 (6).
[41] A.S. 27 (2) (R.C. 230 (3)); see App. II.18.
[42] A.S. 28 (2) (*b*) (R.C. 230 (4) (*b*)).

(c) To a court, public authority or administrative board (whether in the United Kingdom or not) having power to authorise an adoption, on petition by it to the court which granted the original order requesting that information be made available from the process for the purpose of discharging its duties in considering an application for adoption and specifying the precise reasons for which access to the process is required.[43] In a case decided before the operation of the Succession (Scotland) Act 1964, s. 23—which altered the rights of succession between an adopted child and his parent—an adopted child died intestate leaving estate. His adoptive parents did not know the identity of the natural parents of the child. They presented a petition to the court craving access to the process in order to ascertain the names of the natural parents: the petition was granted.[44] In another unreported case the adoptive parents and child were taking up permanent residence in Italy and the Italian authorities required an affidavit from the court narrating the circumstances of the adoption: there the court entertained a petition by the parents to open up the process to enable the clerk to make an affidavit in respect of those matters.

(d) To a person who is authorised in writing by the Secretary of State to obtain information from the process for the purpose of such research as is designed to improve the working of adoption law and practice.[45] In several applications the Secretary of State for Scotland gave written authority to open up processes to enable the author of this book to check a step in procedure in a case where that information could not be got from the official report of the case or from the session papers and to those undertaking research on behalf of the Social Work Services Group of the Scottish Education Department.

There is no express provision in the adoption legislation authorising the opening up of the process when an appeal is marked; but it is a necessary implication of the general provisions governing appeals that in order to transmit the process to the sheriff-principal or to the principal clerk of session the sheriff clerk must open up the process and that all those connected with the appeal must have access to the process. Similarly, where an extract is sought after the process has been sealed up, it is necessarily implied that the court has power to open up the process; and in the Court of Session this power is expressly provided for.[46]

Where there is a subsidiary petition, such as one to revoke a direction to the Registrar General for Scotland or to amend an adoption order, it may be necessary for the court to have access to the original process. It is the practice to seal the subsidiary process and put it with the original process and seal them in a single envelope.

---

[43] A.S. 28 (2) (c) (R.C. 230 (4) (c) and (d)).
[44] *B. & B., Petitioners*, 1950 S.L.T.(Sh.Ct.) 34.
[45] A.S. 28 (2) (d) (R.C. 230 (4) (e)).
[46] R.C. 230 (2) (d); *E. & E., Petitioners*, Edinburgh Sheriff Court, 24 July 1985 (unreported); App. II.18.

CHAPTER 12

Amendment and Revocation

12.01 Scope of amendment and revocation

Amendment and revocation of adoption orders and rectification or cancellation of registers arises in four situations, apart from which the provisions for altering other vital records are to be found in Registration of Births, Deaths and Marriages (Scotland) Act 1965, ss. 42–44.

(a) The court may on the application of the adopter or the adopted person amend the order by the correction of any error in the particulars contained therein.[1] Unlike the situation in the next paragraph, the subject-matter of the application and the time for raising it are not limited. It is envisaged that the kind of situation where this provision would be resorted to would be where the original order recorded the wrong particulars of the child as in the case of a foundling where the true original names and the true date of birth emerged later; or where the court had to determine the probable date of birth,[2] and the actual information came to light later. It is submitted that this paragraph could not be used to correct a situation created by the petitioners or their agents whereby they *per incuriam* inserted the wrong name of the child in the prayer of the petition and that was correctly incorporated in the order and in the Adopted Children Register and failed to make an application under the next paragraph within its time limit of one year, because there is no error in the particulars in the adoption order.

(b) The court may if satisfied on the application of the adopter or the adopted person that within one year beginning with the date of the order any new name has been given to the adopted person (whether in baptism or otherwise), or taken by him, either in lieu of or in addition to the name specified in the particulars required to be entered in the adopted children register in pursuance of the order amend the order by substituting or adding that name in those particulars, as the case may require.[3] Normally, the petitioners state in the crave of the petition the proposed new names of the child and the adoption order and the entry in the Adopted Children Register will follow the crave: nevertheless, this provision permits alteration of these names if the giving or taking of the new name is made within one year of the granting of the order.[4] There are separate provisions of an analogous nature, without prejudice to these provisions, applying to persons whose births are registered in Scotland and to persons in respect of whom there is an entry in the Adopted Children Register.[5]

---

[1] 1978 Act, s. 45 (9), Sched. 1, para. 4 (1); App. II.19.
[2] 1978 Act, s. 45 (9) and Sched. 1, para. 1 (3).
[3] 1978 Act, s. 45 (9), Sched. 1, para. 4 (1) (*a*).
[4] See App. II.20.
[5] Registration of Births, Deaths and Marriages (Scotland) Act 1965, s. 43.

(c) If satisfied on the application of any person concerned that a direction for the marking of an entry in
  (i) the Register of Births, or
  (ii) the Adopted Children Register
was wrongly so included, the court may revoke that direction.[6]

(d) Where any person adopted by his father or mother alone has subsequently become a legitimated person on the marriage of his father and mother, the court by which the adoption order was made may, on the application of any of the parties concerned, revoke that order and the clerk of court must cause the revocation to be communicated to the Registrar General for Scotland who will cause to be cancelled
  (i) the entry in the Adopted Children Register relating to the adopted person, and
  (ii) the marking with the word "Adopted" or, as the case may be, with the word "(England)" of an entry relating to him in the Register of Births.[7]
This procedure is in conformity with the negative provision that where an illegitimate child has been adopted by one of his natural parents as sole adoptive parent and the adopter thereafter marries the other natural parent the provisions conferring legitimacy on an adopted child do not affect any enactment or rule of law whereby, by virtue of the marriage, the child is rendered the legitimate child of both natural parents.[8]

12.02 Procedure

Any application under these sections, apart from the first, is effected by petition to the court which pronounced the adoption order. The court may order such intimation as appears necessary, and in the case of a petition for revocation of an adoption order shall not grant the petition unless it is satisfied that the petition has been served on every parent of the child whose whereabouts can be ascertained.[9] Where appropriate the verification of the matters in the petition would depend on documentary evidence or the oral testimony of the petitioner or his witnesses who have knowledge of the matters. If the matter is in dispute, it may be necessary to have a more formal proof. As has been indicated, the manner of communication to the Registrar General for Scotland of an amendment to an adoption order or of a revocation of an adoption order under these sections is the same as in the case of an adoption order.[10] Where an adoption order is quashed, or an appeal against an adoption order is allowed by any court, the court must give directions to the Registrar General for Scotland to cancel any entry in the Adopted Children Register.[11]

---

[6] 1978 Act, s. 45 (9), Sched.1, para. 4 (1) (*b*); see App. II.21.
[7] 1978 Act, s. 45 (9) and Sched. 1.
[8] 1978 Act, s. 46 (1).
[9] A.S. 29 (R.C. 228).
[10] A.S. 28 (R.C. 229); see above, para. 11.03.
[11] 1978 Act, s. 45 (9) and Sched. 1, para. 4 (3).

CHAPTER 13

Appeal

13.01 Competency

The adoption legislation only mentions obliquely the right of appeal from the decision of a court of first instance[1]: but the general provisions applicable to the sheriff court, namely, the Sheriff Courts (Scotland) Act 1907, ss. 27 and 28, have been consistently adopted with regard to appeals from the sheriff (substitute) to the sheriff-principal[2]; or to the Court of Session[3]; and no doubt a further appeal from the sheriff-principal to the Court of Session, and a reclaiming motion for review of the interlocutor granting an adoption order pronounced in the Outer House in a petition for adoption are also competent.[4] There is a subsequent appeal to the House of Lords.[5] " Every judgment of an inferior Court is subject to review, unless such review is excluded expressly or by necessary implication;"[6] and " the presumption is that the ordinary forms of that Court are to be observed."[7] Surprisingly, in view of considerations of cost, there are very few appeals to the sheriff-principal. Appeals are almost always against the grant[8] or refusal of an adoption order[9] which are by their nature final interlocutors and presumably do not require leave to appeal or reclaim; but in one case the sheriff-substitute granted leave to appeal.[10] No doubt, an order freeing a child for adoption or an order revoking such an order, or an interim order is open to appeal in the same way. There appear to be no examples of appeals on incidental matters; but should such arise and require leave of the court[11] it is most unlikely that in view of the need for expedition and the relative simplicity of a petition for adoption that leave would be readily granted. In the Court of Session the interlocutor of the Lord Ordinary appointing a reporting officer before presentation of the petition " shall be final ".[12] The time for moving for leave to appeal in terms of the rules dealing with ordinary actions is seven days after the date of the interlocutor appealed against.[13] In an adoption process there is seldom any question of an extract

---

[1] e.g. 1978 Act, s. 45 and Sched. 1, para. 4 (3).
[2] A. & B., Petitioners, (1931) 67 Sh.Ct.Rep. 255; 1932 S.L.T.(Sh.Ct.) 37; C. v. D., 1968 S.L.T.(Sh.Ct.) 39.
[3] e.g. K., Petitioner, 1949 S.C. 140.
[4] R.C. 261, 262.
[5] e.g. A. v. B. & C., 1971 S.C.(H.L.) 129, a case which was initiated before the sheriff-substitute.
[6] Central Regional Council v. B., 1985 S.L.T. 413; Harper v. Inspector of Rutherglen (1903) 6 F. 23, per Lord Trayner at p. 25, quoted with approval in Acari v. Dumbartonshire County Council, 1948 S.L.T. 438; 1948 S.C. 62.
[7] Magistrates of Portobello v. Magistrates of Leith (1882) 10 R. 130.
[8] e.g. A. v. B. & C., 1971 S.C.(H.L.) 129.
[9] e.g. A.B. & C.B. v. X.'s Curator, 1963 S.C. 124.
[10] A.B. & C.B. v. X's Curator, 1963 S.C. 124.
[11] Sheriff Courts (Scotland) Act 1907, ss. 27 (f) and 28 (d); R.C. 264 (c).
[12] R.C. 225 (3).
[13] Sheriff Courts (Scotland) Act 1907, Sched. 1, r. 92 (1) (R.C. 264).

being given out—as is normal in an ordinary action—accordingly the time for appealing will not be curtailed by an extract being given out during that time. In England where the petitioners made inadequate inquiry as to the whereabouts of the natural mother, the court allowed the appeal out of time.[14] It may be that an appeal out of time could be made before the sheriff principal or in the Court of Session under the discretionary power of the court to

> "relieve any party from the consequences of any failure to comply with the provisions of these Rules which is shown to be due to mistake, oversight or other cause, not being wilful non-observance of the same, on such terms and conditions as shall appear to be just; and in any such case the Court may make such order as may be just by way of extension of time, lodging or amendment of papers or otherwise so as to enable the cause to proceed as if such failure had not happened."[15]

It would be the appellate court, not the court of first instance, which would exercise this discretion.[16]

13.02 The appellant

Usually the parties in an appeal are the persons who were parties in the court of first instance.[17] The term "party" is referred to in the legislation[18] but it is not defined. Presumably, anyone such as a person whose agreement was required but who did not compear because he was not aware of the proceedings in the court of first instance or of a diet in the proceedings could appeal. In England it has been held that where a natural parent whether or not she was a party within the meaning of the rules of court had her consent dispensed with while she was at a known address in Australia, the court had power to set the decision aside[19]; and a similar situation arose where a natural mother was not a respondent in the lower court because the petitioners had not, in the view of the appeal court, made adequate inquiry into the whereabouts of the natural mother.[20] Beyond that there is less certainty, for in procedure by petition unlike procedure by summons or initial writ there is no necessary contradictor who can become an appellant. It is a question whether other persons on whom notice of a hearing has been served,[21] but did not compear, or even persons on whom a notice could have been served but was not, could be treated as appellants. It would appear to be necessary in the interests of the child that the child or his curator *ad litem* who has the express duty of safeguarding these interests[22] should be able to appeal where, for example, the child's consent had not been given to the making of the adoption order. No doubt the decision of the court of first instance on incidental matters, such as an amendment of an adoption order,

---

[14] *Re F. (R.)* [1970] 1 Q.B. 385.
[15] Act of Sederunt (Rules of Court, Consolidation and Amendment) 1965 (S.I. 1965 No. 321); *cf. Richardson* v. *Minister of Pensions*, 1945 S.C. 363; Sheriff Courts (Scotland) Act 1907, Sched. 1, r. 1, which applies to ordinary actions but would presumably be applied to adoption petitions also: see above, notes 6 and 7.
[16] *Hardy* v. *Robinson; Johnstone* v. *W. Y. Walker*, 1985 S.L.T.(Sh.Ct.) 40.
[17] *e.g. A. B. & C.B.* v. *X's Curator*, 1963 S.C. 124; *A.* v. *B. & C.*, 1971 S.C.(H.L.) 129.
[18] *e.g.* 1978 Act, s. 46 (1); A.S. 24 (R.C. 230 (6) (*a*)).
[19] *Re B.* [1958] 1 Q.B. 12.
[20] *Re F. (R.)* [1970] 1 Q.B. 385.
[21] A.S. 8, 13, 22, (R.C. 220 (12), 221 (8), 222 (5) and 223 (2)).
[22] 1978 Act, s. 58 (1) (*a*).

which are initiated by petition (or note) or the removal of a child from the custody of a petitioner, which is dealt with by a minute, can be reviewed at the instance of those seeking or resisting such motions.[23]

13.03 Procedure

When an appeal is marked in the court of first instance, the clerk of the court will normally transmit the process to the appellate court according to the appropriate rules of court. If the sheriff has not appended a note to his interlocutor, it is anticipated that the appellant at the time of marking the appeal will add to the interlocutor sheet a request that the sheriff write a note: it has been said that it would not be right for the court to proceed to review what purported to be the exercise of a discretion by a sheriff-substitute without knowing whether he exercised his discretion at all or whether he exercised it upon proper grounds.[24] In any event, the sheriff is bound to append a note setting forth the grounds upon which he has proceeded.[25] In addition it is desirable that the reasons of a judge should be written with the least possible delay, lest the passage of time becomes a significant circumstance in the ultimate disposal of the case. No doubt the court can retain a copy or procure a copy of the process from the appeal court to enable the judge to write his note. Sheriffs have given their decision in the form of a Court of Session judgment[26]; or in the form of findings in fact and in law with a note of the grounds on which he has proceeded as was done by the sheriff in *A.B. & C.B.* v. *X.'s Curator*[27] and as is in conformity with rule 89. Once the diet for the appeal has been fixed there are no specialities of procedure except that the hearing takes place behind closed doors and the rules of confidentiality apply equally in the appeal court as in the court of first instance.[28]

13.04 Disposal of the appeal

The consistent unwillingness of the appellate courts to interfere with the decision of the courts of first instance is best illustrated by certain dicta in the House of Lords in English and Scottish decisions:

" Adoption cases depend so much on general impression rather than ascertainment of particular facts that, when the judge at first instance has seen the parties an appeal court must be slow to reverse his decision unless he has misdirected himself as to the law or has otherwise gone clearly wrong."[29]

" Parliament has entrusted the decision of this matter in the first instance to the county court and, for my part, I should be reluctant to disturb a decision without error of law upon a matter which must depend to a large extent upon the impression formed by the trial judge as to the character of the mother and other witnesses."[30]

---

[23] A.S. 29, 30 (R.C. 227, 228).
[24] *Hoggan* v. *McKeachie*, 1960 S.L.T. (Notes) 64.
[25] Sheriff Courts (Scotland) Act 1907, Sched. 1, r. 89.
[26] *A.* v. *B. & C.*, 1971 S.C.(H.L.) 129 and session papers.
[27] 1963 S.C. 124.
[28] 1978 Act, s. 57.
[29] *A.* v. *B. & C.*, 1971 S.C.(H.L.) 129 at 141, *per* Lord Reid.
[30] *Re W.* [1971] A.C. 682 at 724, *per* Lord Guest and quoted with approval in *A.* v. *B. & C.*, 1971 S.C.(H.L.) 129 at 147, *per* Lord Simon of Glaisdale.

"Where there has been no misdirection in law it must be quite exceptional for an appellate court to be justified in interfering with the decision of such a matter by the instance tribunal."[31]

However, in a case where the sheriff had misdirected himself the appeal court regarded itself as free to examine the merits and substitute its own discretion for that initially confided in the sheriff[32]; and in a case where the appeal court found that the sheriff-substitute was wrong in law in not dispensing with the consent of the natural mother, it recalled the interlocutor refusing the adoption order and remitted the case back to the sheriff to review all the considerations,[33] and in other cases where the sheriff-substitute had proceeded by interview of the parties, the appeal court remitted the cause back to him to hold a proof.[34] In another case where it was not clear from his note whether the sheriff had all the relevant considerations in mind the court remitted the cause back to the sheriff to report *quam primum*.[35] The Court of Session does not always issue written opinions in cases where a small point is in issue[36]; in two unreported appeals, the Inner House affirmed the decision of the sheriff without giving opinions[37] but in many other cases opinions have been given.[38]

---

[31] *Re D.* [1977] A.C. 602 at 637, *per* Lord Simon of Glaisdale.
[32] *H. & H., Petitioners*, 1976 S.L.T 80.
[33] *A. B. & C. B.* v. *X's Curator*, 1963 S.C. 124 at 136 and 138.
[34] *A. B.* v. *C. D.*, 1970 S.C. 268; *K., Petitioner*, 1949 S.C. 140; *C.* v. *D.*, 1968 S.L.T. (Sh.Ct.) 30.
[35] *A.* v. *B. & C.*, 1977 S.C. 27 at p. 32.
[36] *A., Petitioner*, 1936 S.C. 255; *B. & B., Petitioners*, 1936 S.C. 256; *C. & C., Petitioners*, 1936 S.C. 257; *D., Petitioner*, 1938 S.C. 223.
[37] Glasgow Sheriff Court, 3B/115/1978, Second Division, 23 Jan. 1981 (unreported); *A. & A.* v. *A.*, Second Division, 16 March 1983 (unreported).
[38] *e.g. A. & B.* v. *C.*, 1977 S.C. 27; *A. B.* v. *C. B.*, 1985 S.L.T. 514.

CHAPTER 14

Expenses

14.01 Expenses

Apart from the common law right inherent in every civil court to award expenses in any cause that comes before it,[1] a court of first instance in an adoption process may make such order with regard to the expenses of the petition, including the expenses of those making reports to the court, as it thinks fit and may modify such expenses or direct them to be taxed on such scale as it may determine.[2] In the normal unopposed petition the petitioners will pay their own expenses including court dues,[3] the account of their solicitor and usually included in that account the fee and expenses of the curator *ad litem* and reporting officer.

Since 1984, every regional council or islands council *must* in certain cases[4]:

(a) defray the expenses incurred by a member of a panel of curators *ad litem* and reporting officers established in their area, and

(b) pay to him such fees and allowances as they think fit.

The effect of the regulations is that from 1986, the local authority must pay these sums in all cases where the curator *ad litem* and reporting officer are appointed from the panel[5]; but there is a significant exception: the local authority is not empowered to pay the fees of the curator *ad litem* or reporting officer if

(a) the child was not placed by an adoption agency; and

(b) the adoption order, or the order to adopt a child abroad[6] is not granted by the court.

In the cases where there is a liability on them, the local authorities have agreed among themselves on a scale of fees both for normal and for extraordinary cases. Normally a curator *ad litem* or reporting officer who was drawn from the panel and who had been required to undertake additional work or to resolve unusual problems would render an account in respect of his extra work to the local authority. Usually the curator *ad litem* or reporting officer would ask the court to approve the additional remuneration either informally or by means of a formal interlocutor. These provisions do not affect the power of the court to deal with the expenses of the whole petition wherein an account of expenses and fee of the curator *ad*

---

[1] MacLaren, *Expenses*, 3.
[2] A.S. 31 (R.C. 230 (7)).
[3] Act of Sederunt (Fees for Sheriff Clerks) 1977, para. 4 (*b*) (iv), Sched., para. 19 (R.C. 346, para. 1).
[4] See above, para. 7.02.
[5] Curators *ad Litem* and Reporting Officers (Panels) (Scotland) Regulations 1984 (S.I. 1984 No. 566), reg. 10 (as amended by Curators *ad Litem* and Reporting Officers (Panels) (Scotland) Amendment Regulations 1985 (S.I. 1985 No. 1556), reg. 4.
[6] See above, para. 7.02.

litem and reporting officer would form only a part. Indeed, the provisions only identify who should pay these sums; they do not detract from the power of the court to make any order with regard to expenses. If the court, on the motion of the curator *ad litem* or the reporting officer, made an order assessing his fee at a sum greater than the local authorities had agreed to pay, no doubt the petitioners would be liable to pay the excess. It is thought, however, that the local authority would respect the court's determination in this matter. In addition to these local authority panels there are in most sheriff courts persons who are not on the local authority panels who (as envisaged in the legislation[7]) may be appointed by the sheriff to act as curators *ad litem* and reporting officers. Courts will no doubt prefer not to use the local authority panel in cases where the child was not placed by an adoption agency because there is no certainty of payment, because liability will only arise if the order is granted.[8] Sometimes the natural parent whose agreement has to be taken, lives in a local authority area different from the area in which the sheriff court dealing with the petition is. Then the court may appoint a member of the panel within its area and he would travel to the other area and look to his own local authority for payment; or the court may appoint a member of the panel in the other area who would look to that local authority for payment. No doubt considerations of economy would determine which course was adopted. Delay in paying the fee of the curator *ad litem* became a problem in some courts; and has been met by indicating to the solicitors at the time of lodging the petition that the court would expect that payment should normally be made as soon as the report had been lodged and suggesting that in cases where the petitioners were not assisted persons they should put the solicitors in funds at least to the extent of the fee in cases where the petitioners (and not the local authority) are liable to pay the fee; in cases where the local authority are liable to pay, arrangements should be made whereby the curator *ad litem* and reporting officer intimate to the local authority that the reports have been lodged. When the reports have been lodged and the curator *ad litem* or reporting officer intimates that fact, then fees should be paid within a matter of days. Although the report is not called for by the petitioner, but by the court, he may be in the first instance responsible for the fees and expenses of the reports:[9] the court could if no explanation for delay in payment were forthcoming make him personally liable. The style of petition includes in the prayer the words " and to pronounce such other or further orders or directions upon such matters, including the expenses of this petition, as the court may think fit."[10] Even in the event of opposition the question of expenses is seldom raised; and each side is liable for his own expenses. In a case where the question of expenses was raised, an unsuccessful respondent might be liable for such additional expenses as were occasioned by his intervention, or an unsuccessful petitioner might be liable for all or part of the expenses depending on the

---

[7] 1975 Act, s. 103 (1); see above, para. 7.02.
[8] See above, para. 7.02.
[9] Court of Session Practice Notes, 13 November 1969 and 9 July 1974, A.S. 18 (R.C. 230 (*f*)).
[10] A.S. Form 7 (R.C. Form 36).

nature of the circumstances. In one appeal which appeared to have little merit the Court of Session found the unsuccessful appellant liable in the expenses of the appeal but his liability was modified at nil.[11]

---

[11] Glasgow Adoption number 3B/115/1978, Second Division, 23 January 1981, unreported. As to legal aid see para. 5.07.

Appendices

Appendices

I Statutes and Acts of Sederunt

1. Adoption (Scotland) Act 1978

(1978 c.28)

An Act to consolidate the enactments relating to adoption in Scotland with amendments to give effect to recommendations of the Scottish Law Commission.   [20th July 1978]

PART I

THE ADOPTION SERVICE

The Adoption Service

Establishment of Adoption Service

[1] **1.**—(1) It is the duty of every local authority to establish and maintain within their area a service designed to meet the needs, in relation to adoption, of—

(*a*) children who have been or may be adopted;

(*b*) parents and guardians or such children; and

(*c*) persons who have adopted or may adopt a child;

and for that purpose to provide the requisite facilities, or secure that they are provided by approved adoption societies.

(2) The facilities to be provided as part of the service maintained under subsection (1) include—

(*a*) temporary board and lodging where needed by pregnant women, mothers or children;

(*b*) arrangements for assessing children and prospective adopters, and placing children for adoption;

(*c*) counselling for persons with problems relating to adoption.

(3) The facilities of the service maintained under subsection (1) shall be provided in conjunction with the local authority's other social services and with approved adoption societies in their area, so that help may be given in a co-ordinated manner without duplication, omission or avoidable delay.

(4) The services maintained by local authorities under subsection (1) may be collectively referred to as "the Scottish Adoption Service", and a local authority or approved adoption society may be referred to as an adoption agency.

NOTE

[1] See the Foster Children (Scotland) Act 1984, s.2(5).

Local authorities' social work

2. The social services referred to in section 1(3) are the functions of a local authority which stand referred to the authority's social work committee, including, in particular but without prejudice to the generality of the foregoing, a local authority's functions relating to—

(*a*) the promotion of the welfare of children by diminishing the need to receive children into care of keep then in care, including (in exceptional circumstances) the giving of assistance in cash;

(*b*) the welfare of children in the care of a local authority;

[1] (*c*) the welfare of children who are foster children within the meaning of the Foster Children (Scotland) Act 1984;

(*d*) children who are subject to supervision orders made in matrimonial or custody proceedings;

(*e*) the provision of residential accommodation for expectant mothers and young children and of day-care facilities;

NOTE

[1] As amended by the Foster Children (Scotland) Act 1984, with effect from 31 January 1985.

(*f*) the regulation and inspection of nurseries and child minders;
(*g*) care and other treatment of children through court proceedings and children's hearings.

Adoption societies

Approval of adoption societies

3.—[1] (1) Subject to regulations under section 9(1), a body which is a voluntary organisation and desires to act as an adoption society or, if it is already an adoption society, desires to continue to act as such may, in the manner specified by regulations made by the Secretary of State, apply to the Secretary of State for his approval to its doing so.

(2) On an application under subsection (1), the Secretary of State shall take into account the matters relating to the applicant specified in subsections (3) to (5) and any other relevant considerations, and if, but only if, he is satisfied that the applicant is likely to make, or, if the applicant is an approved adoption society, is making, an effective contribution to the Scottish Adoption Service, he shall by notice to the applicant give his approval, which shall be operative from a date specified in the notice or, in the case of a renewal of approval, from the date of the notice.

(3) In considering the application, the Secretary of State shall have regard, in relation to the period for which approval is sought, to the following—

(*a*) the applicant's adoption programme, including, in particular, its ability to make provision for children who are free for adoption,
(*b*) the number and qualifications of its staff,
(*c*) its financial resources, and
(*d*) the organisation and control of its operations.

(4) Where it appears to the Secretary of State that the applicant is likely to operate extensively within the area of a particular local authority he shall ask the authority whether they support the application, and shall take account of any views about it put to him by the authority.

(5) Where the applicant is already an approved adoption society or, whether before or after the passing of this Act, previously acted as an adoption society, the Secretary of State, in considering the application, shall also have regard to the record and reputation of the applicant in the adoption field, and the areas within which and the scale on which it is currently operating or has operated in the past.

(6) If after considering the application the Secretary of State is not satisfied that the applicant is likely to make or, as the case may be, is making an effective contribution to the Scottish Adoption Service, the Secretary of State shall, subject to section 5(1) and (2), by notice inform the applicant that its application is refused.

(7) If not withdrawn earlier under section 4, approval given under this section shall last for a period of three years from the date on which it becomes operative, and shall then expire or, in the case of an approved adoption society whose further application for approval is pending at that time, shall expire on the date that application is granted or, as the case may be, refused.

NOTE
[1] As amended by the Health and Social Services and Social Security Adjudications Act 1983, Sched. 2, para. 38.

Withdrawal of approval

4.—(1) If, while approval of a body under section 3 is operative, it appears to the Secretary of State that the body is not making an effective contribution to the Scottish Adoption Service he shall, subject to section 5(3) and (4), by notice to the body withdraw the approval from a date specified in the notice.

(2) If an approved adoption society fails to provide the Secretary of State with information required by him for the purposes of carrying out his

functions under subsection (1), or fails to verify such information in the manner required by him, he may by notice to the society withdraw the approval from a day specified in the notice.

(3) Where approval is withdrawn under subsection (1) or (2) or expires the Secretary of State may direct the body concerned to make such arrangements as to children who are in its care and other transitional matters as seem to him expedient.

Procedure on refusal to approve, or withdrawal of approval from, adoption societies

5. —(1) Before notifying a body which has applied for approval that the application is refused in accordance with section 3(6) the Secretary of State shall serve on the applicant a notice—

(a) setting out the reasons why he proposes to refuse the application;
(b) informing the applicant that it may make representations in writing to the Secretary of State within 28 days of the date of service of the notice.

(2) If any representations are made by the applicant in accordance with subsection (1), the Secretary of State shall give further consideration to the application taking into account those representations.

(3) The Secretary of State shall, before withdrawing approval of an adoption society in accordance with section 4(1), serve on the society a notice—

(a) setting out the reasons why he proposes to withdraw the approval; and
(b) informing the society that it may make representations in writing to the Secretary of State within 28 days of the date of service of the notice.

(4) If any representations are made by the society in accordance with subsection (3), the Secretary of State shall give further consideration to the withdrawal of approval under section 4(1) taking into account those representations.

(5) This section does not apply where the Secretary of State, after having considered any representations made by the applicant in accordance with this section, proposes to refuse approval or, as the case may be, to withdraw approval for reasons which have already been communicated to the applicant in a notice under this section.

Welfare of children

Duty to promote welfare of child

6. In reaching any decision relating to the adoption of a child, a court or adoption agency shall have regard to all the circumstances, first considera-tion being given to the need to safeguard and promote the welfare of the child throughout his childhood; and shall so far as practicable ascertain the wishes and feelings of the child regarding the decision and give due consideration to them, having regard to his age and understanding.

Religious upbringing of adopted child

7. An adoption agency shall in placing a child for adoption have regard (so far as is practicable) to any wishes of the child's parents and guardians as to the religious upbringing of the child.

Supplemental

Inactive or defunct adoption societies

8. —(1) If it appears to the Secretary of State that an approved adoption society, or one in relation to which approval has been withdrawn under section 4 or has expired, is inactive or defunct he may, in relation to any

[121]

child who is or was in the care of the society, direct what appears to him to be the appropriate local authority to take any such action as might have been taken by the society or by the society jointly with the authority; and if apart from this section the authority would not be entitled to take that action, or would not be entitled to take it without joining the society in the action, it shall be entitled to do so.

(2) Before giving a direction under subsection (1) the Secretary of State shall, if practicable, consult both the society and the authority.

Regulation of adoption agencies

9.—(1) The Secretary of State may by regulations prohibit unincorporated bodies from applying for approval under section 3; and he shall not approve any unincorporated body whose application is contrary to regulations made under this subsection.

(2) The Secretary of State may make regulations for any purpose relating to the exercise of its functions by an approved adoption society.

(3) The Secretary of State may make regulations with respect to the exercise by local authorities of their functions of making or participating in arrangements for the adoption of children.

¹ (4) Any person who contravenes or fails to comply with regulations made under subsection (2) shall be guilty of an offence and liable on summary conviction to a fine not exceeding level 5 on the standard scale.

(5) Regulations under this section may make different provisions in relation to different cases or classes of cases and may exclude certain cases or classes of cases.

NOTE
¹ As amended by virtue of the Criminal Procedure (Scotland) Act 1975, ss.289F and 289G.

10. [Repealed by the Health and Social Services and Social Security Adjudications Act 1983, Sched. 2, para. 39 and Sched. 10.]

Restriction on arranging adoptions and placing of children

11.—(1) A person other than an adoption agency shall not make arrangements for the adoption of a child, or place a child for adoption, unless the proposed adopter is a relative of the child.

(2) An adoption society approved as respects England and Wales under section 3 of the Adoption Act 1976, but which is not approved under section 3 of this Act, shall not act as an adoption society in Scotland except to the extent that the society considers it necessary to do so in the interests of a person mentioned in section 1 of that Act.

¹ (3) A person who—
- (*a*) takes part in the management or control of a body of persons which exists wholly or partly for the purpose of making arrangements for the adoption of children and which is not an approved adoption society or a local authority; or
- (*b*) contravenes subsection (1); or
- (*c*) receives a child placed with him in contravention of subsection (1),

shall be guilty of an offence and liable on summary conviction to imprisonment for a term not exceeding three months or to a fine not exceeding level 5 on the standard scale or to both.

(4) In any proceedings for an offence under paragraph (*a*) of subsection

(3), proof of things done or of words written, spoken or published (whether or not in the presence of any party to the proceedings) by any person taking part in the management or control of a body of persons, or in making arrangements for the adoption of children on behalf of the body, shall be sufficient evidence of the purpose for which that body exists.

(5) Section 26 shall apply where a person is convicted of a contravention of subsection (1) as it applies where an application for an adoption order is refused.

NOTE

[1] As amended by virtue of the Criminal Procedure (Scotland) Act 1975, ss.289F and 289G.

PART II

ADOPTION ORDERS

The making of adoption orders

Adoption orders

12.—(1) An adoption order is an order vesting the parental rights and duties relating to a child in the adopters, made on their application by an authorised court.

(2) The order does not affect the parental rights and duties so far as they relate to any period before the making of the order.

(3) The making of an adoption order operates to extinguish—

    (*a*) any parental right or duty relating to the child which immediately before the making of the order was vested in a person (not being one of the adopters) who was—

        (i) a parent of the child, or

        (ii) a tutor, curator or other guardian of the child appointed by a deed or by the order of a court;

    (*b*) any duty owed to or by the child—

        (i) to pay or provide aliment in respect of any period occurring after the making of the order;

        (ii) to make any payment arising out of parental rights and duties in respect of such a period.

(4) Nothing in subsection (3) shall—

    (*a*) extinguish any duty arising under a deed or agreement which constitutes a trust or which expressly provides that the duty is not to be extinguished by the making of an adoption order;

    (*b*) of itself terminate the appointment or functions of any judicial factor loco tutoris or curator bonis appointed to administer the whole or any part of the child's estate.

(5) An adoption order may not be made in relation to a child who is or has been married.

(6) An adoption order may contain such terms and conditions as the court thinks fit.

(7) An adoption order may be made notwithstanding that the child is already an adopted child.

(8) An adoption order shall not be made in relation to a child who is a minor unless with the consent of the minor; except that where the court is satisfied that the minor is incapable of giving his consent to the making of the order, it may dispense with that consent.

Child to live with adopters before order made

13.—(1) Where the applicant, or one of the applicants, is a parent, step-parent or relative of the child, or the child was placed with the applicants by an adoption agency, an adoption order shall not be made unless the child is at least nineteen weeks old and at all times during the preceding thirteen weeks had his home with the applicants or one of them.

[123]

(2) Where subsection (1) does not apply, an adoption order shall not be made unless the child is at least twelve months old and at all times during the preceding twelve months had his home with the applicants or one of them.

(3) An adoption order shall not be made unless the court is satisfied that sufficient opportunities to see the child with the applicant, or, in the case of an application by a married couple, both applicants together in the home environment have been afforded—

(a) where the child was placed with the applicant by an adoption agency, to that agency, or

(b) in any other case, to the local authority within whose area the home is.

Adoption by married couple

14.—(1) Subject to section 53 (1) of the Children Act 1975 (which provides for the making of a custody order instead of an adoption order in certain cases) an adoption order may be made on the application of a married couple where each has attained the age of twenty-one years but an adoption order shall not otherwise be made on the application of more than one person.

(2) An adoption order shall not be made on the application of a married couple unless—

(a) at least one of them is domiciled in a part of the United Kingdom, or in the Channel Islands or the Isle of Man, or

(b) the application is for a Convention adoption order and section 17 is complied with.

Adoption by one person

15.—(1) Subject to section 53 (1) of the Children Act 1975 (which provides for the making of a custody order instead of an adoption order in certain cases) an adoption order may be made on the application of one person where he has attained the age of twenty-one years and—

(a) is not married, or

(b) is married and the court is satisfied that—

(i) his spouse cannot be found, or

(ii) the spouses have separated and are living apart, and the separation is likely to be permanent, or

(iii) his spouse is by reason of ill-health, whether physical or mental, incapable of making an application for an adoption order.

(2) An adoption order shall not be made on the application of one person unless—

(a) he is domiciled in a part of the United Kingdom, or in the Channel Islands or the Isle of Man, or

(b) the application is for a Convention adoption order and section 17 is complied with.

(3) An adoption order shall not be made on the application of the mother or father of the child alone unless the court is satisfied that—

(a) the other natural parent is dead or cannot be found, or

(b) there is some other reason justifying the exclusion of the other natural parent,

and where such an order is made the reason justifying the exclusion of the other natural parent shall be recorded by the court.

Parental agreement

16.—(1) An adoption order shall not be made unless—

(a) the child is free for adoption by virtue of an order made in England and Wales under section 18 of the Adoption Act 1976 and not revoked, or made in Scotland under section 18 and not revoked; or

    (*b*) in the case of each parent or guardian of the child the court is satisfied that—

        (i) he freely, and with full understanding of what is involved, agrees unconditionally to the making of an adoption order (whether or not he knows the identify of the applicants), or

        (ii) his agreement to the making of the adoption order should be dispensed with on a ground specified in subsection (2).

(2) The grounds mentioned in subsection (1) (*b*) (ii) are that the parent or guardian—

    (*a*) cannot be found or is incapable of giving agreement;

    (*b*) is withholding his agreement unreasonably;

    (*c*) has persistently failed without reasonable cause to discharge the parental duties in relation to the child;

    (*d*) has abandoned or neglected the child;

    (*e*) has persistently ill-treated the child;

    (*f*) has seriously ill-treated the child (subject to subsection (5)).

(3) Subsection (1) does not apply in any case where the child is not a United Kingdom national and the application for the adoption order is for a Convention adoption order.

(4) Agreement is ineffective for the purposes of subsection (1) (*b*) (i) if given by the mother less than six weeks after the child's birth.

(5) Subsection (2) (*f*) does not apply unless (because of the ill-treatment or for other reasons) the rehabilitation of the child within the household of the parent or guardian is unlikely.

Convention adoption order

17.—(1) An adoption order shall be made as a Convention adoption order if the application is for a Convention adoption order and the following conditions are satisfied both at the time of the application and when the order is made.

(2) The child—

    (*a*) must be a United Kingdom national or a national of a Convention country, and

    (*b*) must habitually reside in British territory or a Convention country, and

    (*c*) must not be, or have been, married.

(3) The applicant or applicants and the child must not all be United Kingdom nationals living in British territory.

(4) If the application is by a married couple, either—

    (*a*) each must be a United Kingdom national or a national of a Convention country, and both must habitually reside in Great Britain, or

    (*b*) both must be United Kingdom nationals, and each must habitually reside in British territory or a Convention country,

and if the applicants are nationals of the same Convention country the adoption must not be prohibited by a specified provision (as defined in subsection (8)) of the internal law of that country.

(5) If the application is by one person, either—

    (*a*) he must be a United Kingdom national or a national of a Convention country, and must habitually reside in Great Britain, or

    (*b*) he must be a United Kingdom national and must habitually reside in British territory or a Convention country,

and if he is a national of a Convention country the adoption must not be prohibited by a specified provision (as defined in subsection (8)) of the internal law of that country.

(6) If the child is not a United Kingdom national the order shall not be made—

(a) except in accordance with the provisions, if any, relating to consents and consultations of the internal law relating to adoption of the Convention country of which the child is a national, and

(b) unless the court is satisfied that each person who consents to the order in accordance with that internal law does so with full understanding of what is involved.

(7) The reference to consents and consultations in subsection (6) does not include a reference to consent by and consultation with the applicant and members of the applicant's family (including his or her spouse), and for the purposes of subsection (6) consents may be proved in the manner prescribed by act of sederunt and the court shall be treated as the authority by whom, under the law mentioned in subsection (6), consents may be dispensed with and the adoption in question may be effected; and where the provisions there mentioned require the attendance before that authority of any person who does not reside in Great Britain, that requirement shall be treated as satisfied for the purposes of subsection (6) if—

(a) that person has been given a reasonable opportunity of communicating his opinion on the adoption in question to the proper officer or clerk of the court, or to an appropriate authority of the country in question, for transmission to the court; and

(b) where he has availed himself of that opportunity, his opinion has been transmitted to the court.

(8) In subsections (4) and (5) "specified provision" means a provision specified in an order of the Secretary of State as one notified to the Government of the United Kingdom in pursuance of the provisions of the Convention which relate to prohibitions on an adoption contained in the national law of the Convention country in question.

Freeing for adoption

Freeing child for adoption

18.—(1) Where, on an application by an adoption agency, an authorised court is satisfied in the case of each parent or guardian of the child that—

(a) he freely, and with full understanding of what is involved, agrees generally and unconditionally to the making of an adoption order, or

(b) his agreement to the making of an adoption order should be dispensed with on a ground specified in section 16(2),

the court shall, subject to subsection (8), make an order declaring the child free for adoption.

(2) No application shall be made under subsection (1) unless—

(a) it is made with the consent of a parent or guardian of a child, or

(b) the adoption agency is applying for dispensation under subsection (1)(b) of the agreement of each parent or guardian of the child, and the child is in the care of the adoption agency.

(3) No agreement required under subsection (1)(a) shall be dispensed with under subsection (1)(b) unless the child is already placed for adoption or the court is satisfied that it is likely that the child will be placed for adoption.

(4) An agreement by the mother of the child is ineffective for the purposes of this section if given less than six weeks after the child's birth.

(5) On the making of an order under this section the parental rights and duties relating to the child vest in the adoption agency, and subsections (2) and (3) of section 12 apply as if the order were an adoption order and the agency were the adopters.

¹ (6) Before making an order under this section, the court shall satisfy

itself, in relation to each parent or guardian of the child who can be found, that he has been given an opportunity of making, if he so wishes, a declaration that he prefers not to be involved in future questions concerning the adoption of the child; and any such declaration shall be recorded by the court.

(7) Before making an order under this section in the case of an illegitimate child whose father is not its guardian, the court shall satisfy itself in relation to any person claiming to be the father that either—

(a) he has no intention of applying for custody of the child under section 2 of the Illegitimate Children (Scotland) Act 1930, or

(b) if he did apply for custody under that section the application would be likely to be refused.

(8) An order under this section shall not be made in relation to a child who is a minor unless with the consent of the child; except that where the court is satisfied that the minor is incapable of giving his consent to the making of the order, it may dispense with that consent.

NOTE

[1] As amended by the Health and Social Services and Social Security Adjudications Act 1983, Sched. 2, para. 40.

Progress reports to former parent

19.—(1) This section and section 20 apply to any person ("the former parent") who was required to be given an opportunity of making a declaration under section 18(6) but did not do so.

(2) Within the fourteen days following the date twelve months after the making of the order under section 18, the adoption agency in which the parental rights and duties were vested on the making of the order, unless it has previously by notice to the former parent informed him that an adoption order has been made in respect of the child, shall by notice to the former parent inform him—

(a) whether an adoption order has been made in respect of the child, and (if not)

(b) whether the child has his home with a person with whom he has been placed for adoption.

(3) If at the time when the former parent is given notice under subsection (2) an adoption order has not been made in respect of the child, it is thereafter the duty of the adoption agency to give notice to the former parent of the making of an adoption order (if and when made), and meanwhile to give the former parent notice whenever the child is placed for adoption or ceases to have his home with a person with whom he has been placed for adoption.

(4) If at any time the former parent by notice makes a declaration to the adoption agency that he prefers not to be involved in future questions concerning the adoption of the child—

(a) the agency shall secure that the declaration is recorded by the court which made the order under section 18, and

(b) the agency is released from the duty of complying further with subsection (3) as respects that former parent.

Revocation of s.18 order

20.—(1) The former parent, at any time more than 12 months after the making of the order under section 18 when—

(a) no adoption order has been made in respect of the child, and

(b) the child does not have his home with a person with whom he has been placed for adoption,

may apply to the court which made the order for a further order revoking it on the ground that he wishes to resume the parental rights and duties.

(2) While the application is pending the adoption agency having the parental rights and duties shall not place the child for adoption without the leave of the court.

(3) Where an order freeing a child for adoption is revoked under this section—
  (a) the parental rights and duties relating to the child are vested in the individual or, as the case may be, the individuals in whom they vested immediately before that order was made;
  (b) if the parental rights and duties, or any of them, vested in a local authority or voluntary organisation immediately before the order freeing the child for adoption was made, those rights and duties are vested in the individual or, as the case may be, the individuals in whom they vested immediately before they were vested in the authority or organisation; and
  (c) any duty extinguished by virtue of section 12(3)(b) of the Adoption Act 1976 or of section 12(3)(b) is forthwith revived,
but the revocation does not affect any right or duty so far as it relates to any period before the date of the revocation.

(4) Subject to subsection (5), if the application is dismissed on the ground that to allow it would contravene the principle embodied in section 6—
  (a) the former parent who made the application shall not be entitled to make any further application under subsection (1) in respect of the child, and
  (b) the adoption agency is released from the duty of complying further with section 19(3) as respects that parent.

(5) Subsection (4)(a) shall not apply where the court which dismissed the application gives leave to the former parent to make a further application under subsection (1), but such leave shall not be given unless it appears to the court that because of a change in circumstances or for any other reason it is proper to allow the application to be made.

Transfer of parental rights and duties between adoption agencies

21. On the joint application of an adoption agency in which the parental rights and duties relating to a child who is in Scotland are vested under section 18(5) or this section or under section 18(5) or 21 of the Adoption Act 1976, and any other adoption agency, an authorised court may if it thinks fit by order transfer the parental rights and duties to the latter agency.

Supplemental

Notification to local authority of adoption application

22.—(1) An adoption order shall not be made in respect of a child who was not placed with the applicant by an adoption agency unless the applicant has, at least three months before the date of the order, given notice to the local authority within whose area he has his home of his intention to apply for the adoption order.

(2) On receipt of such a notice the local authority shall investigate the matter and submit to the court a report of their investigation.

(3) Under subsection (2), the local authority shall in particular investigate,—
  (a) so far as is practicable, the suitability of the applicant, and any other matters relevant to the operation of section 6 in relation to the application; and
  (b) whether the child was placed with the applicant in contravention of section 11.

(4) A local authority which receives notice under subsection (1) in respect of a child whom the authority know to be in the care of another local authority shall, not more than 7 days after the receipt of the notice, inform that other local authority in writing that they have received the notice.

[128]

Reports where child placed by agency

23. Where an application for an adoption order relates to a child placed by an adoption agency, the agency shall submit to the court a report on the suitability of the applicants and any other matters relevant to the operation of section 6, and shall assist the court in any manner the court may direct.

Restrictions on making adoption orders

24.—(1) The court shall not proceed to determine an application for an adoption order in relation to a child where a previous application for a British adoption order made in relation to the child by the same persons was refused by any court unless—

    (*a*) in refusing the previous application the court directed that this subsection should not apply, or

    (*b*) it appears to the court that because of a change in circumstances or for any other reason it is proper to proceed with the application.

  ¹ (2) The court shall not make an adoption order in relation to a child unless it is satisfied that the applicants have not, as respects the child, contravened section 51.

NOTE

  ¹ As amended by the Health and Social Services and Social Security Adjudications Act 1983, Sched. 2, para. 41.

Interim orders

25.—(1) Where on an application for an adoption order the requirements of sections 16(1) and 22(1) are complied with, the court may postpone the determination of the application and make an order vesting the custody of the child in the applicants for a probationary period not exceeding two years upon such terms for the aliment of the child and otherwise as the court thinks fit.

(2) Where the probationary period specified in an order under subsection (1) is less than two years, the court may by a further order extend the period to a duration not exceeding two years in all.

Care etc. of child on refusal of adoption order

26.—(1) Where on an application for an adoption order in relation to a child under the age of sixteen years the court refuses to make the adoption order then—

    (*a*) if it appears to the court that there are exceptional circumstances making it desirable that the child should be under the supervision of an independent person, the court may order that the child shall be under the supervision of a specified local authority;

    (*b*) if it appears to the court that there are exceptional circumstances making it impracticable or undesirable for the child to be entrusted to either of the parents or to any other individual, the court may by order commit the child to the care of a specified local authority.

(2) Where the court makes an order under subsection (1)(*b*), the order may require the payment by either parent to the local authority, while it has the care of the child, of such weekly or other periodical sum towards the aliment of the child as the court thinks reasonable.

(3) Subsections (2), (4) and (5) of section 11 of the Guardianship Act 1973 (jurisdiction and orders relating to care and custody of children) apply in relation to an order under this section as they apply in relation to an order under that section.

PART III

CARE AND PROTECTION OF CHILDREN AWAITING ADOPTION

Restrictions on removal of children

Restrictions on removal where adoption agreed or application made under s.18

  ¹ **27.**—(1) While an application for an adoption order is pending in a case

where a parent or guardian of the child has agreed to the making of the adoption order (whether or not he knows the identity of the applicant), the parent or guardian is not entitled, against the will of the person with whom the child has his home, to remove the child from the care and possession of that person except with the leave of the court.

(2) While an application is pending for an order freeing a child for adoption and—

(*a*) the child is in the care of the adoption agency making the application, and

(*b*) the application was not made with the consent of each parent or guardian of the child,

no parent or guardian of the child who did not consent to the application is entitled, against the will of the person with whom the child has his home, to remove the child from the care and possession of that person except with the leave of the court.

[2] (3) Any person who contravenes subsection (1) or (2) shall be guilty of an offence and liable on summary conviction to imprisonment for a term not exceeding three months or a fine not exceeding level 5 on the standard scale or both.

(4), (5) [Repealed by the Health and Social Services and Social Security Adjudications Act 1983, Sched. 2, para. 42, and Sched. 10.]

NOTES

[1] As amended by the Health and Social Services and Social Security Adjudications Act 1983, Sched. 2, para. 43.

[2] As amended by virtue of the Criminal Procedure (Scotland) Act 1975, ss.289F and 289G.

Restrictions on removal where applicant has provided home for five years

[1] **28.**—(1) While an application for an adoption order in respect of a child made by the person with whom the child has had his home for the five years preceding the application is pending, no person is entitled, against the will of the applicant, to remove the child from the applicant's care and possession except with the leave of the court or under authority conferred by any enactment or on the arrest of the child.

(2) Where a person ("the prospective adopter") gives notice to the local authority within whose area he has his home that he intends to apply for an adoption order in respect of a child who for the preceding five years has had his home with the prospective adopter, no person is entitled, against the will of the prospective adopter, to remove the child from the prospective adopter's care and possession, except with the leave of the court or under authority conferred by any enactment or on the arrest of the child, before—

(*a*) the prospective adopter applies for the adoption order, or

(*b*) the period of three months from the receipt of the notice by the local authority expires,

whichever occurs first.

(3) In any case where subsection (1) or (2) applies and—

(*a*) the child was in the care of a local authority before he began to have his home with the applicant or, as the case may be, the prospective adopter, and

(*b*) the child remains in the care of a local authority,

the authority in whose care the child is shall not remove the child from the care and possession of the applicant or of the prospective adopter except in accordance with section 30 or 31 or with leave of a court.

(4) Subsection (3) does not apply where the removal of the child is authorised, in terms of Part III of the Social Work (Scotland) Act 1968, by a justice of the peace or a children's hearing.

(5) A local authority which receives such notice as is mentioned in subsection (2) in respect of a child whom the authority know to be in the care

of another local authority or of a voluntary organisation, shall, not more than seven days after the receipt of the notice, inform that other authority or the organisation in writing that they have received the notice.

(6) Subsection (2) does not apply to any further notice served by the prospective adopter on any local authority in respect of the same child during the period referred to in paragraph (*b*) of that subsection or within 28 days after its expiry.

[2] (7) Any person who contravenes subsection (1) or (2) shall be guilty of an offence and liable on summary conviction to imprisonment for a term not exceeding three months or a fine not exceeding level 5 on the standard scale or both.

(8), (9) [Repealed by the Health and Social Services and Social Security Adjudications Act 1983, Sched. 2, para. 42, and Sched. 10.]

(10) The Secretary of State may by order amend subsection (1) or (2) to substitute a different period for the period of five years mentioned in that subsection (or the period which by a previous order under this subsection, was substituted for that period).

(11) In subsections (2) and (3) "a court" means a court having jurisdiction to make adoption orders.

NOTES

[1] As amended by the Health and Social Services and Social Security Adjudications Act 1983, Sched. 2, para. 43.

[2] As amended by virtue of the Criminal Procedure (Scotland) Act 1975, ss.289F and 289G.

Return of child taken away in breach of s.27 or 28

29.—(1) An authorised court may on the application of a person from whose care and possession a child has been removed in breach of section 27 or 28, or section 27 or 28 of the Adoption Act 1976 order the person who has so removed the child to return the child to the applicant.

(2) An authorised court may on the application of a person who has reasonable grounds for believing that another person is intending to remove the child from the applicant's care and possession in breach of section 27 or 28, or section 27 or 28 of the Adoption Act 1976 by order direct that other person not to remove the child from the applicant's care and possession in breach of section 27 or 28, or section 27 or 28 of the Adoption Act 1976.

NOTE

[1] As amended by the Health and Social Services and Social Security Adjudications Act 1983, Sched. 2, paras. 43 and 44.

Return of children placed for adoption by adoption agencies

30.—(1) Subject to subsection (2), at any time after a child has been delivered into the care and possession of any person in pursuance of arrangements made by an approved adoption society or local authority for the adoption of the child by that person, and before an adoption order has been made on the application of that person in respect of the child—

    (*a*) that person may give notice in writing to the society or authority of his intention not to retain the care and possession of the child; or

    (*b*) the society or authority may cause notice in writing to be given to that person of their intention not to allow the child to remain in his care and possession.

(2) No notice under paragraph (*b*) of subsection (1) shall be given in respect of a child in relation to whom an application has been made for an adoption order except with the leave of the court to which the application has been made.

(3) Where a notice is given to an adoption society or local authority by any person, or by such a society or authority to any person, under subsection (1), or where an application for an adoption order made by any person in respect of a child placed in his care and possession by such a society or authority is refused by the court or withdrawn, that person shall,

within seven days after the date on which notice was given or the application refused or withdrawn, as the case may be, cause the child to be returned to the society or authority, who shall receive the child.

(4) Where the period specified in an interim order made under section 25 (whether as originally made or as extended under subsection (2) of that section) expires without an adoption order having been made in respect of the child, subsection (3) shall apply as if the application for an adoption order upon which the interim order was made had been refused at the expiration of that period.

(5) It shall be sufficient compliance with the requirements of subsection (3) if the child is delivered to, and is received by, a suitable person nominated for the purpose by the adoption society or local authority.

(6) Where an application for an adoption order is refused the court may, if it thinks fit at any time before the expiry of the period of seven days mentioned in subsection (3), order that period to be extended to a duration, not exceeding six weeks, specified in the order.

[1] (7) Any person who contravenes the provisions of this section shall be guilty of an offence and liable on summary conviction to imprisonment for a term not exceeding three months or to a fine not exceeding level 5 on the standard scale or to both; and the court by which the offender is convicted may order the child in respect of whom the offence is committed to be returned to his parent or guardian or to the adoption society or local authority which made the arrangements referred to in subsection (1).

NOTE

[1] As amended by virtue of the Criminal Procedure (Scotland) Act 1975, ss.289F and 289G.

Application of s.30 where child not placed for adoption

31.—(1) Where a person gives notice in pursuance of section 22(1) to the local authority within whose area he has his home of his intention to apply for an adoption order in respect of a child who is for the time being in the care of a local authority, not being a child who was delivered into the care and possession of that person in pursuance of such arrangements as are mentioned in section 30(1), that section shall apply as if the child had been so delivered, except that where the application is refused by the court or withdrawn the child need not be returned to the local authority in whose care he is unless that authority so require.

(2) Where notice of intention is given as aforesaid in respect of any child who for the time being in the care of a local authority then, until the application for an adoption order has been made and disposed of, any right of the local authority to require the child to be returned to them otherwise than in pursuance of section 30 shall be suspended.

(3) While the child remains in the care and possession of the person by whom the notice is given no contribution shall be payable (whether under a contribution order or otherwise) in respect of the child by any person liable under section 78 of the Social Work (Scotland) Act 1968 to make contributions in respect of him (but without prejudice to the recovery of any sum due at the time the notice is given), unless twelve weeks have elapsed since the giving of the notice without the application being made or the application has been refused by the court or withdrawn.

Protected children

Meaning of "protected child"

32.—(1) Where a person gives notice in pursuance of section 22(1) to the local authority within whose area he lives of his intention to apply for an adoption order in respect of a child, the child is for the purposes of this Part a protected child while he has his home with that person.

(2) A child shall be deemed to be a protected child for the purposes of this Part if he is a protected child within the meaning of section 32 of the Adoption Act 1976.

[1] (3) A child is not a protected child by reason of any such notice as is mentioned in subsection (1) while—

(*a*) he is in the care of any person in any such school, home or institution as is mentioned in section 2(2) of the Foster Children (Scotland) Act 1984; or

(*b*) he is resident in a residential establishment provided for persons suffering from mental disorder under section 59 of the Social Work (Scotland) Act 1968; or

(*c*) he is liable to be detained or subject to guardianship under section 17 or 39 of the Mental Health (Scotland) Act 1984.

(4) A protected child ceases to be a protected child when—

    (*a*) the application for an adoption order lapses or is withdrawn;

    (*b*) the application for an adoption order is granted or otherwise determined;

    (*c*) an order is made awarding custody of the child;

    (*d*) an order is made appointing a guardian of the child; or

    (*e*) the child attains the age of eighteen years.

NOTE

[1] As amended by the Mental Health (Scotland) Act 1984, Sched. 3, para. 38, and (with effect from 31st January 1985) the Foster Children (Scotland) Act 1984, Sched. 2, para. 7. See *ibid.* s.2(5).

Duty of local authorities to secure well-being of protected children

33.—(1) It shall be the duty of every local authority to secure that protected children within their area are visited from time to time by officers of the authority, who shall satisfy themselves as to the well-being of the children and give such advice as to their care and maintenance as may appear to be needed.

(2) Any officer of a local authority authorised to visit protected children may, after producing, if asked to do so, some duly authenticated document showing that he is so authorised, inspect any premises in the area of the authority in which such children are to be or are being kept.

Removal of protected children from unsuitable surroundings

[1] **34.**—(1) If the sheriff is satisfied, on the complaint of a local authority, that a protected child is being kept or is about to be received by any person who is unfit to have his care or in any premises or any environment detrimental or likely to be detrimental to him, the sheriff may make an order for his removal to a place of safety until he can be restored to a parent, relative or guardian of his, or until other arrangements can be made with respect to him; and on proof that there is imminent danger to the health or well-being of the child the power to make an order under this section may be exercised by a justice of the peace acting on the application of a person authorised to visit protected children.

(2) An order under this section may be executed by any person authorised to visit protected children or by any constable and may be executed on a Sunday.

(3) A local authority may receive into their care under section 15 of the Social Work (Scotland) Act 1968 any child removed under this section, whether or not the circumstances of the child are such that they fall within paragraphs (*a*) to (*c*) of subsection (1) of that section and notwithstanding that he may appear to the local authority to be over the age of seventeen years.

(4) Where a child is removed under this section the local authority shall, if practicable, inform a parent or guardian of the child, or any person who acts as his guardian.

NOTE

[1] See the Foster Children (Scotland) Act 1984, s.7(1)(*f*).

Notices and information to be given to local authorities
  35.—(1) Where a person who has a protected child in his care and possession changes his permanent address he shall, not less than two weeks before the change, or, if the change is made in an emergency, not later than one week after the change, give notice specifying the new address to the local authority in whose area his permanent address is before the change, and if the new address is in the area of another local authority, the authority to whom the notice is given shall inform that other local authority and give them such of the following particulars as are known to them, that is to say—
  (*a*) the name, sex and date and place of birth of the child;
  (*b*) the name and address of every person who is a parent or guardian or acts as guardian of the child or from whom the child has been or is to be received.
  (2) If a protected child dies, the person in whose care and possession he was at his death shall within forty-eight hours give notice of the child's death to the local authority.

Offences relating to protected children
  36.—(1) A person shall be guilty of an offence if—
  (*a*) being required under section 35 to give any notice or information, he fails to give the notice within the time specified in that provision or fails to give the information within a reasonable time, or knowingly makes or causes or procures another person to make any false or misleading statement in the notice or information;
  (*b*) he refuses to allow the visiting of a protected child by a duly authorised officer of a local authority or the inspection under the power conferred by section 33(2), of any premises;
  (*c*) he refuses to comply with an order under section 34 for the removal of any child or obstructs any person in the execution of such an order.
  [1] (2) A person guilty of an offence under this section shall be liable on summary conviction to imprisonment for a term not exceeding three months or a fine not exceeding level 5 on the standard scale or both.

NOTE
  [1] As amended by virtue of the Criminal Procedure (Scotland) Act 1975, ss.289F and 289G.

Miscellaneous provisions relating to protected children
  37.—(1) For the purposes of sections 14 and 323 of the Criminal Procedure (Scotland) Act 1975 (under which a warrant authorising the search for and removal of a child may be issued on suspicion of unnecessary suffering caused to, or certain offences committed against, the child), any refusal to allow the visiting of a protected child or the inspection of any premises by a person authorised to do so under section 33 shall be treated as giving reasonable cause for such a suspicion.
  (2) A person who maintains a protected child shall be deemed for the purposes of the Life Assurance Act 1774 to have no interest in the life of the child.

PART IV

STATUS OF ADOPTED CHILDREN

Meaning of "adoption order" in Part IV
  38.—(1) In this Part "adoption order" means—
  (*a*) an adoption order within the meaning of section 65(1);
  (*b*) an adoption order under the Children Act 1975, the Adoption

Act 1958, the Adoption Act 1950 or any enactment repealed by the Adoption Act 1950;

(c) an order effecting an adoption made in England, Wales, Northern Ireland, the Isle of Man or any of the Channel Islands;

(d) an "overseas adoption" within the meaning of section 65(2); or

(e) any other adoption recognised by the law of Scotland;

and cognate expressions shall be construed accordingly.

(2) The definition of adoption order includes, where the context admits, an adoption order which took effect before the commencement of the Children Act 1975.

Status conferred by adoption

39.—(1) A child who is the subject of an adoption order shall be treated in law—

(a) where the adopters are a married couple, as if he had been born as a legitimate child of the marriage (whether or not he was in fact born after the marriage was constituted);

(b) in any other case, as if he had been born as a legitimate child of the adopter (but not as a child of any actual marriage of the adopter);

and as if he were not the child of any person other than the adopters or adopter.

(2) Where an illegitimate child has been adopted by one of his natural parents as sole adoptive parent and the adopter thereafter marries the other natural parent, subsection (1) shall not affect any enactment or rule of law whereby, by virtue of the marriage, the child is rendered the legitimate child of both natural parents.

(3) This section has effect—

(a) in the case of an adoption before 1st January 1976, from that date, and

(b) in the case of any other adoption, from the date of the adoption.

[1] (4) Subject to the provisions of this Part, this section—

(a) applies for the construction of enactments or instruments passed or made before or after the commencement of this Act so far as the context admits; and

(b) does not affect things done or events occurring before the adoption or, where the adoption took place before 1st January 1976, before that date.

(5) This section has effect subject to the provisions of section 44.

NOTE

[1] Saved by the Insurance Companies Act 1982, s.50(7).

40. [Repealed by the British Nationality Act 1981, Sched. 9.]

Miscellaneous enactments

41.—(1) Section 39 does not apply in determining the forbidden degrees of consanguinity and affinity in respect of the law relating to marriage or in respect of the crime of incest, except that, on the making of an adoption order, the adopter and the child shall be deemed, for all time coming, to be within the said forbidden degrees in respect of the law relating to marriage.

[1] (2) Section 39 does not apply for the purposes of any provision of—

(a) the British Nationality Act 1981,

(b) the Immigration Act 1971,

(c) any instrument having effect under an enactment within paragraph (a) or (b), or (*d*) any other law for the time being in force which determines British citizenship, British Dependent Territories citizenship or British Overseas citizenship.

(3) Section 39 shall not prevent a person being treated as a near relative of a deceased person for the purposes of section 32 of the Social Security Act 1975 (payment of death grant), if apart from section 39 he would be so treated.

(4) Section 39 does not apply for the purposes of section 70 (3) (*b*) or section 73 (2) of the Social Security Act 1975 (payment of industrial death benefit to or in respect of an illegitimate child of the deceased and the child's mother).

(5) Subject to regulations made under section 72 of the Social Security Act 1975 (entitlement of certain relatives of deceased to industrial death benefit), section 39 shall not affect the entitlement to an industrial death benefit of a person who would, apart from section 39, be treated as a relative of a deceased person for the purposes of the said section 72.

NOTE
[1] As amended by the British Nationality Act 1981, Scheds. 7 and 9.

Pensions
42. Section 39 (1) does not affect entitlement to a pension which is payable to or for the benefit of a child and is in payment at the time of his adoption.

Insurance
43. Where a child is adopted whose natural parent has effected an insurance with a friendly society or a collecting society or an industrial insurance company for the payment on the death of the child of money for funeral expenses, the rights and liabilities under the policy shall by virtue of the adoption be transferred to the adoptive parents who shall for the purposes of the enactments relating to such societies and companies be treated as the person who took out the policy.

Effect of s. 39 on succession and inter vivos **deed**
44. Section 39 (status conferred by adoption) does not affect the existing law relating to adopted persons in respect of—

(*a*) the succession to a deceased person (whether testate or intestate), and

(*b*) the disposal of property by virtue of any *inter vivos* deed.

PART V

REGISTRATION AND REVOCATION OF ADOPTION ORDERS AND CONVENTION ADOPTIONS

Adopted Children Register
45.—(1) The Registrar General for Scotland shall maintain at the General Register Office a register, to be called the Adopted Children Register, in which shall be made such entries as may be directed to be made therein by adoption orders, but no other entries.

(2) An extract of any entry in the Adopted Children Register maintained under this section, if purporting to be sealed or stamped with the seal of the General Register Office, shall, without any further or other proof of that entry, be received as evidence of the adoption to which it relates and, where the entry contains a record of the date of the birth or the country of the birth of the adopted person, shall also be received as aforesaid as evidence of that date or country.

(3) The Registrar General for Scotland shall cause an index of the Adopted Children Register maintained under this section to be made and kept in the General Register Office; and the Registrar General for Scotland shall—

    (*a*) cause a search to be made of that index on behalf of any person or permit that person to search the index himself, and

    (*b*) issue to any person an extract of any entry in that register which that person may require,

in all respects upon and subject to the same terms, conditions and regulations as to payment of fees and otherwise as are applicable under the Registration of Births, Deaths and Marriages (Scotland) Act 1965 in respect of searches in other indexes kept in the General Register Office and in respect of the supply from that office of extracts of entries in the registers of births, deaths and marriages.

(4) The Registrar General for Scotland shall, in addition to the Adopted Children Register and the index thereto, keep such other registers and books, and make such entries therein, as may be necessary to record and make traceable the connection between any entry in the register of births which has been marked " Adopted " pursuant to paragraph 1 of Schedule 1 or any enactment at the time in force and any corresponding entry in the Adopted Children Register maintained under this section.

(5) The registers and books kept under subsection (4) shall not be, nor shall any index thereof be, open to public inspection or search, nor, except under an order of the Court of Session or a sheriff, shall the Registrar General for Scotland furnish any information contained in or any copy or extract from any such registers or books to any person other than an adopted person who has attained the age of seventeen years and to whom that information, copy or extract relates or a local authority or an approved adoption society which is providing counselling, under subsection (6), for that adopted person.

(6) Where the Registrar General for Scotland furnishes an adopted person with information under subsection (5), he shall advise that person that counselling services are available—

    (*a*) from the local authority for the area where the adopted person lives; or

    (*b*) if the adopted person's adoption was arranged by an adoption society which is approved under section 3 or under section 3 of the Adoption Act 1976, from that society,

and it shall be the duty of such local authority and approved adoption society to provide counselling for adopted persons who have been furnished with information under subsection (5) and who apply to them for counselling in respect of that information and for adopted persons who apply for information under section 51 (1) of the Adoption Act 1976.

(7) Where an adopted person has arranged to receive counselling under subsection (6), the Registrar General for Scotland shall, on receipt of a request from the local authority or adoption society which is providing that counselling, and on payment of the appropriate fee, send to the authority or society an extract of the entry relating to the adopted person in the register of births.

(8) The provisions of the Registration of Births, Deaths and Marriages (Scotland) Act 1965 with regard to the correction of errors in entries shall apply to the Adopted Children Register maintained by the Registrar General for Scotland and to registration therein in like manner as they apply to any register of births and to registration therein.

(9) Schedule 1 to this Act, which, among other things, provides for the registration of adoptions and the amendment of adoption orders, shall have effect.

Revocation of adoptions on legitimation

46.—(1) Where the natural parents of an illegitimate child, one of whom has adopted him in Scotland, have subsequently married each other, the court by which the adoption order was made may, on the application of any of the parties concerned, revoke that order.

(2) Where a person adopted by his father or mother alone by virtue of a regulated adoption has subsequently become a legitimated person on the marriage of his father and mother, the Court of Session may, upon an application under this subsection by the parties concerned, by order revoke the adoption.

Annulment etc. of overseas adoptions

47.—(1) The Court of Session may, upon an application under this subsection, by order annul a regulated adoption or an adoption effected by a Convention adoption order—

(*a*) on the ground that at the relevant time the adoption was prohibited by a notified provision, if under the internal law then in force in the country of which the adopter was then a national or the adopters were then nationals the adoption could have been impugned on that ground;

(*b*) on the ground that at the relevant time the adoption contravened provisions relating to consents of the internal law relating to adoption of the country of which the adopted person was then a national, if under that law the adoption could then have been impugned on that ground;

(*c*) on any other ground on which the adoption can be impugned under the law for the time being in force in the country in which the adoption was effected.

(2) The Court of Session may, upon an application under this subsection—

(*a*) order that an overseas adoption or a determination shall cease to be valid in Great Britain on the ground that the adoption or determination is contrary to public policy or that the authority which purported to authorise the adoption or make the determination was not competent to entertain the case;

(*b*) decide the extent, if any, to which a determination has been affected by a subsequent determination.

(3) Any court in Great Britain may, in any proceedings in that court, decide that an overseas adoption or a determination shall, for the purposes of those proceedings, be treated as invalid in Great Britain on either of the grounds mentioned in subsection (2).

(4) An order or decision of the High Court on an application under subsection (2) of section 53 of the Adoption Act 1976 shall be recognised and have effect as if it were an order or decision of the Court of Session on an application under subsection (2) of this section.

(5) Except as provided by this section and section 46(2) the validity of an overseas adoption or a determination shall not be impugned in Scotland in proceedings in any court.

Provisions supplementary to ss.46(2) and 47

48.—(1) Any application for an order under section 46(2) or 47 or a decision under section 47(2)(*b*) shall be made in the prescribed manner and within such period, if any, as may be prescribed.

(2) No application shall be made under section 46(2) or 47(1) in respect of an adoption unless immediately before the application is made the person adopted or the adopter habitually resides in Scotland or, as the case may be, both adopters habitually reside there.

(3) In deciding in pursuance of section 47 whether such an authority as is mentioned in section 53 was competent to entertain a particular case, a court shall be bound by any finding of fact made by the authority and stated

[138]

by the authority to be so made for the purpose of determining whether the authority was competent to entertain the case.

(4) In section 47—

"determination" means such a determination as is mentioned in section 53;

"notified provision" means a provision specified in an order of the Secretary of State as one in respect of which a notification to or by the Government of the United Kingdom was in force at the relevant time in pursuance of the provisions of the Convention relating to prohibitions contained in the national law of the adopter; and

"relevant time" means the time when the adoption in question purported to take effect under the law of the country in which it purports to have been effected.

PART VI

MISCELLANEOUS AND SUPPLEMENTAL

Adoption of child abroad

49.—(1) Where on an application made in relation to a child by a person who is not domiciled in England and Wales or Scotland an authorised court is satisfied that he intends to adopt the child under the law of or within the country in which the applicant is domiciled, the court may, subject to the following provisions of this section, make an order vesting in him the parental rights and duties relating to the child.

(2) The provisions of Part II relating to adoption orders, except sections 12(1), 14(2), 15(2), 17 to 21 and 25, shall apply in relation to orders under this section as they apply in relation to adoption orders subject to the modification that in section 13(1) for "nineteen" and "thirteen" there are substituted "thirty-two" and "twenty-six" respectively.

(3) Section 45 and paragraphs 1 and 2(1) and (3) of Schedule 1 shall apply in relation to an order under this section as they apply in relation to an adoption order except than any entry in the register of births or the Adopted Children Register which is required to be marked in consequence of the making of an order under this section shall, in lieu of being marked with the word "Adopted" or "Re-adopted" (with or without the addition of the word "(England)"), be marked with the words "Proposed foreign adoption" or "Proposed foreign re-adoption", as the case may require.

(4) References in sections 27, 28, 30, 31 and 32 to an adoption order include references to an order under this section or under section 55 of the Adoption Act 1976.

Restriction on removal of children for adoption outside Great Britain

50.—[1] (1) Except under the authority of an order under section 49, or under section 55 of the Adoption Act 1976, it shall not be lawful for any person to take or send a child who is a British subject or a citizen of the Republic of Ireland out of Great Britain to any place outside the United Kingdom, the Channel Islands and the Isle of Man with a view to the adoption of the child by any person not being a parent or guardian or relative of the child; and any person who takes or sends a child out of Great Britain to any place in contravention of this subsection, or makes or takes part in any arrangements for transferring the care and possession of a child to any person for that purpose, shall be guilty of an offence and liable on summary conviction to imprisonment for a term not exceeding three months or to a fine not exceeding level 5 on the standard scale or to both.

(2) In any proceedings under this section, a report by a British consular officer or a deposition made before a British consular officer and authenticated under the signature of that officer shall, upon proof that the officer or the deponent cannot be found in the United Kingdom, be sufficient

evidence of the matters stated therein, and it shall not be necessary to prove the signature or official character of the person who appears to have signed any such report or deposition.

(3) A person shall be deemed to take part in arrangements for transferring the care and possession of a child to a person for the purpose referred to in subsection (1) if—

(*a*) he facilitates the placing of the child in the care and possession of that person; or

(*b*) he initiates or takes part in any negotiations of which the purpose or effect is the conclusion of any agreement or the making of any arrangement therefore, or if he causes another person to do so.

NOTE

[1] As amended by virtue of the Criminal Procedure (Scotland) Act 1975, ss.289F and 289G.

Prohibition on certain payments

51.—(1) Subject to the provisions of this section, it shall not be lawful to make or give to any person any payment or reward for or in consideration of—

(*a*) the adoption by that person of a child;

(*b*) the grant by that person of any agreement or consent required in connection with the adoption of a child;

(*c*) the transfer by that person of the care and possession of a child with a view to the adoption of the child; or

(*d*) the making by that person of any arrangements for the adoption of a child.

[1] (2) Any person who makes or gives, or agrees or offers to make or give, any payment or reward prohibited by this section, or who receives or agrees to receive or attempts to obtain any such payment or reward, shall be guilty of an offence and liable on summary conviction to imprisonment for a term not exceeding three months or to a fine not exceeding level 5 on the standard scale or to both; and the court may order any child in respect of whom the offence was committed to be removed to a place of safety until he can be restored to his parents or guardian or until other arrangements can be made for him.

(3) This section does not apply to any payment made to an adoption agency by a parent or guardian of a child or by a person who adopts or proposes to adopt a child, being a payment in respect of expenses reasonably incurred by the agency in connection with the adoption of the child, or to any payment or reward authorised by the court to which an application for an adoption order in respect of a child is made.

(4) This section does not apply to—

(*a*) any payment made by an adoption agency to a person who has applied or proposes to apply to a court for an adoption order or an order under section 49, being a payment of or towards any legal or medical expenses incurred or to be incurred by that person in connection with the application; or

(*b*) any payment made by an adoption agency to another adoption agency in consideration of the placing of a child in the care and possession of any person with a view to the child's adoption; or

(*c*) any payment made by an adoption agency to a voluntary organisation for the time being approved for the purposes of this paragraph by the Secretary of State as a fee for the services of that organisation in putting that adoption agency into contact with another adoption agency with a view to the making of arrangements between the adoption agencies for the adoption of a child.

(5) If an adoption agency submits to the Secretary of State a scheme for the payment by the agency of allowances to persons who have adopted or intend to adopt a child where arrangements for the adoption were made, or are to be made, by that agency, and the Secretary of State approves the

scheme, this section shall not apply to any payment made in accordance with the scheme.

(6) The Secretary of State, in the case of a scheme approved by him under subsection (5), may at any time—

(*a*) make, or approve the making by the agency of, alterations to the scheme;

(*b*) revoke the scheme.

(7) The Secretary of State shall, within seven years of the date on which section 32 of the Children Act 1975 came into force and, thereafter, every five years, publish a report on the operation of the schemes since that date or since the publication of the last report.

(8) Subject to the following subsection, subsection (5) of this section shall expire on the seventh anniversary of the date on which section 32 of the Children Act 1975 came into force.

(9) The Secretary of State may by order made by statutory instrument at any time before the said anniversary repeal subsection (8) of this section.

(10) An order under subsection (9) of this section shall not be made unless a report has been published under subsection (7) of this section.

(11) Notwithstanding the expiry of subsection (5) of this section or the revocation of a scheme approved under this section, subsection (1) of this section shall not apply in relation to any payment made, whether before or after the expiry of subsection (5) or the revocation of the scheme, in accordance with a scheme which was approved under this section to a person to whom such payments were made—

(*a*) where the scheme was not revoked, before the expiry of subsection (5), or

(*b*) if the scheme was revoked, before the date of its revocation.

NOTE
[1] As amended by virtue of the Criminal Procedure (Scotland) Act 1975, ss.289F and 289G.

Restriction on advertisements

52.—(1) It shall not be lawful for any advertisement to be published indicating—

(*a*) that the parent or guardian of a child desires to cause a child to be adopted; or

(*b*) that a person desires to adopt a child; or

(*c*) that any person (not being an adoption agency) is willing to make arrangements for the adoption of a child.

[1] (2) Any person who causes to be published or knowingly publishes an advertisement in contravention of the provisions of this section shall be guilty of an offence and liable on summary conviction to a fine not exceeding level 5 on the standard scale.

NOTE
[1] As amended by virtue of the Criminal Prodcedure (Scotland) Act 1975, ss.289F and 289G.

Effect of determination and orders made in England and Wales and overseas in adoption proceedings

53.—(1) Where an authority of a Convention country or any British territory other than Great Britain having power under the law of that country or territory—

(*a*) to authorise or review the authorisation of a regulated adoption or a specified order; or

(*b*) to give or review a decision revoking or annulling a regulated adoption, a specified order or a Convention adoption order,

makes a determination in the exercise of that power, then, subject to sections 46(2) and 47 and any subsequent determination having effect under this subsection, the determination shall have effect in Scotland for the purpose of effecting, confirming or terminating the adoption in question or confirming its termination, as the case may be.

(2) Subsections (2) and (3) of section 12 shall apply in relation to an order under section 18 of the Adoption Act 1976 (freeing children for adoption in England or Wales) as if the order were an adoption order; and, on the revocation of the order under section 20 of that Act, any duty extinguished by section 12 (3) (*b*) is forthwith revived but the revival does not have effect as respects anything done or not done before the revival.

(3) Sections 12 (3) and (4) and 43 apply in relation to a child who is the subject of an order which is similar to an order under section 49 and is made (whether before or after this Act has effect) in England or Wales, Northern Ireland, the Isle of Man or any of the Channel Islands, as they apply in relation to a child who is the subject of an adoption order.

Evidence of adoption in England, Wales and Northern Ireland

54. Any document which is receivable as evidence of any matter—
>   (*a*) in England and Wales under section 50 (2) of the Adoption Act 1976; or
>   (*b*) in Northern Ireland under section 23 (4) of the Adoption Act (Northern Ireland) 1967 or any corresponding provision contained in a Measure of the Northern Ireland Assembly for the time being in force,

shall also be so receivable in Scotland.

Evidence of agreement and consent

55.—(1) Any agreement or consent which is required by this Act to be given to the making of an order or application for an order (other than an order to which section 17 (6) applies) may be given in writing, and, if the document signifying the agreement or consent is witnessed in accordance with rules, it shall be sufficient evidence without further proof of the signature of the person by whom it was executed.

(2) A document signifying such agreement or consent which purports to be witnessed in accordance with rules, shall be presumed to be so witnessed, and to have been executed and witnessed on the date and at the place specified in the document, unless the contrary is proved.

Courts

56.—(1) In this Act, " authorised court ", as respects an application for an order relating to a child, shall be construed as follows.

(2) Subject to subsections (4) and (5), if the child is in Scotland when the application is made, the following are authorised courts—
>   (*a*) the Court of Session;
>   (*b*) the sheriff court of the sheriffdom within which the child is.

(3) If, in the case of an application for an adoption order or for an order freeing a child for adoption, the child is not in Great Britain when the application is made, the Court of Session is the authorised court.

(4) In the case of an application for a Convention adoption order, paragraph (*b*) of subsection (2) does not apply.

(5) Subsection (2) does not apply in the case of an application under section 29 but for the purposes of such an application the following are authorised courts—
>   (*a*) if there is pending in respect of the child an application for an adoption order or an order freeing him for adoption, the court in which that application is pending;
>   (*b*) in any other case—
>   (i) the Court of Session;
>   (ii) the sheriff court of the sheriffdom within which the applicant resides.

Proceedings to be in private

57. All proceedings before the court under Part II, section 29 or section 49 shall be heard and determined in private unless the court otherwise directs.

Curators ad litem and reporting officers

58.—(1) For the purpose of any application for an adoption order or an order freeing a child for adoption or an order under section 20 or 49, rules shall provide for the appointment, in such cases as are prescribed—

    (*a*) of a person to act as curator *ad litem* of the child upon the hearing of the application, with the duty of safeguarding the interests of the child in the prescribed manner;

    (*b*) of a person to act as reporting officer for the purpose of witnessing agreements to adoption and performing such other duties as the rules may prescribe.

    (2) A person who is employed—

    (*a*) in the case of an application for an adoption order, by the adoption agency by whom the child was placed; or

    (*b*) in the case of an application for an order freeing a child for adoption, by the adoption agency by whom the application was made; or

    (*c*) in the case of an application under section 20, by the adoption agency with the parental rights and duties relating to the child,

shall not be appointed to act as curator *ad litem* or reporting officer for the purposes of the application but, subject to that, the same person may if the court thinks fit be both curator *ad litem* and reporting officer.

    (3) Rules may provide for the reporting officer to be appointed before the application is made.

Rules of procedure

59.—(1) Subject to subsection (4), provision shall be made by act of sederunt with regard to any matter to be prescribed under this Act and generally with regard to all matters of procedure and incidental matters arising out of this Act and for carrying this Act into effect.

    (2) In the case of—

    (*a*) an application for an adoption order in relation to a child who is not free for adoption;

    (*b*) an application for an order freeing a child for adoption,

rules shall require every person who can be found and whose agreement or consent to the making of the order is required to be given or dispensed with under this Act to be notified of a date and place where he may be heard on the application and of the fact that, unless he wishes or the court requires, he need not attend.

    (3) In the case of an application under section 49, rules shall require every person who can be found, and whose agreement to the making of the order would be required if the application were for an adoption order (other than a Convention adoption order), to be notified as aforesaid.

    (4) This section does not apply to sections 9, 10, 11 and 32 to 37.

Orders, rules and regulations

60.—(1) Any power to make orders or regulations conferred by this Act on the Secretary of State or the Registrar General for Scotland shall be exercisable by statutory instrument.

    (2) A statutory instrument containing regulations made under any provision of this Act, except section 3 (1), shall be subject to annulment in pursuance of a resolution of either House of Parliament.

    (3) An order under section 28 (10) or 51 (9) shall not be made unless a draft of the order has been approved by resolution of each House of Parliament.

[143]

(4) An order made under any provision of this Act may be revoked or varied by a subsequent order under that provision.

(5) Any order, rule or regulation made under this Act may make different provision for different circumstances and may contain such incidental and transitional provisions as the authority making the order or regulation considers expedient.

(6) The Registrar General for Scotland shall not make regulations under paragraph 1(1) of Schedule 1 except with the approval of the Secretary of State.

(7) The Statutory Instruments Act 1946 shall apply to a statutory instrument containing regulations made for the purposes of this Act by the Registrar General for Scotland as if the regulations had been made by a Minister of the Crown.

Offences by bodies corporate

61. Where an offence under this Act committed by a body corporate is proved to have been committed with the consent or connivance of or to be attributable to any neglect on the part of, any director, manager, member of the committee, secretary or other officer of the body, he as well as the body shall be deemed to be guilty of that offence and shall be liable to be proceeded against and punished accordingly.

Service of notices etc.

62. Any notice or information required to be given under this Act may be given by post.

Nationality

63.—(1) If the Secretary of State by order declares that a description of persons specified in the order has, in pursuance of the Convention, been notified to the Government of the United Kingdom as the description of persons who are deemed to possess the nationality of a particular Convention country, persons of that description shall, subject to the following provisions of this section, be treated for the purposes of this Act as nationals of that country.

(2) Subject to section 48(3) and subsection (3) of this section, where it appears to the court in any proceedings under this Act, or to any court by which a decision in pursuance of section 47(3) falls to be given, that a person is or was at a particular time a national of two or more countries, then—

(*a*) if it appears to the said court that he is or was then a United Kingdom national, he shall be treated for the purposes of those proceedings or that decision as if he were or had then been a United Kingdom national only;

(*b*) if, in a case not falling within paragraph (*a*), it appears to the said court that one only of those countries is or was then a Convention country, he shall be treated for those purposes as if he were or had then been a national of that country only;

(*c*) if, in a case not falling within paragraph (*a*), it appears to the said court that two or more of those countries are or were then Convention countries, he shall be treated for those purposes as if he were or had then been a national of such one only of those Convention countries as the said court considers is the country with which he is or was then most closely connected;

(*d*) in any other case, he shall be treated for those purposes as if he were or had then been a national of such one only of those countries as the said court considers is the country with which he is or was then most closely connected.

(3) A court in which proceedings are brought in pursuance of section 17, 46(2) or 47 shall be entitled to disregard the provisions of subsection (2)

in so far as it appears to that court appropriate to do so for the purposes of those proceedings; but nothing in this subsection shall be construed as prejudicing the provisions of section 48(3).

(4) Where, after such inquiries as the court in question considers appropriate, it appears to the court in any proceedings under this Act, or to any court by which such a decision as aforesaid falls to be given, that a person has no nationality or no ascertainable nationality, he shall be treated for the purposes of those proceedings or that decision as a national of the country in which he resides or, where that country is one of two or more countries having the same law of nationality, as a national of those countries.

Internal law of a country

64.—(1) In this Act "internal law" in relation to any country means the law applicable in a case where no question arises as to the law in force in any other country.

(2) In any case where the internal law of a country falls to be ascertained for the purposes of this Act by any court and there are in force in that country two or more systems of internal law, the relevant system shall be ascertained in accordance with any rule in force throughout that country indicating which of the systems is relevant in the case in question or, if there is no such rule, shall be the system appearing to that court to be most closely connected with the case.

Interpretation

65.—[1] (1) In this Act, unless the context otherwise requires—

"adoption agency" in sections 11, 13, 18 to 23 and 27 includes an adoption agency within the meaning of section 1 of the Adoption Act 1976 (adoption agencies in England and Wales);

"adoption order" means an order under section 12(1) and, in sections 12(3) and (4), 18 to 20, 27 and 28 and 30 to 32, includes an order under section 12 of the Adoption Act 1976 (adoption orders in England and Wales);

"adoption society" means a body of persons whose functions consist of or include the making of arrangements for the adoption of children;

"approved adoption society" means an adoption society approved under Part I and, in sections 30 and 45, includes an adoption society approved under Part I of the Adoption Act 1976;

"authorised court" shall be construed in accordance with section 56;

"body of persons" means any body of persons, whether incorporated or unincorporated;

"British adoption order" means an adoption order, an order under section 12 of the Adoption Act 1976 or any provision for the adoption of a child effected under the law of Northern Ireland or any British territory outside the United Kingdom;

"British territory" means, for the purposes of any provision of this Act, any of the following countries, that is to say, Great Britain, Northern Ireland, the Channel Islands, the Isle of Man and a colony, being a country designated for the purposes of that provision by order of the Secretary of State or, if no country is so designated, any of those countries;

"child", except where used to express a relationship, means a person who has not attained the age of eighteen years;

"the Convention" means the Convention relating to the adoption of children concluded at The Hague on 15th November 1965 and signed on behalf of the United Kingdom on that date;

"Convention adoption order" means an adoption order made in accordance with section 17(1);

"Convention country" means any country outside British territory, being a country for the time being designated by an order of the Secretary of State as a country in which, in his opinion, the Convention is in force;

"England" includes Wales;

"guardian" means—

   (*a*) a person appointed by deed or will in accordance with the provisions of the Guardianship of Infants Acts 1886 and 1925 or the Guardianship of Minors Act 1971 or by a court of competent jurisdiction to be the guardian of the child, and

   (*b*) in the case of an illegitimate child, includes the father where he has custody of the child by virtue of an order under section 9 of the Guardianship of Minors Act 1971, or under section 2 of the Illegitimate Children (Scotland) Act 1930;

"internal law" has the meaning assigned by section 64;

"local authority" means a regional or islands council and, in sections 13, 22, 28, 30, 31, 35(1) and 45, includes the council of a county (other than a metropolitan county), a metropolitan district, a London borough or the Common Council of the City of London;

"notice" means a notice in writing;

"order freeing a child for adoption" means an order under section 18 and, in section 27(2), includes an order under section 18 of the Adoption Act 1976 (order freeing a child for adoption made in England and Wales);

"overseas adoption" has the meaning assigned by subsection (2);

"place of safety" means any residential or other establishment provided by a local authority, a police station, or any hospital, surgery or other suitable place the occupier of which is willing temporarily to receive a child;

"prescribed" means prescribed by act of sederunt;

"Registrar General for Scotland" means the Registrar General of Births, Deaths and Marriages for Scotland;

"regulated adoption" means an overseas adoption of a description designated by an order under subsection (2) as that of an adoption regulated by the Convention;

"relative" in relation to a child means a grandparent, brother, sister, uncle or aunt, whether of the full blood or half-blood or by affinity and includes, where the child is illegitimate, the father of the child and any person who would be a relative within the meaning of this definition if the child were the legitimate child of his mother and father;

"rules" means rules made by act of sederunt;

"specified order" means any provision for the adoption of a child effected under enactments similar to section 12(1) and 17 in force in Northern Ireland or any British territory outside the United Kingdom;

"United Kingdom national" means, for the purposes of any provision of this Act, a citizen of the United Kingdom and Colonies satisfying such conditions, if any, as the Secretary of State may by order specify for the purposes of that provision;

"voluntary organisation" means a body, other than a public or local authority, the activities of which are not carried on for profit.

(2) In this Act "overseas adoption" means an adoption of such a description as the Secretary of State may by order specify, being a description of adoptions of children appearing to him to be effected under the law of any country outside Great Britain; and an order under this

subsection may contain provision as to the manner in which evidence of an overseas adoption may be given.

(3) For the purposes of this Act, a person shall be deemed to make arrangements for the adoption of a child if he enters into or makes any agreement or arrangement for, or for facilitating the adoption of the child by any other person, whether the adoption is effected, or is intended to be effected, in Great Britain or elsewhere, or if he initiates or takes part in any negotiations of which the purpose or effect is the conclusion of any agreement or the making of any arrangement therefor, or if he causes another person to do so, but the making, under section 44 of the Social Work (Scotland) Act 1968, by a children's hearing of a supervision requirement which, in respect that it provides as to where he is to reside, facilitates his being placed for adoption by an adoption agency, shall not constitute the making of such arrangements.

(4) Except so far as the context otherwise requires, any reference in this Act to an enactment shall be construed as a reference to that enactment as amended by or under any other enactment, including this Act.

(5) In this Act, except where otherwise indicated—

(*a*) a reference to a numbered Part, section or Schedule is a reference to the Part or section of, or the Schedule to, this Act so numbered, and

(*b*) a reference in a section to a numbered subsection is a reference to the subsection of that section so numbered, and

(*c*) a reference in a section, subsection or Schedule to a numbered paragraph is a reference to the paragraph of that section, subsection or Schedule so numbered.

NOTES
[1] As amended by the Health and Social Services and Social Security Adjudications Act 1983, Sched. 2, para. 45.
[2] As amended by the Law Reform (Miscellaneous Provisions) (Scotland) Act 1985, s. 27, with effect from 30th December 1985.

Transitional provisions, amendments and repeals

66.—(1) The transitional provisions contained in Schedule 2 shall have effect.

(2) The enactments specified in Schedule 3 shall have effect subject to the amendments specified in that Schedule, being amendments consequential upon the provisions of this Act.

(3) The enactments specified in Schedule 4 are hereby repealed to the extent specified in column 3 of that Schedule.

Short title, commencement and extent

67.—(1) This Act may be cited as the Adoption (Scotland) Act 1978.

(2) This Act shall come into force on such date as the Secretary of State may by order[1] appoint and different dates may be appointed for different provisions.

(3) Until the date appointed under subsection (2) for sections 3, 4, 5 and 8, in this Act and in the Adoption Act 1958 "adoption agency" means a local authority or a registered adoption society within the meaning of the said Act of 1958.

(4) This Act shall extend to Scotland only.

NOTE
[1] S.I. 1984 No. 1050 brought the whole Act into force on 1st September 1984, with the exception of ss. 1 and 2, which it brought into force on 1st February 1985. See also the Health and Social Services and Social Security Adjudications Act 1983, Sched. 2, para. 1.

SCHEDULES

SCHEDULE 1

REGISTRATION OF ADOPTIONS

Registration of adoption orders

1.—(1) Every adoption order shall contain a direction to the Registrar General for Scotland to make in the Adopted Children Register maintained by him an entry recording the adoption in such form as the Registrar General for Scotland may by regulations specify.

(2) The direction contained in a Convention adoption order in pursuance of this paragraph shall include an instruction that the entry made in that register in consequence of the order shall be marked with the words "Convention order".

(3) For the purposes of compliance with the requirements of subparagraph (1)—

    (*a*) where the precise date of the child's birth is not proved to the satisfaction of the court, the court shall determine the probable date of his birth and the date so determined shall be specified in the order as the date of his birth;

      (*b*) where the country of birth of the child is not proved to the satisfaction of the court, then, if it appears probable that the child was born within the United Kingdom, the Channel Islands or the Isle of Man, he shall be treated as having been born in Scotland, and in any other case the particulars of the country of birth may be omitted from the order and from the entry in the Adopted Children Register;

and the names to be specified in the order as the name and surname of the child shall be the name or names and surname stated in that behalf in the application for the adoption order, or, if no name or surname is so stated, the original name or names of the child and the surname of the applicant.

(4) There shall be produced with every application for an adoption order in respect of a child whose birth has been registered under the Registration of Births, Deaths and Marriages (Scotland) Act 1965 or under any enactment repealed by that Act an extract of the entry of the birth.

(5) Where on an application to a court for an adoption order in respect of a child (not being a child who has previously been the subject of an adoption order made by a court in Scotland under this Act or any enactment at the time in force) there is proved to the satisfaction of the court the identity of the child with a child to whom an entry in the register of births relates, any adoption order made in pursuance of the application shall contain a direction to the Registrar General for Scotland to cause the entry in that register to be marked with the word " Adopted ".

(6) Where an adoption order is made in respect of a child who has previously been the subject of an adoption order made by a court in Scotland under this Act or any enactment at the time in force, the order shall contain a direction to the Registrar General for Scotland to cause the previous entry in the Adopted Children Register to be marked with the word " Re-adopted ".

(7) Where an adoption order is made, the clerk of the court which made the order shall cause the order to be communicated to the Registrar General for Scotland and upon receipt of the communication the Registrar General for Scotland shall cause compliance to be made with the directions contained in the order.

Registration of adoptions in England, Northern Ireland, the Isle of Man and the Channel Islands

2.—(1) Where the Registrar General for Scotland is notified by the Registrar General that an adoption order has been made by a court in England in respect of a child to whom an entry in the register of births or the Adopted Children Register relates, the Registrar General for Scotland shall cause the entry to be marked " Adopted (England) " or, as the case may be, " Re-adopted (England) ".

(2) Where the Registrar General for Scotland is notified by the authority maintaining a register of adoptions in Northern Ireland, the Isle of Man or any of the Channel Islands that an order has been made in that country authorising the adoption of a child to whom an entry in the register of births or the Adopted Children Register relates, he shall cause the entry to be marked " Adopted " or " Re-adopted ", as the case may be, followed by the name in brackets of the country in which the order was made.

(3) Where, after an entry has been marked under the foregoing provisions of this paragraph, the Registrar General for Scotland is notified as aforesaid that the order has been quashed, that an appeal against the order has been allowed or that the order has been revoked, he shall cause the marking to be cancelled; and an extract of an entry in any register, being an

entry the marking of which is cancelled under this sub-paragraph, shall be deemed to be accurate if and only if both the marking and the cancellation are omitted therefrom.

(4) The foregoing provisions of this paragraph shall apply in relation to orders corresponding to orders under section 49 as they apply in relation to orders authorising the adoption of a child; but any marking of an entry required by virtue of this sub-paragraph shall consist of the words " proposed foreign adoption " or, as the case may require, " proposed foreign re-adoption " followed by the name in brackets of the country in which the order was made.

Registration of overseas adoptions

3. If the Registrar General for Scotland is satisfied that an entry in the register of births relates to a person adopted under an overseas adoption and that he has sufficient particulars relating to that person to enable an entry, in the form specified for the purposes of this paragraph in regulations made under paragraph 1 (1), to be made in the Adopted Children Register in respect of that person, he shall—

(a) make such an entry in the Adopted Children Register; and

(b) if there is a previous entry in respect of that person in that register, mark the entry (or if there is more than one such entry the last of them) with the word " Re-adopted " followed by the name in brackets of the country in which the adoption was effected; and

(c) unless the entry in the register of births is already marked with the word " Adopted " (whether or not followed by other words), mark the entry with that word followed by the name in brackets of the country aforesaid.

Amendment of orders and rectification of registers

4.—(1) The court by which an adoption order has been made may, on the application of the adopter or of the adopted person, amend the order by the correction of any error in the particulars contained therein, and may—

(a) if satisfied on the application of the adopter or the adopted person that within one year beginning with the date of the order any new name has been given to the adopted person (whether in baptism or otherwise), or taken by him, either in lieu of or in addition to a name specified in the particulars required to be entered in the Adopted Children Register in pursuance of the order, amend the order by substituting or adding that name in those particulars, as the case may require;

(b) if satisfied on the application of any person concerned that a direction for the marking of an entry in the register of births or the Adopted Children Register included in the order in pursuance of sub-paragraph (5) or (6) of paragraph 1 was wrongly so included, revoke that direction.

(2) Where an adoption order is amended or a direction revoked under subparagraph (1), the clerk of the court shall cause the amendment to be communicated in the prescribed manner to the Registrar General for Scotland who shall as the case may require—

(a) cause the entry in the Adopted Children Register to be amended accordingly; or

(b) cause the marking of the entry in the register of births or the Adopted Children Register to be cancelled.

(3) Where an adoption order is quashed or an appeal against an adoption order allowed by any court, the court shall give directions to the Registrar General for Scotland to cancel any entry in the Adopted Children Register, and any marking of an entry in that Register, or the register of births as the case may be, which was effected in pursuance of the order.

(4) If the Registrar General for Scotland is satisfied—

(a) that a Convention adoption order or an overseas adoption has ceased to have effect, whether on annulment or otherwise; or

(b) that any entry or mark was erroneously made in pursuance of paragraph 3 in any register mentioned in that paragraph,

he may cause such alterations to be made in any such register as he considers are required in consequence of the cesser or to correct the error; and where an entry in such a register is amended in pursuance of this sub-paragraph, an extract of the entry shall be deemed to be accurate if and only if it shows the entry as amended but without indicating that it has been amended.

Marking of entries on re-registration of birth

5. Without prejudice to any other provision of this Act where, after an entry in the register of births has been marked in accordance with paragraph 2 or 3, the birth is re-registered under section 20 (1) of the Registration of Births, Deaths and Marriages (Scotland) Act 1965 (re-registration of birth in certain cases), the entry made on re-registration shall be marked in the like manner.

[149]

Appendix I

Cancellations in registers on legitimation

6. Where an adoption order is revoked under section 46 (1) the clerk of the court shall cause the revocation to be communicated in the prescribed manner to the Registrar General for Scotland who shall cause to be cancelled—

    (*a*) the entry in the Adopted Children Register relating to the adopted person; and

    (*b*) the marking with the word " Adopted " (or, as the case may be, with that word and the word " (England) ") or any entry relating to him in the register of births;

and an extract of an entry in any register, being an entry the marking of which is cancelled under this paragraph shall be deemed to be accurate if and only if both the marking and the cancellation are omitted therefrom.

7. In this Schedule, " Registrar General " means the Registrar General for England and Wales.

Section 66   SCHEDULE 2

TRANSITIONAL PROVISIONS AND SAVINGS

General

1. In so far as anything done under an enactment repealed by this Act could have ben done under a corresponding provision of this Act it shall not be invalidated by the repeal but shall have effect as if done under that provision.

2. Where any period of time specified in an enactment repealed by this Act is current at the commencement of this Act, this Act shall have effect as if the corresponding provision thereof had been in force when that period began to run.

3. Nothing in this Act shall affect the enactments repealed by this Act in their operation in relation to offences committed before the commencement of this Act.

4. Any reference in any enactment or document, whether express or implied, to an enactment repealed by this Act shall, unless the context otherwise requires, to be construed as a reference to the corresponding enactment in this Act.

Existing adoption orders

5.—(1) Without prejudice to paragraph 1, an adoption order made under an enactment at any time before this Act comes into force shall not cease to have effect by virtue only of a repeal effected by this Act.

(2) Paragraph 4(1) and (2) of Schedule 1 shall apply in relation to an adoption order made before this Act came into force as if the order had been made under section 12, but as if, in sub-paragraph (1)(*b*) of the said paragraph 4, there were substituted for the reference to paragraph 1(5) and (6) a reference—

    (*a*) in the case of an order under the Adoption Act 1950, to section 20(4) and (5) of that Act,

    (*b*) in the case of an order under the Adoption Act 1958, to section 23(4) and (5) of that Act.

(3) The power of the court under the said paragraph 4(1) to amend an order includes power in relation to an order made before 1st April 1959, to make on the application of the adopter or adopted person any such amendment of the particulars contained in the order as appears to be required to bring the order into the form in which it would have been made if paragraph 1 of Schedule 1 had applied to the order.

(4) Section 46(1) and paragraph 6 of Schedule 1 shall apply in relation to an adoption order made under an enactment at any time before this Act came into force as they apply in relation to an adoption order made under this Act.

Payments relating to adoptions

6. Section 51(8), (9) and (10) shall not have effect if, immediately before section 51 comes into force, there is in force in Scotland an order under section 50(8) of the Adoption Act 1958.

Registers of adoptions

7. Any register or index to a register kept under the Adoption Act 1958, or any register or index deemed to be part of such a register, shall be deemed to be part of the register or index kept under section 45.

Commencement of Act

8. An order under section 67(2) may make such transitional provision as appears to the Secretary of State to be necessary or expedient in connection with the provisions thereby brought into force, including such adaptations of those provisions or any provision of this Act then in force or any provision of the Adoption Act 1958 or the Children Act 1975 as appear to him to be necessary or expedient in consequence of the partial operation of this Act.

2. Act of Sederunt (Adoption of Children) 1984

(S.I. 1984 No. 1013)

[13th July 1984]

The Lords of Council and Session, under and by virtue of the powers conferred on them by section 32 of the Sheriff Courts (Scotland) Act 1971, section 59 of the Adoption (Scotland) Act 1978 and of all other powers competent to them in that behalf, after consultation with the Sheriff Court Rules Council, do hereby enact and declare:—

Citation and commencement

1.—(1) This Act of Sederunt may be cited as the Act of Sederunt (Adoption of Children) 1984 and shall come into operation on 1st September 1984.

(2) This Act of Sederunt shall be inserted in the Books of Sederunt.

(3) In this Act of Sederunt—

"the 1978 Act" means the Adoption (Scotland) Act 1978;

"adoption agency" means a local authority or an approved adoption society;

"Her Majesty's Forces" means the Royal Navy, the regular armed forces as defined by section 225 of the Army Act 1955, the regular air force as defined by section 223 of the Air Force Act 1955, the Queen Alexandra's Royal Naval Nursing Service and the Women's Royal Naval Service; and

"Registrar General" means the Registrar General of Births, Deaths and Marriages for Scotland.

(4) Expressions used in this Act of Sederunt which are used in the 1978 Act have the same meaning as in the 1978 Act.

(5) In this Act of Sederunt a form referred to by number means the form so numbered in the Schedule to this Act of Sederunt or a form substantially to the like effect, with such variation as circumstances may require.

Revocation

2. The Act of Sederunt (Adoption of Children) 1959 is revoked.

Appendix I

APPLICATION FOR AN ORDER DECLARING A CHILD FOR ADOPTION

Petition
3.—(1) An application under section 18(1) of the 1978 Act for an order declaring a child free for adoption shall be made by petition in form 1.

(2) There shall be lodged in process at the same time as the lodging of a petition under sub-paragraph (1)—

    (*a*) an extract of the entry in the Register of Births relating to the child who is the subject of the application;

    (*b*) a report of the adoption agency on the proposed adoption proceedings and the prospects for adoption, if such report is available;

    (*c*) the consent of a parent or guardian of the child to the petition (unless application for dispensation of consent is sought by the petitioner); and

    (*d*) any other document founded upon by the petitioner in support of the terms of the petition.

Consents and agreements to order freeing child for adoption
4.—(1) An agreement to an order under paragraph 3(1) required by section 18(1)(*a*), or a consent required by section 18(8), of the 1978 Act shall be in form 2 or 9 as appropriate and such form duly executed shall be sufficient evidence of such agreement or consent whether the document is executed before or after the commencement of proceedings.

(2) A form of consent or agreement under sub-paragraph (1) shall, if not available at the time of lodging the petition, be lodged so soon as is practicable thereafter.

(3) A form of consent or agreement executed outwith the United Kingdom shall be sufficient evidence of consent if it is executed—

    (*a*) if the person by whom the document is executed is serving in Her Majesty's forces, by an officer holding a commission in any of those forces; or

    (*b*) in any other case, by a British consular official, or by any person for the time being authorised by the law of the country in which the form is executed to administer an oath for any judicial or legal purpose.

Appointment of curator ad litem *and reporting officer*
5.—(1) The sheriff shall, after the lodging of a petition under paragraph 3, appoint a curator *ad litem* and reporting officer or reporting officers and, where reasonably practicable, shall appoint the same person as curator *ad litem* and reporting officer in the same petition.

(2) The sheriff may appoint a person who is not a member of a panel established under the Curators *Ad Litem* and Reporting Officers (Panels) (Scotland) Regulations 1984 to be a curator *ad litem* or a reporting officer.

(3) The sheriff may, on cause shown, appoint a reporting officer prior to the lodging of a petition.

(4) An application for an appointment under sub-paragraph (3) shall be made by letter addressed to the sheriff clerk specifying the reasons for the appointment, and shall not require to be intimated to any other person.

Duties of reporting officer and curator ad litem
6.—(1) A reporting officer appointed under this part of this Act of Sederunt shall—

[152]

(*a*) witness any agreement executed within the United Kingdom by a parent or guardian to the making of an adoption order in respect of his child and shall lodge the agreement in process;

(*b*) investigate the giving by a parent or guardian of his consent to the lodging of the petition;

(*c*) ascertain that each parent or guardian who can be found understands that the effect of an adoption order would be to deprive him permanently of his parental rights;

(*d*) ascertain whether there is any person other than those mentioned in the petition upon whom notice of the petition should be served;

(*e*) where a parent or guardian can be found, ascertain whether alternatives to adoption have been discussed with him;

(*f*) confirm that each parent or guardian who can be found understands the implications of an order freeing the child for adoption;

(*g*) confirm that each parent or guardian who can be found understands that he may withdraw his agreement at any time before an order under paragraph 3 is made;

(*h*) confirm that each parent or guardian who can be found is aware that he may in certain circumstances apply to the court for revocation of the order freeing the child for adoption and the appropriate procedure for such an application;

(*i*) confirm that each parent or guardian who can be found has been given an opportunity to make a declaration in terms of section 18(6) of the 1978 Act (declaration of preference not to be involved in future questions concerning the adoption of the child); and

(*j*) in the case of an illegitimate child, consider the likelihood of any person reputed to be the father of the child successfully raising proceedings for custody of, or access to, the child,

and shall report to the sheriff thereon.

(2) A curator *ad litem* appointed under this part of this Act of Sederunt shall—

(*a*) generally safeguard the interests of the child who is the subject of the petition and ensure that consideration has been given to the interests of the child required by section 6 of the 1978 Act (duty to promote welfare of child);

(*b*) ascertain whether the facts stated in the petition are correct except where investigation of such facts falls within the duties of the reporting officer;

(*c*) confirm that the child, if he is a minor, consented to the application;

(*d*) ascertain whether an order freeing the child for adoption would promote the child's well-being; and

(*e*) report on the current circumstances and care of the child,

and shall report to the sheriff thereon.

Declaration made under section 18(6) of the 1978 Act

7.—(1) A declaration made under section 18(6) of the 1978 Act shall be in form 3, be signed by each parent or guardian of the child and shall be witnessed by the reporting officer.

(2) The reporting officer shall provide a copy of the form of declaration to each parent or guardian of the child for signature and shall explain to him the consequences of signing the declaration and of the terms of section 19 of the 1978 Act (progress reports to former parents).

(3) The reporting officer shall submit the executed declaration to the sheriff clerk who shall thereafter record the declaration in the manner prescribed in paragraph 10.

Hearing
8.—(1) When the reports of the reporting officer and the curator *ad litem* have been received by the court, the sheriff shall order a diet of hearing to be fixed.

(2) Intimation of the diet of hearing shall be made in form 11 by the petitioner to every person who can be found and whose agreement or consent to the making of the order freeing the child for adoption is required to be given or dispensed with.

(3) If no person entitled to appear at such a hearing appears to be heard, the sheriff may make an order freeing the child for adoption on the motion of the petitioner.

(4) If a person, entitled to appear, appears and wishes to be heard, the sheriff may hear him or may order a further diet to be fixed at which he may be heard and evidence given at any such diet shall be given in the presence of the petitioner or his solicitor.

Confidentiality
9.—(1) All documents lodged in process, including the reports of the reporting officer and curator *ad litem* shall, unless the sheriff otherwise directs, be available only to the court, the reporting officer, the curator *ad litem* and the parties. Such documents shall be treated as confidential by any persons involved in, or a party to, the proceedings and by the sheriff clerk.

(2) The reporting officer or curator *ad litem* shall treat all information obtained by him in the exercise of his duties as confidential and shall not disclose any such information to any person unless disclosure of such information is necessary for the proper discharge of his duties.

Register of Adoptions
10.—(1) The sheriff clerk shall maintain a register known as the "Adoption Register".

(2) The sheriff clerk shall enter any declaration made under section 18(6) of the 1978 Act submitted to him by the reporting officer in the Adoption Register.

(3) A declaration under section 19(4) of the 1978 Act (declaration by former parent not to be involved in future questions concerning the adoption) shall be made in form 3 and the adoption agency shall submit the declaration to the sheriff clerk who shall enter it in the Adoption Register.

PART II

REVOCATION ORDERS, ETC.

Application for revocation
11.—(1) An application for revocation, under section 20(1) of the 1978 Act, of an order freeing a child for adoption shall be made by minute in the process of the original application in form 4 and shall specify detailed proposals for the future well-being of the child.

(2) On the lodging of a minute under sub-paragraph (1), the sheriff shall make an order requiring the applicant to intimate the minute to the petitioner in the original application and to such other person as shall to the sheriff seem appropriate.

(3) Any person to whom intimation has been made under sub-paragraph (2) may, within 14 days after the date on which intimation is made, lodge answers to the minute.

Appointment of curator ad litem

12. On the lodging of a minute under paragraph 11(1) the sheriff may appoint a curator *ad litem* who shall—

(*a*) investigate the facts contained in the minute, and

(*b*) investigate the circumstances and care of the child with regard to the promotion of his welfare throughout his childhood and, so far as practicable, ascertain his wishes and feelings regarding the minute, having regard to his age and understanding.

and shall report to the sheriff thereon.

Hearing

13.—(1) Where answers to the minute have been lodged, the sheriff shall order a diet of hearing to be fixed.

(2) Where no answers to the minute have been lodged, the sheriff may either—

(*a*) order a diet of hearing to be fixed, or

(*b*) order the relevant adoption agency to submit a report to him.

Application to place a child

14.—(1) An application by an adoption agency under section 20(2) of the 1978 Act (leave of court to place a child) shall be made by minute in the original process in form 5.

(2) A minute under sub-paragraph (1) shall be intimated by the applicant to such persons as shall to the sheriff seem appropriate.

Further applications with leave of the court

15. Any further application made with leave of the sheriff in terms of section 20(5) of the 1978 Act (further application by former parent with leave of the court) shall be made by minute in the original process and such minute shall be in form 6, and the provisions of paragraphs 11(2) and (3), 12 and 13 shall apply to an application under this paragraph as they apply to an application under paragraph 11(1).

Part III

Adoption Orders

Application for adoption order

16.—(1) An application for an adoption order, or for an order vesting parental rights and duties relating to a child under section 49(1) of the 1978 Act (adoption of children abroad), shall be made by petition in form 7 or 8 as appropriate.

(2) A petition under sub-paragraph (1) shall specify—

(*a*) the date upon which the child was received into the care and possession of the petitioner;

(*b*) whether the child has since that date been continously in the care and possession of the petitioner;

(*c*) the date upon which the petitioner notified the local authority for the area in which he was then resident of this intention to apply for an adoption order in respect of the child;

(*d*) whether the petitioner has received or given any reward or payment for or in consideration of the adoption of the child or for the giving of agreement or consent to the making of an adoption order;

(*e*) What persons have taken part in the arrangement for placing the child in his care; and

(*f*) particulars of any order freeing the child for adoption.

(3) There shall be iodged in process along with the petition—

(*a*) an extract of the entry in the Register of Births relating to the child who is the subject of the application;

(*b*) in the case of a joint peitition by a married couple, an extract of the entry in the Register of Marriages relating to their marriage;

(*c*) a medical certificate of the health of the petitioner or each of the joint petitioners except where the petitioner or one of the joint petitioners is a parent of the child;

(*d*) any report by the adoption agency required by section 23 of the 1978 Act (report on the suitability of the applicants);

(*e*) any report by the local authority required by section 22(2) of the 1978 Act (investigation by local authority on receipt of notice of intention to apply for adoption order);

(*f*) subject to the terms of paragraph 18(2), any consent required by section 12(8) (consent of minor), or any agreement required by section 16(1) (parental agreement), of the 1978 Act; and

(*g*) any other document founded upon by the petitioner in support of the terms of his petition.

(4) If no report by the adoption agency under sub-paragraph (3)(*d*) is available to be lodged along with the petition, the petitioner shall intimate the petition to the adoption agency concerned with a request that such a report be produced.

Additional requirements where child to be adopted abroad

17.—(1) In a petition for an order under section 49(1) of the 1978 Act, the petitioner shall, in addition to complying with paragraph 16, adduce evidence of the law of adoption in the country in which he is domiciled.

(2) The evidence of the law of adoption required under sub-paragraph (1) may be in the form of an affidavit by a person who is conversant with the law of adoption of that country and who practises or has practised law in that country or is a duly accredited representative of the government of that country in the United Kingdom.

Consents and agreement to adoption orders

18.—(1) A consent to an order under paragraph 16 required by section 12(8) or an agreement required by section 16(1), of the 1978 Act shall be in form 9 or 10 as appropriate and such form duly executed shall be sufficient evidence of such consent or agreement whether the document is executed before or after the commencement of proceedings.

(2) A form of consent or agreement under sub-paragraph (1) shall, if not available at the time of lodging the petition, be lodged so soon as is practicable thereafter.

(3) A form of consent or agreement executed outwith the United Kingdom shall be sufficient evidence of consent if it is executed—

(*a*) if the person by whom the document is executed is serving in Her Majesty's forces, by an officer holding a commission in any of those forces; or

(*b*) in any other case, by a British consular official, or by any person for the time being authorised by the law of the country in which the form is executed to administer an oath for any judicial or legal purpose.

Protection of identity of petitioner

19.—(1) When any person who proposes to apply for an order under paragraph 16 wishes to prevent his identity being disclosed to any person whose agreement to the order is required, he may, before presenting his petition, apply to the sheriff clerk for a serial number to be assigned to him for all purposes connected with the petition.

(2) On receipt of an application for a serial number, the sheriff clerk shall assign such a number to the applicant and shall enter a note of it opposite the name of the applicant in a register of such serial numbers.

(3) The contents of the register of serial numbers and the names of the persons to whom each number relates shall be treated as confidential by the sheriff clerk and shall not be disclosed to any person other than the sheriff.

(4) Where a serial number has been assigned to an applicant in terms of sub-paragraph (2), any form of agreement to an adoption order which is required shall not contain the name or designation of the petitioner but shall refer to him by means of the serial number assigned to him and shall specify the year in which, and by which court, such serial number has been assigned.

Appointment of reporting officer and curator ad litem

20.—(1) The sheriff shall, after the lodging of a petition under paragraph 16, appoint a curator *ad litem* and a reporting officer or reporting officers, and, where reasonably practicable, appoint the same person as curator *ad litem* and reporting officer in the same petition.

(2) The sheriff may appoint a person who is not a member of a panel established under the Curators *Ad Litem* and Reporting Officers (Panels) (Scotland) Regulations 1984 to be curator *ad litem* or a reporting officer.

Duties of reporting officer and curator ad litem

21.—(1) A reporting officer appointed under this part of this Act of Sederunt shall—

(a) witness any agreement executed within the United Kingdom by a parent or guardian to the making of an adoption order in respect of his child and shall lodge the agreement in process;

(b) ascertain that each parent or guardian whose agreement is required or may be dispensed with understands that the effect of the adoption order would be to deprive him permanently of his parental rights;

(c) ascertain whether there is any person other than those mentioned in the petition upon whom notice of the petition should be served;

(d) where a parent or guardian whose agreement is required or may be dispensed with can be found, ascertain whether alternatives to adoption have been discussed with him; and

(e) confirm that each parent or guardian whose agreement is required understands that he may withdraw his agreement at any time before an order under paragraph 16 is made,

and shall report to the sheriff thereon.

(2) A curator *ad litem* under this part of this Act of Sederunt shall—

(a) generally safeguard the interests of the child whose adoption is the subject of the petition;

(b) ascertain whether the facts stated in the petition are correct and if they are not establish the true facts;

(c) obtain particulars of the accommodation in the home of the petitioner and the condition of the home;

(d) obtain particulars of all members of the household of the petitioner and their relationship to the petitioner;

(e) in the case of a petition by one of two spouses, the reasons of the other spouse for not joining in the application;

(f) ascertain whether the means and status of the petitioner are sufficient to enable him to maintain and bring up the child suitably;

(g) ascertain what rights or interests in property the child has;

(*h*) establish that the petitioner understands the nature and effect of an adoption order and in particular that the making of the order will render him responsible for the maintenance and upbringing of the child;

(*i*) ascertain when the mother of the child ceased to have the care and possession of the child and to whom care and possession was then transferred;

(*j*) ascertain whether any payment or other reward in consideration of the adoption has been given or agreed upon;

(*k*) establish whether the adoption is likely to safeguard and promote the welfare of the child throughout his childhood;

(*l*) ascertain whether the life of the child has been insured and for what sum;

(*m*) ascertain whether it is in the interests of the welfare of the child that the sheriff should make any interim order or make the adoption order subject to particular terms and conditions or require the petitioner to make special provision for the child and if so what provision;

(*n*) where the petitioner is not ordinarily resident in the United Kingdom, establish whether a report has been obtained on the home and living conditions of the petitioner from a suitable agency in the country in which he is ordinarily resident;

(*o*) establish the reasons of the petitioner for wishing to adopt the child;

(*p*) establish to which religion, if any the petitioner subscribes;

(*q*) assess the considerations which might arise where the difference in ages as between the petitioner and the child is greater or less than the normal difference in age as between parents and their children;

(*r*) consider such other matters, including the personality of the petitioner and, where appropriate, that of the child, which might affect the suitability of the petitioner and the child for the relationship created by adoption and affect the ability of the petitioner to bring up the child; and

(*s*) ascertain, so far as practicable, the wishes and feelings of the child regarding the proposed adoption,

and shall report to the sheriff thereon.

Hearing

22.—(1) When the reports of the reporting officer and the curator *ad litem* in respect of a child who is not free for adoption have been received by the court, the sheriff shall order a diet of hearing to be fixed.

(2) Intimation of the diet of hearing shall be made in form 11 by the petitioner to the following persons—

(*a*) in a petition for an adoption order, every person who can be found and whose agreement or consent to the making of such an order is required to be given or dispensed with, or

(*b*) in a petition for an order under section 49(1) of the 1978 Act, every person who can be found and whose agreement to the making of such an order would be required if the application were for an adoption order.

(3) The sheriff may, if he considers it appropriate, ordain the petitioner to serve notice of the date of the hearing in form 11, on the following persons—

(*a*) any person or body having the rights and powers of a parent of the child or having the custody or care of the child or a local authority having the child committed to its care by virtue of section 5 of the Guardianship of Infants Act 1886, section 10 of the Matrimonial Proceedings (Children) Act 1958, sections 16 and 17 of the Social Work (Scotland) Act 1968, section 9 of the Guardianship of Minors

Act 1971, section 43 of the Matrimonial Causes Act 1973, or sections 2(2)(*b*) and (11)(1)(*a*) of the Guardianship Act 1973;

(*b*) any person liable by virtue of any order or agreement to contribute to the maintenance of the child;

(*c*) the local authority to whom the petitioner has given notice of his intention to apply for an adoption order;

(*d*) any other person or body who in the opinion of the sheriff ought to be served with notice of the hearing.

(4) If no person entitled to appear at such a hearing appears to be heard, the sheriff may grant an adoption order on the motion of the petitioner.

(5) If a person, entitled to appear, appears and wishes to be heard, the sheriff may hear him or may order a further diet to be fixed at which he may be heard. Evidence given at such diets shall be given in the presence of the petitioner or his solicitor.

Insufficient evidence

23. If the sheriff is not satisfied that the facts stated in the petition are supported by the documents lodged along with the petition or by the reports of the curator *ad litem* and reporting officer, or if for any reason he considers it appropriate, he may refuse to grant any adoption order or interim order without production of further documents or hearing oral evidence and may order that such productions be lodged or evidence led.

Confidentiality

24.—(1) Unless the sheriff otherwise directs, all documents lodged in process including the reports by the curator *ad litem* and the reporting officer shall be available only to the sheriff, the curator *ad litem*, the reporting officer and the parties. Such documents shall be treated as confidential by all persons involved in, or a party to, the proceedings and by the sheriff clerk.

(2) The reporting officer or curator *ad litem* shall treat all information obtained by him in the exercise of his duties as confidential and shall not disclose any such information to any person unless disclosure of such information is necessary for the proper discharge of his duties.

Adoption by married couples

25. A married couple may petition for an adoption order in respect of a child who has already been adopted by one of them.

Communications to the Registrar General

26. The communication to the Registrar General of an adoption order or order for the revocation of an adoption order required to be made by the sheriff clerk shall be made by sending a certified copy of the order to the Registrar General either by recorded delivery post in an envelope marked "Confidential" or by personal delivery by the sheriff clerk in a sealed envelope marked "Confidential".

Adoption orders

27.—(1) An adoption order granted by the sheriff shall specify the name and address of the adoption agency, if any, which has taken part in the arrangements for placing the child in the care of the petitioner.

(2) No extract of an adoption order shall be issued except with the authority of the sheriff who made the order.

(3) The authority required by sub-paragraph (2) shall be obtained by lodging a petition setting forth the reasons for which the extract is required.

Final procedure

28.—(1) After the granting of an order under this part of this Act of Sederunt the court process shall, immediately upon the communication under paragraph 26 being made or, in the event of an extract of the order being issued under paragraph 27, immediately upon the issue of such extract, be sealed by the sheriff clerk in an envelope marked "Confidential".

(2) The envelope referred to in sub-paragraph (1) shall not be unsealed by the sheriff clerk or any other person having control of the records of that or any court, and the process shall not be made accessible to any person, for 100 years after the date of the granting of the adoption order except—

    (*a*) to an adopted child who has attained the age of 17 years and to whose adoption the process refers;

    (*b*) to the sheriff clerk, on an application made to him by an adoption agency and with the consent of the adopted person for the purpose only of ascertaining the name of the agency, if any, responsible for the placement of that person and informing the applicant of that name;

    (*c*) to a court, public authority or administrative board (whether in the United Kingdom or not) having power to authorise an adoption, on petition by it to the court which granted the original order requesting that information be made available from the process for the purpose of discharging its duties in considering an application for adoption and specifying the precise reasons for which access to the process is required; or

    (*d*) to a person who is authorised by the Secretary of State to obtain information from the process for the purposes of such research as is intended to improve the working of adoption law and practice.

Amendment of adoption order

29—(1) An application under paragraph 4(1) of Schedule 1 to (amendment of orders and rectification of Registers), or section 46(1) of (revocation where adoptive parent marries other parent), the 1978 Act shall be by petition to the court which pronounced the adoption order.

(2) The sheriff may order the petitioner to intimate the petition to such persons as to the sheriff may seem appropriate.

(3) In an application for revocation of an adoption order the sheriff shall not grant a petition unless he is satisfied that the petition has been served upon every parent of the child whose whereabouts can be ascertained.

Application for removal of child pending adoption

30.—(1) An application under section 27(1) (restrictions on removal where adoption agreed or application made under section 18(1)), section 28 (restrictions on removal where applicant has provided home for five years), section 29 (return of child taken away in breach of section 27 or 28), or section 30(2) (return of children placed for adoption), of the 1978 Act shall be made by minute lodged in the process of the original adoption petition.

(2) A minute under paragraph (1) shall set forth the relevant facts and the crave which the minuter wishes to make.

(3) On receipt of the minute the sheriff shall order a diet of hearing to be fixed and shall ordain the minuter to send a notice of such hearing in form 12 together with a copy of the minute by registered post or by recorded delivery letter to the petitioner or petitioners in the original petition, to the curator *ad litem* in the original petition, to any person who may have care and possession of the child and to such other persons as the sheriff may deem appropriate.

PART IV

EXPENSES

Expenses
31. The sheriff may make such order with regard to the expenses of an application under this Act of Sederunt as he thinks fit and may modify such expenses or direct them to be taxed on such scale as he may determine.

Appendix I

SCHEDULE

Paragraph 3(1)   Form 1

APPLICATION FOR AN ORDER DECLARING A CHILD FREE FOR ADOPTION UNDER THE ADOPTION (SCOTLAND) ACT 1978 SECTION 18

PETITION OF

A.B. (address), Petitioner

For an order in relation to the child, C.D.

(Full Name)
(Date of Birth)

Presently residing at

(Address)

The Petitioner craves the court [(1)] to make an order declaring the child, C.D., free for adoption [; and (2) to dispense with the agreement [or consent] of
on the ground that

].

The following documents are produced herewith:

     a.   An extract of the entry in the Register of Births relating to the child;

     b.   *Consent of *(name and address)* to the making of this application;

     c.   *Consent by the child dated   ;

     d.   *Adoption agency report dated

                                    Signed ....
                                      and designation

                                      Date ....

*Delete as appropriate.

Paragraph 4(1)   Form 2

FORM OF PARENTAL AGREEMENT UNDER THE ADOPTION (SCOTLAND) ACT 1978 SECTION 18

In the petition by *(adoption agency, name and address)*

for an order declaring the child—
                     —*(full name of child)*

free for adoption,

I, *(name, address)*

confirm that I am the mother/father/guardian of the child. I fully understand that on the making of an order under section 18 of the Adoption (Scotland) Act 1978 any parental right or duty which I have at present relating to the child vests in the petitioners and that the effect of an adoption order will be permanently to deprive me of these parental rights or duties. I freely agree generally and unconditionally to the making of an adoption order in relation to the child.

[162]

I have signed this agreement at (*place of signing*)

on the   day of   Nineteen
hundred and   years.

(*Signature*) ....

This agreement was signed in the presence of:—

(*Signature of reporting officer*) ....

Full name

Address

Paragraph 7(1) or 10(3)   Form 3

DECLARATION UNDER SECTION 18(6) OR SECTION 19(4) OF THE ADOPTION (SCOTLAND) ACT 1978

In the petition by (*adoption agency, name and address*)

for an order declaring the child (*full name*)

free for adoption,

I/We,

being the

of the child, hereby declare that I/we prefer not to be involved in future questions concerning the adoption of the child.

In witness whereof I/we have signed this declaration on the
                              day of   , Nineteen hundred
and

               Signature ....
               Signature ....

Signed in presence of

(*Signature*) ....
Full name

Designation   and Reporting Officer

Address

FOR OFFICIAL USE ONLY

The foregoing declaration was received at the Sheriff Clerk's Office,

                                     on   19   , and has
been duly entered in the adopted register of that court.

                                   Signature ....

                                   Sheriff Clerk Depute

[163]

Paragraph 11(1)   Form 4

APPLICATION TO REVOKE AN ORDER FREEING A CHILD FOR ADOPTION UNDER THE ADOPTION (SCOTLAND) ACT 1978 SECTION 20(1)

MINUTE

by

(full name, address)

in relation to the child

(full name and date of birth)

The minuter craves the court to revoke the order declaring the child free for adoption on the ground that he/she wishes to resume parental rights and duties and condescends as follows:

1. An order freeing the child for adoption was made on
2. More than 12 months have elapsed since the child was freed for adoption
3. No adoption order has been made in respect of the child
4. The child at present resides at
   and does not have his home with a person with whom he had been placed for adoption
5. The minuter makes the following proposals for the future well-being of the child:—

Signed ....
and designation

Date ....

Paragraph 14(1)   Form 5

APPLICATION (FOR LEAVE OF COURT) TO PLACE CHILD FOR ADOPTION UNDER THE ADOPTION (SCOTLAND) ACT 1978 SECTION 20(2)

MINUTE BY

(full name, address)

in relation to the child

(full name and address and date of birth)

presently residing at

The minuters crave leave of the court to place the child for adoption and condescend as follows:

a. An order in terms of section 18 of the Adoption (Scotland) Act 1978 declaring the child free for adoption was made by the court on   19   , in a petition by the minuters.

b. An application to revoke the aforesaid order was lodged on   19   , by and application for revocation has not yet been determined by the court.

c. *(Set out here the circumstances justifying the placing of the child)*

Date ....   Signature ....
and designation

Act of Sederunt (Adoption of Children) 1984

Paragraph 15   Form 6

FURTHER APPLICATION BY FORMER PARENT TO REVOKE AN ORDER FREEING A CHILD FOR ADOPTION UNDER THE ADOPTION (SCOTLAND) ACT 1978 SECTION 20(5)

MINUTE BY

(full name and address)

in relation to the child

(full name and address) born on *(date of birth)*

The minuter craves leave of the court to make this further application on the ground that:— *(narrate the change in circumstances or other proper reason for application)*

The minuter craves the court to revoke the order declaring the child free for adoption on the ground that he wishes to resume parental rights and duties and condescends as follows:

a.   An order freeing the child for adoption was made on

b.   An application to the court to revoke the order was made
     on   , but was refused on

c.   More than 12 months have elapsed since the child was freed for adoption.

d.   No adoption order has been made in respect of the child.

e.   The child at present resides at
     and does not have his home with a person with whom he has been placed for adoption.

f.   The minuter makes the following proposals for the future well-being of the child:—

Signature ....
and designation

Date ....

Paragraph 16(1)   Form 7

PETITION FOR ADOPTION ORDER UNDER THE ADOPTION (SCOTLAND) ACT 1978 SECTION 12

Petition of

A.B. *(full name)*

[and *(full name of spouse)*

Maiden surname

Any previous married surname]

(Address)

For authority to adopt the child

(Full name of child as shown on birth certificate), born on

(Child's date of birth)

(Child's present address)

1. The petitioner(s) crave(s) the court [(1)] to make an adoption order in his/her/their favour under section 12 of the Adoption (Scotland) Act 1978, in relation to the child [; and to dispense with the agreement [*or* consent] of   on the ground that   ] and condescends as follows:

[165]

a. The petitioner(s) is/are domiciled in
                                        and reside(s) at
   [*or* the male/female petitioner is domiciled in
   and both petitioners reside at   ].

b. The occupation(s) of the petitioner(s) is/are

c. The petitioner(s) is/are married [*or* unmarried *or* widow *or* widower]. (*If married, state whether spouse resides with, or apart, from, the petitioner.*)

d. The petitioner(s) is/are [respectively]   [and]
   years of age.

e. The petitioner(s) has/have resident with him/her/them the following persons, namely

f. The child was received into the care and possession of the petitioners on (*date*)

g. The child has been continuously in the care and possession of the petitioner(s) since the date shown above.

h. The petitioner(s) notified (*give name of local authority notified*) of his/her/their intention to apply for an adoption order in relation to the child on (*date*)

i. *Arrangements for placing the child in the care of the petitioner(s) were made by (*give full name and address of agency or authority or person making such arrangements*)

   (*Delete this statement if it does not apply)

j. An order freeing the child for adoption was made at
                                        Sheriff Court on (*date*)
   [*or* An order declaring the child free for adoption has not been made.]

k. No reward or payment has been given or received by the petitioner(s) for or in consideration of the adoption of the child or the giving of consent to the making of an adoption order.

2. a. The child is   years of age, having been born on the   day of
                              19 , at
       in the County of

    b. The child is not and never has been married and is male/female.

    c. The child's natural mother is
       (*full name and address*)

    d.* The child's natural father is
       (*full name and address*)

    e.* Paternity of the child has not been admitted or established by decree of any court.

       (*Delete either d. or e. as appropriate)

    f. The child is of British/or   nationality.

    g. The child is entitled to the following property, namely

    h. The child has the following tutors, curators or guardians. (*Either give full names and addresses or delete the paragraph if it does not apply*).

3.   is/are liable to contribute to
the support of the child.

4. The child has not been the subject of an adoption order or of a petition for an adoption order save that

5. The petitioner(s) is/are prepared to undertake, if any order is made on this petition, to make for the said child the following provisions, namely:—

[166]

6. There is lodged along with this application the following documents

    (i)   extract birth certificate relating to the child

    (ii)   extract marriage certificate relating to the petitioner(s)
        (Note: this need be lodged only in the case of a joint application by spouses)

    (iii)   medical certificate relating to the health of the male petitioner

    (iv)   medical certificate relating to the health of the female petitioner
        (Note: medical certificate need not be produced where either the petitioner or one of the joint petitioners is a parent of the child)

    (v)*   agreement to the adoption by the child's natural mother

    (vi)*   agreement to the adoption by the child's natural father

    (vii)*   consent to the adoption by the child

    (viii)* consent to the adoption by the tutor or curator

    (ix)*   acknowledgement by local authority of letter by petitioner(s) intimating intention to apply for adoption order

    (x)*   report by local authority in terms of section 22(2) of the Adoption (Scotland) Act 1978

    (xi)*   report by the adoption agency in terms of section 23 of the Adoption (Scotland) Act 1978

    (xii)* any other document not referred to above.

        (*Delete as appropriate)

7.   have taken part in the arrangements for placing the child in the care of the petitioner(s)

The petitioner(s) humbly crave(s) the court to dispense with intimation and to order notice of this petition to be served on such persons, if any, as the court may think proper, and thereafter, on resuming consideration hereon, to make

an adoption order in favour of the petitioner(s) under the Adoption (Scotland) Act 1978 section 12 on such terms and conditions (if any) as the court may think fit, and to direct the Registrar General for Scotland to make an entry regarding the adoption in the Adopted Children Register in the form prescribed by him, giving   as the forename(s), and the surname of the adopter(s) as the surname, of   in the form; and further, upon proof to the satisfaction of the court in the course of the proceedings to follow hereon, that *(name of child)*
was born on the   day of
in the year nineteen hundred and
and is identical with the
to whom any entry numbered   and made on the day of
                        in the year 19   , in the Register of Births for the Registration District of   in the   relates, to direct the said Registrar General to cause such birth entry to be marked with the word "adopted" and to include the above-mentioned date of birth in the entry recording the adoption in the manner indicated in the Schedule to the   and to pronounce such other or further orders or directions upon such matters, including the expenses of this petition, as the court may think fit.

                        ....
                        Signature of male petitioner

                        ....
                        Signature of female petitioner

                        or

                        ....
                        Signature of solicitor with designation and address
                        ....

                        ....

Appendix I

Paragraph 16(1)   Form 8

PETITION FOR AN ORDER UNDER THE ADOPTION (SCOTLAND) ACT 1978
SECTION 49

Petition of

A.B. (*full name*)

[and (*full name of spouse*)

Maiden surname

Any previous married surname]

(*Address*)

For an order vesting in him/her/them the parental rights and duties relating to the child.

(*Full name of child as shown on birth certificate*), born on

(*Child's date of birth*)

(*Child's present address*)

1. The petitioner(s) crave(s) the court [(1)] to make an order under section 49 of the Adoption (Scotland) Act 1978 vesting in him/her/them the parental rights and duties relating to the child [; and to dispense with the agreement [*or* consent] of   on the ground that   ] and condescends as follows:

    a. The petitioner(s) is/are domiciled in
                              and reside(s) at

    b. The occupation(s) of the petitioner(s) is/are

    c. The petitioner(s) is/are married [*or* unmarried *or* widow *or* widower]. (*If married, state whether spouse resides with, or apart from, the petitioner.*)

    d. The petitioner(s) is/are [respectively]   [and]
       years of age.

    e. The petitioner(s) has/have resident with him/her/them the following persons, namely

    f. The child was received into the care and possession of the petitioners on (*date*)

    g. The child has been continuously in the care and possession of the petitioner(s) since the date shown above.

    h. The petitioner(s) notified (*give name of local authority notified*) of his/her/their intention to apply for an adoption order in relation to the child on (*date*)

    i. *Arrangements for placing the child in the care of the petitioner(s) were made by (*give full name and address of agency or authority or person making such arrangements*)

      (*Delete this statement if it does not apply)

    j. An order freeing the child for adoption was made at
                      Sheriff Court on (*date*)
      [*or* an order declaring the child free for adoption has not been made.]

    k. No reward or payment has been given or received by the petitioner(s) for or in consideration of the adoption of the child or the giving of consent to the making of an adoption order.

2. a. The child is   years of age, having been born on the   day of
       19 , at   in the County of

    b. The child is not and has never been married and is male/female.

    c. The child's natural mother is (*full name and address*)

[168]

d.* The child's natural father is (*full name and address*)

OR

e.* Paternity of the child has not been admitted or established by decree of any court.

(*Delete either d. or e. as appropriate)

f.   The child is of British/or   nationality.

g.   The child is entitled to the following property, namely

h.   The child has the following tutors, curators or guardians. (*Either give full names and addresses or delete the paragraph if it does not apply*).

3.   is/are liable to contribute to the support of the child.

4. The child has not been the subject of an adoption order or of a petition for an adoption order save that

5. The petitioner(s) is/are prepared to undertake, if any order is made on this petition, to make for the said child the following provision, namely:—

6. There is lodged along with this application the following documents

(i)   extract birth certificate relating to the child

(ii)   extract marriage certificate relating to the petitioner(s)
(*Note: this need be lodged only in the case of a joint application by spouses*)

(iii)   medical certificate relating to the health of the male petitioner

(iv)   medical certificate relating to the health of the female petitioner
(*Note: medical certificates need not be produced where either the petitioner or one of the joint petitioners is a parent of the child*)

(v)*   agreement to the adoption by the child's natural mother

(vi)*   agreement to the adoption by the child's natural father

(vii)* consent to the adoption by the child

(viii)* consent to the adoption by the tutor or curator

(ix)*   acknowledgement by local authority of letter by petitioner(s) intimating intention to apply for adoption order

(x)*   report by local authority in terms of section 22(2) of the Adoption (Scotland) Act 1978

(xi)*   report by the adoption agency in terms of section 23 of the Adoption (Scotland) Act 1978

(xii)* an affidavit by   who is conversant with the law of
         adoption of   and has practised law as a
                                      [*or* represents that country as (*state capacity*)
                       in the United Kingdom].

(*Delete where appropriate)

7.   have taken part in the arrangement for placing the child in the care of the petitioner(s).

The petitioner(s) humbly crave(s) the court to dispense with intimation and to order notice of this petition to be served on such persons, if any, as the court may think proper, and thereafter, on resuming consideration hereof, to make

[169]

an order under the Adoption (Scotland) Act 1978 section 49, vesting in the petitioners the parental rights and duties relating to (*name of child*)   on such terms and conditions (if any) as the court may think fit; to authorise removal of the child for the purpose of adoption under the laws of   ; to find the petitioners entitled to the custody of the child pending such adoptions and to direct the Registrar General for Scotland to make an entry regarding the order in the Adopted Children Register in the form prescribed by him, giving

as the forename(s), and the surname of the proposed adopters as the surname, of   in the form; and further, upon proof to the satisfaction of the court in the course of the proceedings to follow hereon, that the child

was born on the   day of

in the year Nineteen hundred and

and is identical with the

to whom any entry numbered   and made on the

day of   in the year 19   , in the Register of Births for the

Registration District of   in the   relates, to direct the said Registrar General to cause such birth entry to be marked with the words "proposed foreign adoption" and to include the above-mentioned date of birth in the entry recording the order in the manner indicated in the Schedule to the said Act; and to pronounce such other or further orders or directions upon such matters, including the expenses of this petition, as the court may think fit.

....

Signature of male petitioner or agent

....

Signature of female petitioner or agent

or

....

Signature of solicitor with designation and address

....

....

Paragraph 4(1) or 18(1)   Form 9

FORM OF CONSENT UNDER THE ADOPTION (SCOTLAND) ACT 1978
SECTION 12(8) OR SECTION 18(8)

in the

Petition

by

(*Name and address*)   Petitioner

I, (*full name of child*) confirm that I understand the nature and effect of any order declaring me free for adoption/adoption order for which application is made. I hereby consent to the making of such an order in the petitioners' favour in respect of myself.

I have signed this consent at (*place of signing*)

on the   day of   Nineteen

hundred and   years.

(*Signature*)

This consent was signed in the presence of:—

[170]

1st Witness	2nd Witness
Signature	Signature
Full Name	Full Name
Designation	Designation
Address	Address

Paragraph 18(1)   Form 10

FORM OF PARENTAL AGREEMENT UNDER THE ADOPTION (SCOTLAND) ACT 1978 SECTION 16(1)

In the petition relating to the adoption of

(Insert the full name of the child as it is given in the birth certificate)

to which petition the court has assigned the serial number

I, *(name and address)*

confirm that I am the mother/father/guardian of the child. I fully understand that the effect of the adoption order for which application has been made will be permanently to deprive me of any parental right or duty which I have at present over the child. I freely agree generally and unconditionally to the making of an adoption order in relation to the child.

I have signed this agreement at *(place of signing)*

on the   day of   Nineteen

hundred and   years.

(Signature)

This agreement was signed in the presence of:—

(Signature of reporting officer)

Full name

Address

Appendix I

FORM OF INTIMATION OF DIET OF HEARING UNDER THE ADOPTION (SCOTLAND) ACT 1978 SECTION 12 OR SECTION 18

To:—

(Full name and address of person to whom this intimation is to be sent)

Notice is given that a hearing will take place at

Sheriff Court

(Name of sheriff court)

(Full address of court)

on   at

       (date)   *(time)*

in relation to the child *(full name of child as given in the birth certificate)*

when the court will consider an application for an order declaring the child free for adoption [*or an application for adoption of the child*].

You do not need to attend this hearing if you do not wish to be heard by the court.

If you do not attend this hearing the court may make an order as noted above.

Signature
and designation ....
Date

Paragraph 30(3)   Form 12

FORM OF INTIMATION OF DIET OF HEARING UNDER THE ADOPTION (SCOTLAND) ACT 1978 SECTION 27, 28, 29 OR 30

Notice of hearing of minute in petition for authority to adopt:

(Full name of child as given in the birth certificate)

To:—

(Full name and address of person to whom this intimation is to be sent)

Notice is hereby given that a hearing in the petition for authority to adopt the child, which hearing will be restricted to matters bearing upon the crave of the minute, a copy of which is attached hereto, will take place at *(name of sheriff court)*

Sheriff Court (*address*)

on

(*date*) at   (*time*) when, if so advised, you may appear
and be heard personally or by solicitor or counsel.

Signature

....

Designation

Date

3. Act of Sederunt (Rules of Court, consolidation and amendment) 1965

(S.I. 1965 No. 321)

[10th November 1964]

CHAPTER IV

PETITIONS

[1] SECTION 4—ADOPTION OF CHILDREN

ADOPTION ACTS 1958 TO 1964 AND CHILDREN ACT 1975

NOTE
[1] Substituted by S.I. 1984 No. 997.

Interpretation
   219.—(1) In this section, unless the context otherwise requires—
   "the 1978 Act" means the Adoption (Scotland) Act 1978;
   "adoption agency" means a local authority or an approved adoption society;
   "Her Majesty's Forces" means the Royal Navy, the regular armed forces as defined by section 225 of the Army Act 1955, the regular air force as defined by section 223 of the Air Force Act 1955, the Queen Alexandra's Royal Naval Nursing Services and the Women's Royal Naval Service; and
   "Registrar General" means the Registrar General of Births, Deaths and Marriages for Scotland.

(2) Expressions which are used in this section and are also used in the 1978 Act have the same meaning as in that Act.

(3) In this section, a form referred to by number means the form so numbered in the Appendix to the rules or a form substantially to the like effect, with such variation as circumstances may require.

Freeing for adoption
220.—(1) An application by an adoption agency for an order freeing a child for adoption under section 18(1) of the 1978 Act shall be made by petition in the Outer House.

(2) Rules 192 and 195 to 197 shall not apply to a petition under this rule, and the petition shall not be intimated on the walls or in the minute book or advertised.

(3) A petition under paragraph (1) shall include averments about, or refer to a report or other documents produced which deal with, the following matters—

   (a) whether the petition is presented with the consent of a parent or guardian;
   (b) whether the petitioner is applying for dispensation of the agreement of a parent or guardian under section 18(1)(b) of the 1978 Act and on what ground in section 16(2) of the 1978 Act dispensation is sought;
   (c) how the needs of the child came to the notice of the petitioner;
   (d) any relevant family circumstances of the child;
   (e) a description of the physical and mental health of the child (including any special needs) and his emotional, behavioural and educational development;
   (f) an account of the discussion by the petitioner with the parents or guardians of the child and, if appropriate, with the child about their wishes and the alternatives to adoption;
   (g) the knowledge of the petitioner of the position of other relatives or persons likely to be involved;
   (h) an account of the search by the petitioner for any parent or guardian who cannot be found;
   (i) the likelihood of placement of the child for adoption and whether a petition for an adoption order is likely in the near future;
   (j) the arrangements of the petitioner to care for the child after the granting of the prayer of the petition for an order freeing a child for adoption;
   (k) whether the petitioner has given each parent or guardian who can be found an opportunity to make a declaration under section 18(6) of the 1978 Act that he prefers not to be involved in future questions concerning the adoption of the child;
   (l) an account of the inquiries by the petitioner into the circumstances of any reputed father;
   (m) the intentions of the petitioner about giving notice to a former parent or guardian under section 19(2) and (3) of the 1978 Act; and
   (n) any other information which may be of assistance to the court.

(4) Where a petition is presented with the consent of a parent or guardian, there shall be appended to the petition a consent in Form 37 duly signed by that parent or guardian and witnessed.

(5) There shall be lodged in process with the petition—

   (a) an extract of the entry, if any, in the Register of Births relating to the child; and
   (b) any other document founded on by the petitioner for the purpose of vouching averments in the petition.

(6) On presentation of the petition, the court—
- (*a*) shall appoint a reporting officer with the duties in Rule 224(1);
- (*b*) shall appoint a curator *ad litem* with the duties in Rule 224(4) where it appears that a parent or guardian of the child is unwilling to agree to the making of an adoption order; and
- (*c*) may appoint a curator *ad litem* with the duties in Rule 224(4) in any case where it appears to the court to be desirable in the circumstances of the case in order to safeguard the interests of the child.

(7) Where a curator *ad litem* is appointed, the court may order the petitioner, a local authority or the reporting officer to make available to the curator *ad litem* any report or information in relation to the child and the natural father and mother of the child.

(8) The reporting officer shall, on completion of his report, lodge three copies of it in process together with—
- (*a*) any agreement under section 18(1)(*a*) of the 1978 Act in Form 37A;
- (*b*) any consent under section 18(8) of the 1978 Act in Form 38; and
- (*c*) any declaration under section 18(6) of the 1978 Act in Form 37A.

(9) The curator *ad litem* shall, on completion of his report, lodge three copies of it in process.

(10) On receipt of the report of the reporting officer and, where one has been appointed, the report of the curator *ad litem*, the petition department shall—
- (*a*) inform the petitioner that the reports have been lodged and that a motion for a hearing to determine the application must be enrolled within seven days; and
- (*b*) make available to the petitioner, and to any other party, a copy of the report.

(11) At the motion for a hearing to determine the application, the court shall consider—
- (*a*) whether to require any person, whose agreement or consent is required to be given or dispensed with, to attend the hearing to determine the application;
- (*b*) whether to require intimation of the date of the hearing to determine the application to any other person; and
- (*c*) whether to require the reporting officer or a curator *ad litem* to perform any other duties.

(12) On a date being fixed for a hearing to determine the application, the petitioner shall intimate the date of the hearing in Form 39—
- (*a*) to every person who can be found whose agreement or consent is required to be given or dispensed with;
- (*b*) to the reporting officer and, where one has been appointed, to the curator *ad litem*; and
- (*c*) to any person upon whom intimation has been ordered by the court under paragraph (11)(*b*).

(13) At the hearing to determine the application—
- (*a*) the petitioner, the reporting officer and, where one has been appointed, the curator *ad litem* shall, if required by the court, appear and may be represented;
- (*b*) any person required by the court to attend the hearing shall appear and may be represented; and
- (*c*) any other person upon whom intimation was made under paragraph (12)(*a*) or (*c*) may appear or be represented.

(14) The court shall, where a declaration has been made under section 18(6) of the 1978 Act, record the fact of that declaration in the interlocutor making the order freeing a child for adoption.

Revocation of freeing for adoption order

221.—(1) An application by a former parent under section 20(1) of the

1978 Act for revocation of an order freeing a child for adoption shall be made by note in the process of the petition for that order.

(2) Rules 191 to 196 and 198 shall apply to a note under this Rule as they apply to a petition, except that a note under this Rule shall not be intimated on the walls or in the minute book or advertised.

(3) On presentation of the note, the court—

(*a*) shall make an order for service upon—

(i) the petitioner;

(ii) any person upon whom the petition was intimated, except a parent or guardian who has made a declaration under section 18(6) or 19(4) of the 1978 Act;

(iii) any adoption agency in which parental rights and duties relating to the child are vested by virtue of section 21 of the 1978 Act; and

(*b*) shall appoint a curator *ad litem* with the duties in Rule 224(5) where it appears to the court to be desirable in the circumstances of the case in order to safeguard the interests of the child.

(4) Where a curator *ad litem* is appointed, the court may order the adoption agency, a local authority or the reporting officer to make available to the curator *ad litem* any report or information in relation to the child and the natural father and mother of the child.

(5) The curator *ad litem* shall, on completion of his report, lodge three copies of it in process.

(6) On receipt of the report of the curator *ad litem*, where one has been appointed, the petition department shall—

(*a*) inform the noter that the report has been lodged and that a motion for a hearing to determine the application must be enrolled within seven days; and

(*b*) make available to the noter and to any other party, a copy of the report.

(7) At the motion for a hearing to determine the application, the court shall consider, in an application to which section 20(5) of the 1978 Act applies, whether to grant leave to allow the application to proceed.

(8) On a date being fixed for a hearing to determine the application, the noter shall intimate the date of the hearing in Form 39A to the adoption agency and, where one has been appointed, to the curator *ad litem*.

(9) At the hearing to determine the application, the noter, the adoption agency and, where one has been appointed, the curator *ad litem* shall appear and may be represented.

(10) An application, by an adoption agency having the parental rights and duties relating to a child, for leave under section 20(2) of the 1978 Act to place that child for adoption while the application under this Rule for revocation of an order freeing that child for adoption is pending, shall be made by motion in the process for revocation of that order.

Adoption orders
222.—(1) An application for an adoption order shall be made by petition in the Outer House by the proposed adopter in Form 36.

(2) Rules 191, 192 and 195 to 197 shall not apply to a petition under this Rule, and a petition shall not be intimated on the walls or in the minute book or advertised.

(3) Where a person, who proposes to present a petition for an adoption order, desires that his identity should not be disclosed to any person whose agreement is required under section 16(1) of the 1978 Act, he may apply in writing to the clerk of court before presenting the petition for a serial number to be assigned to him, and in such a case—

(*a*) the record of the serial number assigned and the person to whom it applies shall be confidential and open only to the court; and (*b*) an agreement under section 16(1) of the 1978 Act in Form 37B shall not name the petitioner but shall refer to him as the petitioner to whom that serial number has been assigned and shall specify the year in which that serial number was applied.

(4) There shall be lodged in process with the petition—

(*a*) an extract of the entry, if any, in the Register of Births relating to the birth of the child;

(*b*) an extract of the entry in the Register of Births relating to the birth of the petitioner;

(*c*) in the case of a petition by a married couple, an extract of the entry in the Register of Marriages relating to their marriage;

(*d*) where the child was not placed for adoption with the applicant by an adoption agency, three copies of a medical report showing the physical and mental health of the child (including any special needs) and his emotional, behavioural and educational development; and

(*e*) any other document founded on by the petitioner for the purpose of vouching averments in the petition.

(5) On presentation of the petition, the court—

(*a*) shall make an order requiring the petitioner to give notice in Form 39B—

(i) where the child has been placed for adoption, to the adoption agency which placed the child; or

(ii) where the child has not been placed for adoption, to the local authority within whose area the petitioner lives;

(*b*) shall appoint a reporting officer with the duties in Rule 224(2);

(*c*) shall appoint a curator *ad litem* with the duties in Rule 224(6) where the child is not free for adoption and it appears that a parent or guardian is unwilling to agree to the making of an adoption order; and

(*d*) may appoint a curator *ad litem* with the duties in Rule 224(6) where it appears to the court to be desirable in the circumstances of the case in order to safeguard the interests of the child.

(6) Where a curator *ad litem* is appointed, the court may order the adoption agency, a local authority or the reporting officer to make available to the curator *ad litem* any report or information in relation to the child and the natural father and mother of the child.

(7) A report by a local authority under section 22(2), or an adoption agency under section 23, of the 1978 Act shall include the following matters—

(*a*) information about how the needs of the child came to the notice of the agency;

(*b*) the family circumstances of the child;

(*c*) where the child was placed for adoption by an adoption agency, a description of the physical and mental health of the child (including any special needs) and his emotional, behavioural and educational development;

(*d*) an account of the discussion with the parents or guardians of the child and, if appropriate, with the child about their wishes and the alternatives to adoption;

(*e*) the position of other relatives or persons likely to be involved;

(*f*) an account of the search for a parent or guardian who cannot be found;

(*g*) information about the mutual suitability of the petitioner and the child for the relationship created by adoption and the ability of the petitioner to bring up the child including an assessment of the personality of the petitioner and, where appropriate, that of the child;

(*h*) particulars of all members of the household of the petitioner and their relationship to the petitioner;

(*i*) a description of the accommodation in the home of the petitioner;

(*j*) in a petition by one of two spouses, why the other spouse has not joined in the petition;

(*k*) whether the petitioner understands the nature and effect of an adoption order and in particular that the order, if made, will make the petitioner responsible for the maintenance and upbringing of the child;

(*l*) whether the means and standing of the petitioner are such as to enable him to maintain and bring up the child suitably, and what right or interest in property the child has;

(*m*) whether any payment or other reward in consideration of the adoption, other than an approved adoption allowance, has been received or agreed upon;

(*n*) what insurance has been offered on the life of the child;

(*o*) the religious persuasion of the petitioner;

(*p*) considerations arising from the difference in age between the petitioner and the child if this is more or less than the normal difference in age between parents and children;

(*q*) whether adoption is likely to safeguard and promote the welfare of the child throughout its childhood; and

(*r*) any other information which may be of assistance to the court.

(8) On completion of a report under section 22(2) or 23 of the 1978 Act, the local authority or adoption agency shall—

(*a*) lodge three copies of the report in process; and

(*b*) send a copy of the report to the reporting officer and, where one has been appointed, to the curator *ad litem*.

(9) The reporting officer shall, on completion of his report, lodge three copies of it in process together with—

(*a*) any agreement under section 16(1) of the 1978 Act in Form 37B; and

(*b*) any consent under section 12(8) of the 1978 Act in Form 38A.

(10) The curator *ad litem* shall, on completion of his report, lodge three copies of it in process.

(11) On receipt of the reports of the reporting officer, the local authority or adoption agency and, where one has been appointed, the report of the curator *ad litem*, the petition department shall—

(*a*) inform the petitioner that the reports have been lodged and that a motion for a hearing to determine the application must be enrolled within seven days; and

(*b*) make available to the petitioner, and to any other party, a copy of each report.

(12) At the motion for a hearing to determine the application, the court shall consider—

(*a*) whether to require any person, whose agreement or consent is required to be given or dispensed with, to attend the hearing to determine the application;

(*b*) whether to require intimation of the date of the hearing to determine the application to any other person; and

(*c*) whether to require the reporting officer or a curator *ad litem* to perform any other duties.

(13) On a date being fixed for a hearing to determine the application, the petitioner shall intimate the date of the hearing in Form 39C—

(*a*) to every person who can be found whose agreement or consent is required to be given or dispensed with;

(*b*) to the local authority or adoption agency which lodged the report under paragraph (8), the reporting officer and, where one has been appointed, to the curator *ad litem*; and

(*c*) to any person upon whom intimation has been ordered by the court under paragraph (12)(*b*).

(14) At the hearing to determine the application—

(*a*) the petitioner, the adoption agency, the reporting officer and, where one has been appointed, the curator *ad litem* shall, if required by the court, appear and may be represented;

(*b*) any person required by the court to attend the hearing shall appear and may be represented; and

(*c*) any other person upon whom intimation was made under paragraph (13)(*a*) or (*c*) may appear or be represented.

(15) Where the court has made an *interim* order, the petitioner shall, before the expiry of the period specified in the *interim* order, enrol the cause for a further hearing.

(16) Where, in relation to a child under 16, the court refuses to make an adoption order and considers—

    (i) that the child should be placed under the supervision of a specified local authority; or

    (ii) that the child should be committed to the care of a specified local authority,

the following provisions of this rule shall apply—

(*a*) the court shall appoint intimation to be made to the local authority and give the local authority an opportunity to make representations;

(*b*) any representations of a local authority shall be made by minute in the petition process;

(*c*) on a minute being lodged in process, the court shall order service of the minute upon the parties to the petition who may lodge answers within such period as the court may allow; and

(*d*) after the period for answers has expired, the court shall put the cause out by order for a hearing to determine the matter.

Adoption of children abroad

223.—(1) An application for an order under section 49(1) of the 1978 Act shall be made by petition in the Outer House.

(2) The provisions of Rule 222, except paragraph (5)(*b*), shall apply to an application under this Rule as they apply to an application under that Rule.

(3) On presentation of the petition, the court shall appoint a reporting officer with the duties in Rule 224(3).

Duties of reporting officer and curator ad litem

224.—(1) A reporting officer appointed under Rule 220(6) (freeing for adoption) shall have the following duties—

(*a*) to inquire into the facts and circumstances averred in the petition;

(*b*) to ascertain the whereabouts of each parent or guardian and, if practicable, to meet them;

(*c*) to witness any agreement by a parent or guardian who is within Scotland to the freeing for adoption under section 18(1) of the 1978 Act in Form 37A; and to ensure that the agreement is given freely, unconditionally and with full understanding of what is involved;

(*d*) where a parent or guardian is furth of Scotland, to confirm his views in writing and to ensure that any agreement under section 18(1) of the 1978 Act is witnessed in accordance with Rule 230(1).

(*e*) to witness any consent of a minor under section 18(8) of the 1978 Act in Form 38 and to ensure that he understands the consequences of that consent;

(*f*) where the agreement or consent of a parent or guardian or the consent of a minor is sought to be dispensed with, to consider whether the ground of dispensation has been made out;

(*g*) to consider whether the petitioner has made every reasonable effort to find every person whose agreement is required;

(*h*) to consider whether other persons with a relevant interest should be informed of the petition;

(*i*) to inquire whether the petitioner has considered the position of any reputed father;

(*j*) where the child is illegitimate, to consider the prospect of any application by a reputed father for a custody order and whether such an application would be likely to be refused;

(*k*) to discuss alternatives to adoption with each parent or guardian who can be found;

(*l*) to explain the implications of a freeing order to each parent or guardian who can be found;

(*m*) to ensure that each parent or guardian who can be found understands he may be able to apply under section 20 of the 1978 Act and Rule 221 for revocation of an order under section 18 of the 1978 Act, and the procedure for making such application;

(*n*) to ensure that each parent or guardian who can be found has been given an opportunity to make a declaration under section 18(6) of the 1978 Act that he prefers not to be involved in future questions concerning the adoption of the child;

(*o*) to consider whether the account by the petitioner of why the application is for a freeing order and not a full adoption order is satisfactory;

(*p*) to consider whether the account by the petitioner of the prospects of arranging adoption after a freeing order is correct;

(*q*) to consider whether any payment prohibited by section 51 of the 1978 Act has been made or received;

(*r*) to ensure that each parent or guardian who can be found is aware of the date of the hearing to determine the application if he wishes to appear;

(*s*) to draw to the attention of the court any matter which may be of assistance; and

(*t*) to prepare a report in relation to the exercise of the above duties.

(2) A reporting officer appointed under Rule 222(5) (adoption) shall have the following duties—

(*a*) to inquire into the facts and circumstances averred in the petition and the report of the adoption agency;

(*b*) to ascertain the whereabouts of each parent or guardian and, if practicable, to meet them;

(*c*) to witness any agreement by a parent or guardian who is within Scotland to the adoption under section 16(1) of the 1978 Act in Form 37B, and to ensure that the agreement is given freely, unconditionally and with full understanding of what is involved;

(*d*) where a parent or guardian is furth of Scotland, to confirm his views in writing and to ensure that any agreement under section 16(1) of the 1978 Act is witnessed in accordance with Rule 230(1);

(*e*) to witness any consent of a minor under section 12(8) of the 1978 Act in Form 38A and to ensure that he understands the consequences of that consent;

(*f*) to ensure that each parent or guardian whose agreement is required understands that in agreeing to the adoption he is giving up all future claims to the child and that all parental rights and duties will vest in the adopter;

(*g*) where the agreement of a parent or guardian or the consent of a minor is sought to be dispensed with, to consider whether the ground of dispensation has been made out;

(*h*) in the case of a child not free for adoption, to consider whether the adoption agency has made every reasonable effort to find every person whose agreement is required;

(*i*) to consider whether other persons with a relevant interest should be informed of the petition;

(*j*) in the case of a child not free for adoption, that the adoption agency has considered the position of any reputed father;

(*k*) where the child is illegitimate, to ascertain whether the father has a custody order and, if not, is not applying for one;

(*l*) to ascertain the wishes of the child, if practicable;

(*m*) to ascertain whether the requirements of section 13 of the 1978 Act have been complied with;

(*n*) to consider whether it is desirable for the welfare of the child that an interim order should be made or whether conditions should be imposed in any adoption order or whether an order for custody should be made;

(*o*) where a previous application for adoption has been refused to which section 24(1) of the 1978 Act applies, to report on whether there has been any change of circumstances or other reason which might lead the court to allow the application to proceed;

(*p*) in the case of a child not free for adoption, to consider whether there has been any payment or reward in consideration of the adoption;

(*q*) to ensure that each parent or guardian whose agreement is required or may be dispensed with is aware of the date of the hearing to determine the application if he wishes to appear;

(*r*) to draw to the attention of the court any matter which may be of assistance; and

(*s*) to prepare a report in relation to the exercise of the above duties.

(3) A reporting officer appointed under Rule 223(3) (adoption of children abroad) shall have the following duties—

(*a*) the duties in paragraph (2) of this rule; and

(*b*) to obtain a statement from a qualified person in the country in which the petitioner is intending to adopt the child whether there is any legal obstacle to the adoption taking place.

(4) A curator *ad litem* appointed under Rule 220(6) (freeing for adoption) shall have the following duties—

(*a*) to inquire into, so far as he considers necessary, the matters averred in the petition;

(*b*) to inquire into any other matters which appear to him to be relevant to the making of an order freeing the child for adoption;

(*c*) to consider whether, in his opinion, the child should be present at the hearing to determine the application;

(*d*) to perform such other duties as appear to him to be necessary or as the court may require; and

(*e*) to prepare a report in relation to the exercise of the above duties.

(5) A curator *ad litem* appointed under Rule 221(3) (revocation of freeing for adoption order) shall have the following duties—

(*a*) to inquire into the facts and circumstances averred in the note;

(*b*) to determine whether 12 months have elapsed between the making of the freeing order and the date of presentation of the note;

(*c*) where a previous application under section 20 of the 1978 Act was refused, to inquire whether there has been any change of circumstances or other reason which the court should know about when considering whether to allow the application to proceed;

(*d*) to inquire into any other matters which appear to him to be relevant to the revocation of the order freeing the child for adoption;

(*e*) to consider whether, in his opinion, the child should be present at the hearing to determine the application;

(*f*) to perform such other duties as appear to him to be necessary or as the court may require; and

(g) to prepare a report in relation to the exercise of the above duties.

(6) A curator *ad litem* appointed under Rule 222(5) (adoption) shall have the following duties—

    (a) to inquire into, so far as he considers necessary, the matters averred in the petition and in any report under Rule 222(7);

    (b) to inquire into any other matters which appear to him to be relevant to the making of an adoption order;

    (c) to consider whether, in his opinion, the child should be present at the hearing;

    (d) to perform such other duties as appear to him to be necessary or as the court may require; and

    (e) to prepare a report in relation to the exercise of the above duties.

Special application for appointment of reporting officer

225.—(1) Where a person intends to present a petition under Rules 220, 222 or 223 and seeks the appointment of a reporting officer before that petition is presented, he may apply under this Rule for the appointment of a reporting officer.

(2) An application shall be made by letter addressed to the deputy principal clerk together with any necessary supporting documents and shall be dealt with by a Lord Ordinary in chambers.

(3) The interlocutor of the Lord Ordinary shall be written on an interlocutor sheet and shall be final.

(4) The letter of application and interlocutor sheet shall be kept in the petition department and subsequently added to the process in the petition.

Application for transfer of parental rights and duties between adoption agencies

226.—(1) An application for transfer of parental rights and duties between adoption agencies under section 21 of the 1978 Act shall be made by note in the process of the petition for an order freeing a child for adoption.

(2) Rules 191 to 198 shall apply to a note under this Rule as they apply to a petition except that a note under this Rule shall not be intimated on the walls or in the minute book or advertised.

Application for return, removal or prohibition of removal, of child

227.—(1) An application for an order to return a child to, or to ordain a person not to remove a child from, the custody of the applicant under section 29 of the 1978 Act shall be made—

    (a) in relation to section 27(1) or 28(1) of the 1978 Act, by note in the process of the petition for an adoption order or of the petition for an order under section 49(1) of the 1978 Act;

    (b) in relation to section 27(2) of the 1978 Act, by note in the process of the petition for an order freeing a child for adoption; and

    (c) in relation to section 28(3) of the 1978 Act, by petition in the Outer House.

(2) An application for leave—

    (a) to remove a child under section 27(1) or 28 of the 1978 Act, shall be made by note in the process of the petition for an adoption order or of the petition for an order under section 49(1) of the 1978 Act;

    (b) to remove a child under section 27(2) of the 1978 Act, shall be made by note in the process of the petition for an order freeing a child for adoption;

    (c) to give notice under section 30(2) of the 1978 Act (of intention under section 30(1)(b)), shall be by note in the process of the petition for an adoption order or of the petition for an order under section 49(1) of the 1978 Act.

(3) Rules 191 to 198 shall apply to a petition or note under this Rule as they apply to a petition except that a petition or note under this Rule shall not be intimated on the walls or in the minute book or advertised.

Application to amend or revoke a direction in, or revoke an, adoption order
228.—(1) An application—
    (*a*) to amend, or to revoke a direction in, an adoption order under paragraph 4(1) of Schedule 1 to the 1978 Act; or
    (*b*) to revoke an adoption order under section 46(1) of the 1978 Act,
shall be made by petition in the Outer House.
    (2) Rules 191 to 198 shall apply to a petition under this Rule as they apply to a petition except that a petition under this Rule shall not be intimated on the walls or in the minute book or advertised.

Registration
229.—On the making of—
    (*a*) an adoption order, an amendment to, or a revocation of, an adoption order; or
    (*b*) an order under section 49(1) of the 1978 Act,
a certified copy of the order of the court shall be transmitted by the clerk of court to the Registrar General by personal delivery in a sealed envelope marked "confidential".

Miscellaneous provisions
230.—(1) An agreement under section 16(1) or 18(1) of the 1978 Act by a parent or guardian, or a consent under section 12(8) or 18(8) of the 1978 Act by a minor, who is furth of Scotland shall be witnessed—
    (*a*) if the agreement or consent is executed in England and Wales or Northern Ireland, by a justice of the peace;
    (*b*) if the agreement or consent is executed outside the United Kingdom—
        (i) by a British consular officer;
        (ii) by a notary public;
        (iii) by a person authorised to administer an oath for any judicial or legal purpose in the country in which it is executed; or
        (iv) where the person making the agreement or consent is serving in any of Her Majesty's Forces, by an officer holding a commission in any of those forces.
    (2) Where a declaration is made by a former parent under section 19(4) of the 1978 Act to the adoption agency in whose favour an order has been made under section 18 of the 1978 Act—
    (*a*) the adoption agency shall—
        (i) lodge the declaration in process;
        (ii) enrol a motion to have the declaration recorded; and
    (*b*) the court shall record the declaration by pronouncing an interlocutor recording the fact of that declaration.
    (3) An extract of an adoption order or an order under section 49(1) of the 1978 Act shall not be issued except by order of the court on application by petition in the Outer House setting forth the reasons for which the extract is required.
    (4) After an order referred to in Rule 229 has been transmitted to the Registrar General or an extract has been issued under paragraph (3) of this rule, the clerk of court or the extractor, as the case may be, shall place the whole process in a sealed envelope marked "confidential" bearing only the name of the petitioner and the name and surname of the child to whom the order relates and the date of the order; and the envelope shall not be opened by or made accessible to any person within 100 years after the date of the adoption order or the order under section 49(1) of the 1978 Act except—

(*a*) to an adopted child who has reached the age of 17 years and to whom the order refers;

(*b*) by or to the deputy principal clerk of session or the extractor, as the case may be, on the written application to him by an adoption agency with the agreement of the adopted person for the purpose of ascertaining the name of the adoption agency, if any, responsible for placing that person for adoption and informing that person of the name of that adoption agency;

(*c*) by order of the court on application by petition in the Outer House by another court or authority (whether within the United Kingdom or not) having power to authorise an adoption which requests that information be made available from the process for the purpose of discharging its duties in considering an application for adoption;

(*d*) by order of the court on application by petition in the Outer House by a person setting forth the reasons for which access to the process is required; or

(*e*) to a person who is authorised in writing by the Secretary of State to obtain information from the process for the purpose of such research as is designed to improve the working of adoption law and practice.

(5) In any cause to which this section applies, the court may, before determining the application, order—

(*a*) production of further documents (including affidavits); or

(*b*) parole evidence.

(6) Unless the court otherwise directs, in any cause to which this section applies—

(*a*) all documents lodged in process, including a report by an adoption agency, a reporting officer or a curator *ad litem* shall be treated as confidential and open only to the court, the parties, the reporting officer and the curator *ad litem*; and

(*b*) a reporting officer or curator *ad litem* shall regard all information obtained by him in relation to the cause as confidential, and not to be divulged to any person except to a person to whom it may be necessary to do so for the proper execution of his duties.

(7) In any cause to which this section applies, the court may make such order as to liability for expenses, including the expenses of an adoption agency which prepared a report, a reporting officer, a curator *ad litem* and any other person who attends the hearing to determine the application, as it thinks fit and may—

(*a*) modify those expenses; or

(*b*) direct those expenses to be taxed on such scale as it may determine.

(8) Where a reporting officer or a curator *ad litem* is to be appointed by the court, such person shall be appointed from a panel established under the Curators *Ad Litem* and Reporting Officers (Panels) (Scotland) Regulations 1984 except where the court considers, in exceptional circumstances, that it would be appropriate to appoint a person who is not a member of a panel other than an employee of an adoption agency, which is a party to the proceedings, or who has been involved in making any arrangements for the adoption of the child.

SECTION 4A—CONVENTION ADOPTION ORDERS

(ADOPTION (SCOTLAND) ACT 1978)

Interpretation
[1] **230A.**—(1) In this section, unless the context otherwise requires—

(*a*) "the 1978 Act" means the Adoption (Scotland) Act 1978;

"Convention proceedings" means proceedings on an application for a

Convention adoption order under section 17, and proceedings under section 47, of the 1978 Act;

"Registrar General" means the Registrar General of Births, Deaths and Marriages for Scotland;

(*b*) Expressions which are used in this section and are also used in the 1978 Act, have the same meaning as in that Act.

(2) Any reference in this section to any enactment shall be construed as a reference to that enactment as amended, extended or applied by any other enactment.

(3) Any reference in this section to the nationality of a person who is not solely a United Kingdom national means that person's nationality as determined in accordance with section 63 of the 1978 Act.

NOTE
[1] Added by S.I. 1978 No. 1373, and as amended by S.I. 1984 No. 997.

Extent and application
[1] **230B.**—(1) This section applies to Convention proceedings.

(2) Subject to paragraph (1), Rules 223, 224(2) and (6), 225, 227, 229 and 230 (except paragraph (2) of that Rule) apply to Convention proceedings as they apply to proceedings in applications under those rules.

NOTE
[1] Added by S.I. 1978 No. 1373, and as amended by S.I. 1984 No. 997.

Applications
[1] **230C.**—(1) All applications for a Convention Adoption Order shall be by way of petition to the Inner House, and shall, subject to the provisions of this rule, be in the form set out in Form 36 with the substitution for any reference to an Adoption Order of a reference to a Convention Adoption Order.

(2) A petitioner in a petition under paragraph (1) shall include averments stating—

(*a*) that he is applying for a Convention Adoption Order;
(*b*) the country of which he is a national;
(*c*) the country of which the child he proposes to adopt is a national;
(*d*) the place where he habitually resides and the country in which it is;
(*e*) the place where the child habitually resides and the country in which it is;
(*f*) whether any country mentioned is a Convention country;
(*g*) whether the child is, or has been, married;
(*h*) in a case where the petitioner is a national of a Convention country, or in a case where both petitioners are nationals of the same Convention country, whether there are specified provisions in respect of that country, and if there are, that the adoption is not prohibited by any such specified provision;
(*i*) in a case where the child is not a United Kingdom national, the provisions, if any, relating to consents and consultations of the internal law relating to adoption of the Convention country of which the child is a national.

(3) (*a*) Those averments shall be fully investigated by the curator *ad litem* and the results of his investigation shall be included in his report.

(*b*) Where in the course of these investigations the curator *ad litem* requires a report from any authority outside Great Britain, he shall request the local authority to request that other authority to provide that report.

(4) The prayer of the petition shall request the court to direct the Registrar-General—

(*a*) to insert the words "Convention Order" in the entry to be made by him in the Adopted Children Register regarding the adoption;

(*b*) to intimate the terms of the order to the authorities mentioned in Rule 230H or 230I, as the case may be.

NOTE
[1] Added by S.I. 1978 No. 1373.

Documentary evidence
[1] **230D.** For the purposes of proceedings in petitions brought under the provisions of this section, written statements (including affidavits) and reports are admissible in place of parole evidence, if the court, on the application of the party proposing to rely on such a statement or report, so directs.

NOTE
[1] Added by S.I. 1978 No. 1373.

Evidence of nationality
[1] **230E.**—(1) Any document which is to be used for the purpose of satisfying the court as to the nationality of a petitioner or of the child shall be lodged together with the petition, or as soon as possible thereafter.

(2) Where a petitioner claims that for the purposes of section 17(2)(*a*), (4)(*a*) or (5)(*a*) of the 1978 Act he or the child is a national of a Convention country, he shall lodge together with the petition or as soon as possible thereafter, a written statement by an expert in the law of that country as to the law of that country relating to the nationality applicable to that person.

NOTE
[1] Added by S.I. 1978 No. 1373, and as amended by S.I. 1984 No. 997.

Evidence of consents, etc.
[1] **230F.**—(1) This rule applies to Convention proceedings in which the child it is proposed to adopt is not a United Kingdom national.

(2) A petitioner shall lodge together with the petition, or as soon as possible thereafter, a written statement by an expert in the law of the country of which the child is a national setting out the consents and consultations (if any) required by that law for the purposes of an adoption, and whether and on what conditions they may be dispensed with, and in the case of consents, the form in which they may be given.

(3) Any document signifying the consent of a person to, or otherwise containing the opinion of a person with respect to the making of, the Convention Adoption Order shall be in a form which complies with the internal law relating to adoption of the Convention country of which the child is a national, but where the court is not satisfied that a person consents with full understanding of what is involved, it may call for further evidence.

(4) A document referred to in paragraph (3) shall, if sufficiently attested, be admissible as evidence of the consent or, as the case may be, of the opinion it contains without further proof of the signature of the person by whom it is executed.

(5) A petitioner in proceedings to which this rule applies, shall, in any case in which a hearing is ordered, serve a notice of hearing in terms of Form 38 upon—

(*a*) all persons whose consent to the making of the order is required and who are not petitioners;

(*b*) all persons who, in accordance with the internal law relating to adoption of the country of which the child is a national, have to be consulted about, but do not have to consent to, the adoption.

(6) For the purposes of section 17(7)(*a*) of the 1978 Act, the proper officer of the court to whom any person whose consent is required under or who is consulted in pursuance of the internal law relating to adoption of the Convention country of which the child is a national may communicate his

opinion on the adoption is the Deputy Principal Clerk of the Court of Session.

NOTE
  [1] Added by S.I. 1978 No. 1373, and as amended by S.I. 1984 No. 997.

Dispensing power
  [1] **230G.** Where under Rule 230F any consent or consultation is not duly signified to the court as having been given or undertaken, and the court is satisfied that under the internal law of the country concerned that consent or consultation could properly be dispensed with, the court may dispense with that consent or consultation in accordance with the provisions of that law.

NOTE
  [1] Added by S.I. 1978 No. 1373.

Notice to Registrar General
  [1] **230H.**—(1) The Deputy Principal Clerk shall send to the Registrar General—
  (*a*) together with any Convention Adoption Order made under the provisions of this section, a notice specifying and requesting him to inform the authorities mentioned in paragraph 2 of the terms of the order;
  (*b*) together with any order made under section 46(2) of the 1978 Act revoking a Convention Adoption Order, a notice specifying and requesting him to inform the authorities mentioned in paragraph 3 of the terms of the order.
  (2) The authorities referred to in paragraph (1)(*a*) are the designated authorities of any Convention country—
  (*a*) of which the child is a national;
  (*b*) in which the child was born;
  (*c*) in which a petitioner habitually resides;
  (*d*) of which a petitioner is a national.
  (3) The authorities referred to in paragraph (1)(*b*) are the designated authorities of any Convention country—
  (*a*) of which the adopted person is a national;
  (*b*) in which the adopted person was born.

NOTE
  [1] Added by S.I. 1978 No. 1373, and as amended by S.I. 1984 No. 997.

Revocation, etc., of regulated adoptions
  [1] **230I.**—(1) This rule applies to applications for an order under section 46(2) and 47 of the 1978 Act.
  (2) An application shall be made by way of petition to the Inner House.
  (3) An application under section 47(1) of the 1978 Act (annulment) shall not, except with the leave of the court, be made later than two years after the date of the regulated adoption to which it relates.
  (4) Where the adopted person is under the age of 18 on the date of the presentation of a petition under this rule, the court shall appoint a curator *ad litem* and Rule 224(6) shall apply to the petition as it applies to a petition under that rule.
  (5) (*a*) Where the court has ordered that a regulated adoption be annulled or revoked or that an overseas adoption or a determination shall cease to be valid in Great Britain, the Deputy Principal Clerk shall serve notice of the order on the Registrar General, and shall specify in the notice—
  (i) the date of the adoption;
  (ii) the name and address of the authority which granted the adoption;

    (iii) the names of the adopter or adopters and of the adopted person as given in the petition;
    (iv) the country in which the adoption was granted;
    (v) the country of which the adopted person is a national;
    (vi) the country in which the adopted person was born,

and where any country so specified is a Convention country shall request the Registrar General to inform the designated authorities of that country of the terms of the order.

NOTE
   [1] Added by S.I. 1978 No. 1373, and as amended by S.I. 1984 No. 997.

Order
  [1] **230J.** Where the applicant is a national or both applicants are nationals of a Convention country, the court shall take account of any specified provision (as defined in section 17(8) of the 1978 Act of the internal law of that country before any decision is made to postpone the determination of the application and to make an interim order.

NOTE
   [1] Added by S.I. 1978 No. 1373, and as amended by S.I. 1984 No. 997.

Attestation
  [1] **230K.** A document shall be sufficiently attested for the purpose of this section if it is attested by any of the following persons:—
    (*a*) if it is executed in the United Kingdom—
        (i) a justice of the peace; or
        (ii) if it is executed in Scotland, a sheriff; or
        (iii) if it is executed in England or Wales, an officer of a county court appointed for the purposes of section 87 of the County Courts Act 1959, or a justice's clerk within the meaning of section 21 of the Justices of the Peace Act 1949.
    (*b*) if it is executed elsewhere, any person mentioned in Rule 230(1).

NOTE
   [1] Added by S.I. 1978 No. 1373, and as amended by S.I. 1984 No. 997.

Translations
  [1] **230L.** Where any document is served outside the United Kingdom in a country in which English is not an official language, the petitioner shall provide and send with the document a translation of it in the official language of the country in which service is to be effected or, if there is more than one official language of the country, in any one of those languages which is appropriate to the place in that country where service is to be effected.

NOTE
   [1] Added by S.I. 1978 No. 1373.

4. Children Act 1975

(1975 c.72)

An Act to make further provision for children.

                  [12th November 1975.]

PART I

ADOPTION

[Repealed by the Adoption (Scotland) Act 1978, Sched. 4.]

PART II

CUSTODY

. . . . . .

Custody order on application for adoption in Scotland

53.—(1) Without prejudice to the provisions of section 19 (power to make an interim order giving custody), where on an application for an adoption order in respect of a child the applicant is a person qualified to apply for custody of the child, and the court is of opinion—

(*a*) in the case of an applicant who is a relative of the child or a husband or wife of the mother or father of the child (whether applying alone or jointly with his or her spouse)—

   (i) that the child's welfare would not be better safeguarded and promoted by the making of an adoption order in favour of the applicant than it would be by the making of a custody order in his favour; and

   (ii) that it would be appropriate to make a custody order in favour of the applicant; or

(*b*) in any other case, that the making of a custody order in favour of the applicant would be more appropriate than the making of an adoption order in his favour,

the court shall direct that the application is to be treated as if it had been made for custody of the child; but where such a direction is made the court shall not cease to have jurisdiction by reason only that it would not have had jurisdiction to hear an application by the applicant for custody of the child.

(2) In the application of this Part of this Act to any case where a direction under subsection (1) has been made—

(*a*) for references in section 47(2) to the making of an application for custody there shall be substituted references to the making of an application for an adoption order;

(*b*) for the references in section 49 and paragraph (*a*) of subsection (1) of section 51 to the making of an application there shall be substituted references to the making of a direction in terms of subsection (1) of this section;

(*c*) in section 51(1) for the words "for custody of" there shall be substituted the words "for an adoption order in respect of".

(3) For the purposes of section 11 of the Guardianship Act 1973, any application in respect of which a direction has been made under subsection (1) of this section, is an application for custody of a child.

. . . . . .

PART V

MISCELLANEOUS AND SUPPLEMENTAL

. . . . . .

Panel for curators ad litem **and reporting officers**

[1] **103.**—(1) The Secretary of State may by regulations[2] make provision for the establishment of one or more panels of persons from whom—

    (*a*) curators *ad litem* and reporting officers may in accordance with rules or rules of court be appointed for the purposes of—

        [3] (i) section 58 of the Adoption (Scotland) Act 1978;

        (ii) section 32B of the Children and Young Persons Act 1969;

    [4] (iii) section 7 of the Child Care Act 1980;

    (*b*) persons may be appointed for the purposes of section 18A or 34A of the Social Work (Scotland) Act 1968.

(2) Regulations under subsection (1) may provide—

    (*a*) for the defrayment by local authorities of expenses incurred by members of a panel established by virtue of that subsection; and

    (*b*) for the payment by local authorities of fees and allowances for members of such a panel.

(3) In relation to Scotland, the reference in subsection (1) to guardians *ad litem* shall be construed as a reference to curators *ad litem*.

NOTES

[1] As amended by the Health and Social Services and Social Security Adjudications Act 1983, Sched. 2, para. 28.

[2] See S.I. 1984 No. 566.

[3] As amended by the Adoption (Scotland) Act 1978, Sched. 3, para. 17.

[4] Substituted by the Child Care Act 1980, Sched. 5, para. 37.

. . . . . .

II Styles and Interlocutors

1. Oath of curator *ad litem* and reporting officer (*to be administered at the time of appointment*)

(a) Edinburgh,   1986. In presence of AB sheriff of   at Compeared CD who declared his acceptance of the office of curator *ad litem* and reporting officer in such cases as are remitted to him by the sheriff for the purpose of investigating and reporting to the court in terms of the Adoption (Scotland) Act 1978. (*To be signed by the curator* ad litem *and reporting officer and witnessed by the sheriff.*)

(b) Edinburgh,   1986. In presence of AB sheriff of   at Compeared CD who took an oath in the following terms: I, CD swear by almighty God (*or affirms*) that I will faithfully perform the duties of the office of curator *ad litem* and reporting officer in all petitions for adoption in which I may be appointed by the sheriff of   at   to act as curator *ad litem* and reporting officer. (*To be signed by the curator* ad litem *and reporting officer and witnessed by the sheriff.*)

2. Interlocutor nominating a curator *ad litem* and reporting officer[1]

Edinburgh,   1986. The sheriff having considered the cause, Appoints CD to be curator *ad litem* and reporting officer in the petition for the purpose of investigating and reporting to the court in terms of the Adoption (Scotland) Act 1978 and Act of Sederunt (Adoption of Children) 1984, on or before (*being a date four weeks ahead*).

3. Final interlocutor[2]

Edinburgh,   1986. The sheriff having resumed consideration of the cause, grants the prayer of the petition.

4. Interlocutor freeing a child for adoption

Grants the prayer of the petition; makes an order freeing the child AB for adoption.

5. Interlocutor making an interim order[3]

Edinburgh,   1986. The sheriff having resumed consideration of the cause postpones the determination of the cause until   (*being a date not exceeding two years*); appoints the curator *ad litem* to furnish a supplementary report on or before   (*being a date about eight weeks before the end of the interim order*); finds the petitioners entitled to custody of the child AB during the period of postponement; ordains the petitioners jointly and severally to aliment the child (*and add such other conditions as to education and supervision of the child as the court thinks fit*); appoints the clerk of court to send a copy of this interlocutor to the curator *ad litem*.

---

[1] See para. 7.01.
[2] See para. 11.01.
[3] See paras. 8.05 (m) and 11.01.

6. Adoption order[4]

SHERIFFDOM OF LOTHIAN AND BORDERS AT EDINBURGH
Adoption
Order

Under the Adoption (Scotland) Act 1978

ADOPTION ORDER

in

PETITION

of

AB (*name and designation*) and CB (*name and designation*)

for

AUTHORITY TO ADOPT

DB (*name as in birth certificate or name by which
the child is ordinarily known*) residing with the petitioners

---

Edinburgh,   1986. The sheriff authorises the petitioners AB and CB to adopt the male (*or* female) child DB who was born in Scotland (*or such other country as may be*) on 17 September 1980 and is identical with DB to whom an entry numbered 123 was made on 1 November 1980 in the Register of Births for the registration district of Johnstone in the County of Renfrew relates, in terms of the Adoption (Scotland) Act 1978 (*if any conditions, insert them; if no conditions, insert " No conditions "*); directs the Registrar General for Scotland to make an entry regarding the said adoption in the Adopted Children Register in the form prescribed by him, giving the name R as the forename, and B as the surname of the child in that form, and to include the above mentioned date and country of birth in the entry recording the adoption; and directs the Registrar General for Scotland to cause the entry of the birth of the child in the Register of Births to be marked with the word " adopted."

(1) Relationship of the petitioners to the child: The female petitioner is the mother of the child (*or as the case may be; if there is no relationship, insert " None "*).

(2) Adoption Agency which has taken part in the arrangements for placing the child in the care of the petitioners: (*insert name and address of adoption agency; if none, insert " None "*).

7. Order to adopt child abroad[5]

SHERIFFDOM OF LOTHIAN AND BORDERS AT EDINBURGH

Order to
adopt
a child
abroad

Under the Adoption (Scotland) Act 1978

ORDER UNDER SECTION 49

in

PETITION

of

AB (*name and designation*) and CB (*name and designation*)

for

AUTHORITY TO ADOPT ABROAD

DB (*name as in birth certificate, or name by which
the child is ordinarily known*) residing with the petitioners

---

[4] See para. 11.01.
[5] See paras. 1.03 (d) and 11.01.

Edinburgh,   1986. The sheriff authorises the petitioners AB and CB to remove the male child DB who was born in Scotland (*or such other country as may be*) on 17 September 1980 and is identical with DB to whom an entry numbered 123 was made on 1 November 1980 in the Register of Births for the registration district of Johnstone in the County of Renfrew from Great Britain for the purpose of adopting the child under the law of the State of   in the Country of   ; finds the petitioners entitled, pending his adoption, to the custody of the child in terms of the Adoption (Scotland) Act 1978 (*if any conditions, insert them; if no conditions insert* "*None*"); directs the Registrar General for Scotland to make an entry regarding the provisional adoption in the Adopted Children Register in the form prescribed by him, giving R as the forename and B as the surname of the child in that form, and to include the above-mentioned date and country of birth in the entry recording the provisional adoption; and directs the Registrar General for Scotland to cause the entry of the birth of the child (*or* the Adopted Children Register) to be marked with the words " Proposed foreign adoption " (*or* proposed foreign re-adoption) " provisionally adopted."

(1) Relationship, etc. (*as in style 6*)

8. Interlocutor appointing statutory hearing
Edinburgh,   1986. The sheriff having resumed consideration of the cause, Assigns (*date, time and place*) as diet of hearing in terms of Act of Sederunt (Adoption of Children) 1984, paragraph 8 (*petition to free a child for adoption*), *or* paragraph 22 (*petition for adoption*); appoints the petitioners to intimate the diet of hearing in terms of Form 11 to the natural parents of the child (*or other persons as the case may be*).

9. Interlocutor appointing a hearing on a particular point[6]
Edinburgh,   1986. The sheriff appoints the petitioners and their solicitors (*or* the solicitors of the petitioners) to be heard on the question of the care and possession of the child (*or whatever other matter*) and appoints (*time and place*) as a diet therefor.

10. Interlocutor appointing a proof[7]
Edinburgh,   1986. The sheriff on motion of parties (*or ex proprio motu*) allows parties a proof and appoints (*time and place*) as a diet therefor.

11. Interlocutor dispensing with the agreement of a parent[8]
Edinburgh,   1986. The sheriff having resumed consideration of the cause, finds that natural father is withholding his agreement unreasonably; therefore dispenses with the same in terms of the Adoption (Scotland) Act 1978, section 16(2)(*b*) (*or* sections 16(2)(*b*) and 18(1)(*b*)) (*or such other ground as the case may be*).

12. Interlocutor making an adoption order justifying the exclusion of one parent[9]
Edinburgh,   1986. The sheriff having resumed consideration of the cause and in particular the letter of the natural father (no.   of process) finds that the natural father does not wish to take part in the adoption at the instance of the natural mother; therefore finds that there is reason justifying

---

[6] See paras. 5.11 and 11.01.
[7] See para. 6.05.
[8] See para. 11.01.
[9] See para. 11.01.

the exclusion of the natural father in terms of the Adoption (Scotland) Act 1978, section 15(3).

13. Declaration in terms of section 18(6)

(a) I, MN (*design*), the mother of the child, declare that I prefer not to be involved in future questions concerning the adoption of the child (*to be witnessed in the presence of the reporting officer.*)

(b) The foregoing declaration was received at the office of the sheriff clerk on   and has been recorded in the adoption register of the court.

14. Interlocutor revoking a freeing order

Edinburgh,   1986. The sheriff having resumed consideration of the cause revokes the freeing order dated   in respect of the child AB.

15. Interlocutor where child seeks access to the process (assuming that the court has a locus in the matter)[10]

Edinburgh,   1986. The sheriff having considered the letter of AB dated   , having seen the sealed envelope containing the process of serial number 1234 (relating to the adoption of the child AB at the instance of CB and DB) which was granted on   and being satisfied that AB is the person to whom the adoption relates, and that he is now 17 years of age authorises the sheriff clerk to make available to AB for inspection the process upon proof of her identity to the satisfaction of the clerk of court, all in terms of the Act of Sederunt 1984, paragraph 28(2)(*a*); and thereafter to reseal the process. (*In any event the clerk of court should make a minute narrating that the process was opened up and a similar note on the outside of the envelope.*)

16. Petition for access to the process[11]

XY for the petitioner states to the court that:

(1) On   an adoption order with serial number 1234 was granted in Edinburgh Sheriff Court.

(2) On   AB appeared on petition in that court charged at the instance of the present petitioner with *inter alia* perjury in respect that on   at Edinburgh Sheriff Court in a proof in the proceedings to which the process relates falsely he deponed on oath that (*take in the false statement*) whereas the truth as he well knew was (*take in true statement*).

(3) The petitioner is of the opinion that it is necessary for the purposes of his investigation for him to have access to the process, (*or other reason as the case may be*).

> Therefore the petitioner craves the court to ordain the clerk of the court or other person having control of the records of the court to open up the process to furnish the petitioner with the process or a certified copy thereof in terms of the Act of Sederunt 1984, paragraph 28(2)(*c*).[12]

17. Letter to the Secretary of State seeking information from a process[13]

CONFIDENTIAL: ADOPTIONS

Dear Sir,
Adoption of children: Rules of Court, Rule 230 (4)(e);
A. v. B. 1955 S.C. 378

I am presently engaged in writing a textbook on adoption in Scotland. It is not clear from the law report of this case (1955 S.C. 378) or from the

---

[10] See para. 11.05 (a).
[12] *Cf. B. & B.*, 1950 S.L.T.(Sh.Ct.) 34.
[13] See para. 11.05 (d).

Session Papers (which only relate to the custody aspect of the case) under what power the associated sheriff court case was transmitted to the Court of Session: I feel it would be necessary to see the motion sheet and interlocutor sheets to find this out. I understand that the process in its sealed state will now have been transmitted to the Keeper of the Records of Scotland.

In terms of rule 230 (4)(*e*) it is necessary to have your authority in writing to open up the process and make it accessible to me so that I may obtain this information from the process. I would submit that the writing of such a textbook falls within the terms of the rule, *viz.*, "for the purpose of such research as is designed to improve the working of adoption law and practice." I have of course no interest at all in the identity of any of the parties to the petition.

If you are agreeable to my request, please let me know where and when the process may be seen.

18. Petition for extract of an adoption order[14]

XY for the petitioners states to the court that:

(1) On   an adoption order with serial number 1234 was granted in Edinburgh Sheriff Court in favour of the petitioners.

(2) The petitioners and their family including the adopted child intend to emigrate to   and take up the nationality of that country.

(3) The immigration authorities there require an extract of the adoption order relating to the adopted child as appears from their letter of   which is produced (*or other reason as the case may be*).

> Therefore the petitioners crave the court to authorise the clerk of court or other person having control of the records to open up the process and give out an extract of the adoption order and transmit the extract to the petitioners on payment of the dues thereof; in terms of the Act of Sederunt 1984, paragraph 27(3).

19. Petition to correct an error in adoption order[15]

XY for the petitioners states to the court that:

(1) On   an adoption order with serial number 1234 was granted in Edinburgh Sheriff Court in favour of the petitioners.

(2) It was stated in the petition for the adoption order and incorporated in the adoption order that the date of birth of the child was 15 March 1970 whereas the correct date of birth of the child is 29 August 1969 (*or other reason as the case may be*).

> Therefore the petitioners crave the court to open up the process and to amend the adoption order dated   by altering the date of birth of the child from 15 March 1970 to 29 August 1969; and direct the Registrar General for Scotland to cause the entry in the Adopted Children Register to be amended accordingly, in terms of the Adoption (Scotland) Act 1978, Schedule 1, paragraph 4 (1) and Act of Sederunt 1984, paragraph 29 (1); and therafter to re-seal the process.

20 (a). Petition to alter the name of an adopted child[16]

XY for the petitioners states to the court that:

---

[14] See para. 13.01, *E. & E., Petitioners*, Edinburgh Sheriff Court, E 195/74, July 24, 1985 (unreported).
[15] See para. 12.01 (a), *K. & K., Petitioners*, Edinburgh Sheriff Court, October 3, 1985 (unreported).
[16] See para. 12.01 (b).

(1) On   an adoption order with serial number 1234 was granted in Edinburgh Sheriff Court in favour of the petitioners in which the name of the child by which she was to be known was specified in the prayer of the petition as John Smith.

(2) The petitioners are desirous that the child should be known as James Smith.

(3) Less than a year has elapsed since the granting of the order and the child being given this new name.

Therefore the petitioners crave the court to open up the process and to amend the adoption order dated   by altering the name of the child from John Smith to James Smith; and direct the Registrar General for Scotland to cause the entry in the Adopted Children Register to be amended accordingly, in terms of the Adoption (Scotland) Act 1978, Schedule 1, paragraph 4 (1) and Act of Sederunt 1984, paragraph 29 (1); and thereafter to re-seal the process.

(b) Interlocutor following thereon

The sheriff having resumed consideration of the cause, grants the prayer of the petition; directs the Registrar General for Scotland to cause the entry relating to the child John Smith (volume 123, entry 456 registered on 20 March 1980) to be amended by deleting the forename "John" and substituting therefor the forename " James"; appoints the clerk of court to send a certified copy of the amended order to the Registrar General for Scotland in terms of Adoption (Scotland) Act 1978, Schedule 1, paragraph 4 (1) and Act of Sederunt 1984, paragraph 29 (1); and thereafter to re-seal the process.

21. Petition to revoke a direction wrongly included in an adoption order

XY for the petitioners states to the court that:

(1) On   an adoption order with serial number 1234 was granted in Edinburgh Sheriff Court in favour of the petitioners.

(2) The adoption order wrongly included the name of the child as John Smith whereas the correct name of the child as was specified in the prayer of the petition is James Smith.

(3) The Registrar General for Scotland has in conformity with the adoption order made an entry in the Adopted Children Register in the name of John Smith.

(4) The error only came to the notice of the petitioners when they procured an extract from the Adopted Children Register relative to the child.

Therefore the petitioners crave the court to open up the process and to amend the adoption order dated   by substituting for the name John Smith the name James Smith; and direct the Registrar General for Scotland to cause the entry in the Adopted Children Register to be amended accordingly, in terms of the Adoption (Scotland) Act 1978, Schedule 1, paragraph 4 (1) and Act of Sederunt 1984, paragraph 29 (1); and therafter to re-seal the process.

22. Petition to revoke an adoption order on the marriage of the parents of the child[17]

XY for the petitioners states to the court that:

(1) On   an adoption order to which serial number 1234 had been

---

[17] See paras. 1.04 and 12.02.

assigned was made in Edinburgh Sheriff Court whereby the first petitioner adopted the child DB who was born at   on   .

(2) The child was the illegitimate child of the petitioners.

(3) The petitioners were married to each other at   on   and the child was thereby legitimated.

(4) The petitioners wish that the adoption order be revoked in terms of the Adoption (Scotland) Act 1978, section 46.

Therefore the petitioners crave the court to revoke the adoption order of serial number 1234 dated   ; direct the Registrar General for Scotland to cancel the entry in the Adopted Children Register relating to the child DB and also the marking with the word " adopted " (*or, as the case may be, with that word and the word " (Scotland)" or " (England)")* of any entry relating to him in the Register of Births.

23. Minute for leave to remove a child from custody of a person with whom the child has his home[18]

XY for the minuter states to the court that:

(1) On   a petition for adoption (*or to free a child for adoption*) with serial number 1234 was presented and is presently pending in respect of the child AB.

(2) The minuter is the mother of the child.

(3) On or about   the minuter gave her agreement to the making of the adoption order at a time when she felt that she was unable to look after the child properly.

(4) The minuter now believes that she can give a good home to the child and she wishes to withdraw her agreement and take the child back into her custody.

Therefore the minuter craves the court to fix a date for the hearing of the minute and to ordain the minuter to intimate the same and to serve a notice in Form 12 together with a copy of the minute by registered post or recorded delivery to the petitioners, the curator *ad litem*, to any person who may have the care and possession of the child and to such other person or persons as the sheriff shall deem appropriate, in terms of Adoption (Scotland) Act 1978 section 27 (1) (*or* section 27 (2)) and Act of Sederunt 1984, paragraph 30 (if any) as the court shall think proper in terms of the Adoption Act 1958, section 34 and Act of Sederunt 1959, paragraph 17 (*b*).

24. Minute for leave to remove a child where the applicant has provided a home for five years[19]

(*Adapt style 23 as required by Adoption (Scotland) Act 1978, section 28.*)

25. Minute for return of a child taken away in breach of section 27 or section 28 of 1978 Act[20]

(*Adapt style 23 as required by Adoption (Scotland) Act 1978, section 28.*)

26. Minute for return of child placed for adoption by an adoption agency[21]

XY for the minuters states to the court that:

---

[18] See para. 5.06 (a).
[19] See para. 5.06 (b).
[20] See para. 5.06.
[21] See para. 5.06.

(1) On   the child was delivered into the care and possession of the petitioners in pursuance of arrangements made by the minuters for the adoption of the child.

(2) No adoption order has been made in respect of the child.

(3) The minuters are apprehensive about the safety of the child while in the care and possession of the petitioners, in respect that (*state the circumstances*).

(4) The minuters wish to give notice in writing of their intention not to allow the child to remain in the care and possession of the petitioners.

> Therefore the minuters crave the court to fix a date for hearing of the minute, etc. (*as in style 23*) in terms of Adoption (Scotland) Act 1978, section 30 (2) and Act of Sederunt 1984, paragraph 30.

27. Interlocutor appointing local authority to provide a report under section 22[22]

Edinburgh,   1986. The sheriff having resumed consideration of the cause, Appoints   Regional Council, being the appropriate local authority, to submit a report of their investigations to the sheriff clerk of Edinburgh on or before (*a date three or four weeks ahead*) in terms of Adoption (Scotland) Act 1978, section 22, and appoints the sheriff clerk to send a copy of this interlocutor to the   Regional Council.

---

[22] 1978 Act, s. 22; A.S. 16 (3) (e) (R.C. 222 (8)); see above, para. 8.09.

III Forms of Reports[1]

Preamble

It is desirable for the clerk of court to make available to curators *ad litem*, reporting officers, and others information about their duties, as follows:

(1) The curator *ad litem* or reporting officer should not take up this appointment if he is employed by or has been recently employed by:

    (a) the adoption agency which placed the child for adoption;

    (b) the adoption agency which are the petitioners in a freeing for adoption;

    (c) the adoption agency, which in a minute to revoke, have the parental rights and duties in relation to the child;

    (d) the local authority which must report to the court under section 22;

but should be in touch with the clerk of court.

(2) The fees of the curator *ad litem* and reporting officer become due when the report is lodged with the sheriff clerk; and are the responsibility of the solicitor for the petitioners (or if the petitioners have no solicitor, the petitioners themselves) *or* the local authority in terms of Statutory Instrument 1984 No. 566, paragraph 10 (*delete which is inapplicable*).

(3) Where the report is called for by the court, the report should begin with the interlocutor of the court at the top of the first page. In all cases the instance should be on the first page, with the report proper beginning on a fresh page which should be headed by the register number only. In the report no reference should be made to the child or parties by name, or in any other way whereby they may be identified. The style of the first page is as follows:

SHERIFFDOM OF LOTHIAN AND BORDERS AT EDINBURGH

Edinburgh,   January 1986. The sheriff [*take in interlocutor appointing curator* ad litem *or reporting officer or both*]

REPORT

by

NM (*design*)

Curator *ad litem* (*or reporting officer*)

in

PETITION

of

AB and CB (*design*)

PETITIONERS

To free for adoption (*or* to adopt) the child, CD (*design*) (which petition has assigned to it serial number SN 222/85 (if any) and register number E999/85)

---

[1] See above, Chap. 8.

Appendix III

A. PETITION TO FREE CHILD FOR ADOPTION

1. Report by reporting officer[2]

(a) The reporting officer has witnessed the agreement to the making of an adoption order in respect of the child in the petition by the natural mother and the natural father. The agreements are lodged in process.

(b) The natural mother   gave her consent to the lodging of this petition on   1985. She wishes the child to be adopted. (*Similarly, in relation to the natural father.*)

(c) The natural mother (*or* natural father) understands that the effect of the adoption order will be to deprive her (*or* him) of all parental rights; *or* the natural mother (*or* father) cannot be found (*state the efforts made to trace the parent and produce copy letters or returned postal packets, or as the case may be.*)

(d) There is no person other than those mentioned in the petition upon whom notice of the petition should be served, *or* notice of the petition should be served upon (*state the persons and the reason for such notice*).

(e) The natural mother (*or* father) told me that alternatives to adoption had been with her (*or* him).

(f) The natural mother (*or* father) understands the implication of an order freeing the child for adoption.

(g) The natural mother understands that she may withdraw her agreement at any time before an order under paragraph 3 is made. (*Similarly, in relation to natural father.*)

(h) The natural parents are aware that they may in certain circumstances apply to the court for revocation of the order freeing the child for adoption and they are aware of the appropriate procedure for such an application.

(i) Each parent has been given an opportunity to make a declaration in terms of section 18 (6) of the 1978 Act, declaring a preference not to be involved in future questions relating to the adoption of the child.

(j) XY claims to be the father of the child who is illegitimate. He has no intention of applying for custody of the child under the Illegitimate Children (Scotland) Act 1930, section 2: and if he did apply for custody under that section, the application is likely to be refused, because he has not seen the child for ten years (*or as the case may be*).

Edinburgh,   1986   " NM "
                                                                                          Reporting Officer

2. Report of curator *ad litem*[3]

(a) In the opinion of the curator *ad litem* the interests of the child have been safeguarded. In the circumstances narrated in this report, the curator is of the opinion that the freeing of the child is likely to safeguard and promote the welfare of the child throughout his childhood; *or* the curator is of the opinion that the freeing of the child for adoption would not safeguard and promote the welfare of the child. Particular reference is made to paragraphs   and   hereof (*or, as the case may be*).

(b) Apart from the facts which fall within the duties of the reporting officer the facts stated in the petition are correct except (*state any exceptions*).

(c) The child, who is a minor, has consented to the application: form of consent has been lodged in process; *or*, the child is incapable of giving his consent, because he is suffering from mental illness, (*or as the case may be*).

(d) In my view the freeing of the child for adoption would promote the well-being of the child (*or as the case may be*).

---

[2] A.S. 6 (1) (R.C. 224 (1)); see above, para. 8.07.
[3] A.S. 7 (2) (R.C. 224 (4)).

(e) The child is presently in the care of   (*describe briefly the care
and circumstances of the child*).
Edinburgh,   1986   " NM "
                                                                  Curator *ad Litem*

3. Report of adoption agency[4]

(*The adoption agency petitioning to free the child for adoption must report
on the background and circumstances of the child, his family and (where
appropriate) the persons proposing to adopt him, and on any other matter
relevant to the duty to promote the welfare of the child. The terms of the report
will depend on the circumstances of the case.*)

B. MINUTE TO REVOKE FREEING ORDER

4. Report of curator *ad litem*[5]

(a) The curator *ad litem* has investigated the facts and found them to be
correct except (*take in any exceptions, and narrate the true facts*).

(b) The child is   years old, having been born on   at   .
The child was in the care and possession of the natural mother from birth
until   when the child was transferred to the care of   .

(c) Since the order freeing the child for adoption was made on   ,
this child has been in the care of   at   .

(d) In the opinion of the curator *ad litem*, the promotion of the welfare
of the child throughout his childhood would be best achieved by refusing (*or
granting*) this application because (*state briefly the reasons*). The child is a
minor and it is impracticable to ascertain his wishes or feelings, *or* the child is
          years old and is able to understand what is being proposed: he wishes
to remain with   or he wishes to be returned to the care of his mother.
Edinburgh,   1986   " NM "
                                                                  Curator *ad Litem*

C. PETITION FOR ADOPTION

5. Report by reporting officer[6]

(a) The reporting officer has witnessed the agreement to the making of
an adoption order in respect of the child in the petition by the natural
mother. The agreement is lodged in process, *or* she declines to give her
agreement, *or* the reporting officer has been unable to trace the natural
mother (*state efforts to trace the natural mother and produce copy letters or
returned postal packets, or as the case may be*). Similarly in relation to the
natural father.

(b) The natural mother (*or* natural father) understands that the effect of
the adoption order would be to deprive her (*or* him) permanently of her (*or*
his) parental rights.

(c) There is no other person other than those mentioned in the petition
upon whom the notice of the petition should be served; *or* notice of the
petition should be served on

(d) The reporting officer has ascertained that alternatives to adoption
have been discussed with the natural mother (*or* the natural father).

(e) The natural mother (*or* natural father) understands that she (*or* he)

---

[4] Adoption Agencies (Scotland) Regulations 1984 (S.I. 1984 No. 988), para. 23; see above,
para. 8.10.
[5] A.S. 12 (R.C. 224 (5)); see above, para. 5.14.
[6] A.S. 21 (1) (R.C. 224 (2)); see above, para. 8.08.

may withdraw the agreement at any time before the order sought is made.
(*This paragraph will require to be adapted depending on the circumstances.*)
Edinburgh, 1986 "NM"
Reporting Officer

6. Report of curator *ad litem*[7]

(a) In the opinion of the curator *ad litem* the interests of the child have
been safeguarded.

(b) The statements in the petition have been investigated and it appears
that they are true, except (*state any exceptions*) and the true facts are (*state
the true facts*).

(c) The petitioners are joint owners of a semi-detached villa of four (*or
as the case may be*) apartments with kitchen and bathroom in the
district of the city. The house is well furnished and maintained.

(d) The household consists of the petitioners, the child and the father of
the female petitioner. The petitioners are related to the child in that the
female petitioner is the mother of the child; *or* the petitioners are not related
to the child. The other members of the household are   and their
relationship to the petitioners is   .

(e) This is a joint petition; and both petitioners confirmed that they wish
to adopt the child; *or* one spouse is not a petitioner because (*state the
reason*).

(f) The male petitioner is a   and earns £   ; the female
petitioner is a housewife and has no separate income apart from child
allowance of £   . The petitioners have a building society loan over their
house in respect of which the monthly repayments are £   ; they also pay
rates of £   . It appears that their means are sufficient to enable them to
maintain and bring up the child suitably.

(g) The child has no right to, or interest in, any property; *or* the child is
the owner of (*take in a brief description of the property*).

(h) The petitioners understand the nature and effect of an adoption
order and in particular that the order if granted will render them responsible
for the maintenance and upbringing of the child.

(i) The child is   years of age having been born on   at
          . The child was in the care and possession of the natural mother from
birth until about six weeks thereafter, when she left the child in the care of
the petitioners who have had the care and possession of the child since then;
or the child has been in the care and possession of the female petitioner since
birth and in the joint care and possession of the petitioners since their
marriage. The adoption arrangements were undertaken privately; *or* were
undertaken by the   Adoption Society (*take in address*).

(j) No payment or other reward appears to have been given or agreed
upon in consideration of the adoption; except that the adoption agency has
resolved to pay an adoption allowance to the petitioners of £   per
week in respect of the child, in terms of their scheme which has been
approved by the Secretary of State, beginning on   .

(k) In the circumstances narrated in this report the curator is of the
opinion that the adoption is likely to safeguard and promote the welfare of
the child throughout his childhood. The welfare of the child would be better
safeguarded and promoted by the making of an adoption order, than it
would be by the making of a custody order in favour of the petitioners; and it
would not be appropriate to make a custody order (*or as the case may be*); *or*
in view of the shiftless character of the male petitioner *or* his animosity to the
child (*or as the case may be*) the curator is of the opinion that the adoption is
not likely to safeguard and promote the welfare of the child throughout his
childhood.

---

[7] A.S. 21 (2) (R.C. 224 (6)); see above, para. 8.05.

(l) No insurance appears to have been effected over the life of the child; *or* life policy number   for £   has been effected over the life of the child by the petitioners and the premiums are kept up by them.

(m) The curator is of the opinion that there is no need to make an interim order to impose any particular terms and conditions in making the order; *or* to make special provision for the child; *or*, in view of the obvious immaturity of the petitioners, the curator feels that the court may wish to proceed in the first instance by way of an interim order of one (*or* two) years.

(n) The petitioners are ordinarily resident in the United Kingdom, and are of   nationality; *or* the male petitioner is ordinarily resident in West Germany and a report is produced on his home and living conditions there from the local authority there.

(o) The petitioners wish to adopt the child so that both of them may have full parental rights over the child, *or* because the female petitioner is unable to have children herself (*or as the case may be*).

(p) The petitioners are members of the Church of Scotland and intend to bring up the child in that persuasion (*or as the case may be*).

(q) The male petitioner is   years old and the female petitioner is , and the child is   : the curator is of the opinion that the petitioners are within the normally accepted age-range of parenthood; *or* notwithstanding the age of the female petitioner, she is very active and has already coped well with the child for almost a year (*or as the case may be*).

(r) (The contents of this paragraph must be so peculiar to the circumstances of each case that it would be of little value to do more than enumerate the matters set forth in the Act of Sederunt, para. 21 (2) (*r*), *viz.* such other questions or matters, including an assessment of the personalities of the petitioners and (where appropriate) the child, as having a bearing on (i) the mutual suitability of the petitioners and the child for the relationship created by adoption, and (ii) the ability of the petitioners to bring up the child.)

(s) It is impracticable in view of the age of the child to ascertain his wishes and feelings, but the petitioners intend to inform the child that he is adopted as soon as possible when a suitable moment arises; *or* from his discussion with the petitioners and the child the curator feels that the child is of sufficient understanding to state his wishes and feelings and these are in favour of him being adopted; *or* the child is a minor who has consented in writing to the adoption and he has confirmed his consent to the curator.

(t) The curator *ad litem* has been able to consider the report of the local authority (under section 22) *or* of the Adoption Agency (under section 23) and has no observations to make (*or as the case may be*); *or* such report has not been made.

Edinburgh,   1986

" NM "
Curator *ad Litem*

7. **Report of local authority** (*section 22*)[8]

(1) The petitioners in this case gave notice to the local authority on   of their intention to apply for an adoption order. The matter has been investigated by EF (*insert name of officer and designation*).

(2) The male petitioner is a   and earns £   ; The female petitioner is a housewife and has no separate income apart from child allowance of £   .

(3) The petitioners are joint owners of a semi-detached villa/flat of   apartments with kitchen and bathroom in the   district of the city. The house is well furnished and maintained.

(4) The household consists of the petitioners, the child and three other children of the petitioners (*or as the case may be*).

---

[8] 1978 Act, s. 22; see above, para. 8.10.

(5) The petitioners are emotionally and materially well able to look after the child.

(6) In the circumstances narrated in this report it appears that the adoption is likely to safeguard and promote the welfare of the child throughout his childhood.

(7) The child was placed by the adoption agency, *or* the female petitioner is the mother of the child (*or as the case may be*). Accordingly the child has not been placed with the petitioners in contravention of section 11.

(8) The child is not in the care of another local authority *or* the child is in the care of the   local authority and this authority has informed that authority by letter dated   that they have received a notice of intention to apply for an adoption order.

Edinburgh,   1986   (Signed) " EF "

8. Report of adoption agency *(section 23)*[9]

(1) The matter has been investigated by GH (*insert name of officer and designation*).

(2) The male petitioner is a   and earns £   ; The female petitioner is a housewife and has no separate income apart from child allowance of £   . The adoption agency in terms of their adoption allowance scheme, which has been approved by the Secretary of State, has resolved to pay to the petitioners in respect of the child an adoption allowance of £   per week, beginning on   .

(3) The petitioners are joint owners of a semi-detached villa/flat of   apartments with kitchen and bathroom in the   district of the city. The house is well furnished and maintained.

(4) The household consists of the petitioners, the child and three other children of the petitioner (*or as the case may be*).

(5) The petitioners are emotionally and materially well able to look after the child (*or otherwise as the case may be*).

(6) In the circumstances narrated in this report it appears that the adoption is likely to safeguard and promote the welfare of the child throughout his childhood, *or* because of the character of the male petitioner (*or as the case may be*), the adoption is not likely to safeguard and promote the welfare of the child throughout his childhood. The child has consented to the making of the adoption order (*or as the case may be*).

(7) The child was placed by the   adoption agency, *or* the female petitioner is the mother of the child (*or as the case may be*). Accordingly the child has not been placed with the petitioners in contravention of section 11.

(8) The child is not in the care of another local authority *or* the child is in the care of the   local authority and this authority has informed that authority by letter dated   that they have received a notice of intention to apply for an adoption order.

Edinburgh,   1986   " GH "

9. Report of adoption agency *(regulation 23)*[10]

(*The adoption agency placing the child must report on the background and circumstances of the child, his family and the persons proposing to adopt him, and on any other matters relevant to the duty to promote the welfare of the child. The terms of the report will depend on the circumstances of the case.*)

---

[9] 1978 Act, s. 23; see above, para. 8.09.

[10] Adoption Agencies (Scotland) Regulations 1984 (S.I. 1984 No. 988), reg. 23; see above, para. 8.10.

IV Overseas Registers[1]

The countries in the list which follows are those in respect of which orders in council have been made under Evidence (Foreign, Dominion and Colonial Documents) Act 1933 and Oaths and Evidence (Overseas Authorities and Countries) Act 1963 whereby an official copy of an entry in the public registers of those countries is admissible in the courts in the United Kingdom in so far as it conforms with the terms of the order. After each country is the year and number of the statutory instrument which incorporates the order in council relating to that country.

Aden 1965/1527
Australia (Commonwealth) 1938/739
Antigua 1965/312
Bahamas 1961/2041
Barbados 1962/641
Basutoland 1965/1719
Bechuanaland 1965/1720
Belgium 1933/383
Belize. *See* British Honduras, below.
Bermuda 1961/2042
Botswana. *See* Bechuanaland, above.
British Antarctic Territory 1962/2605
British Guiana 1961/2043
British Honduras 1961/2044
British Indian Ocean Territory 1984/857
Canada 1962/2606
Cayman Islands 1965/313
Denmark 1969/144
Dominica 1961/2045
Falkland Islands 1962/2607
Fiji 1961/2046
France 1937/515
Germany (Federal Republic) 1970/819
Gibraltar 1961/2047
Grenada 1966/82

Guyana. *See* British Guiana, above.
Hong Kong 1962/642
Ireland (Republic) 1969/1059
Italy 1969/145
Jamaica 1962/643
Kenya 1965/1712
Lesotho. *See* Basutoland, above.
Luxembourg 1972/116
Mauritius 1961/2048
Montserrat 1962/644
Netherlands 1970/284
New Zealand 1959/1306
St. Helena 1961/2049
St. Lucia 1965/1721
Sarawak 1961/2050
Seychelles 1962/2608
Sierra Leone 1962/2609
Swaziland 1965/1865
Tanganyika 1961/2051
Tanzania. *See* Tanganyika, above and Zanzibar, below.
Turks and Caicos Islands 1966/83
Uganda 1961/2052
U.S.A. 1969/146
Zanzibar 1961/2053

---

[1] See para. 5.10.

Index

[References are generally to paragraph numbers. References preceded by a roman numeral (II) are to e.g. Appendix II.
References consisting only of a roman numeral are to a complete Appendix.]

207

Index

Welfare—*cont.*
  illegitimacy, removal of stigma of, 8.05 (k)
  material welfare, 8.05 (k)
  relevant,
    to merits, 10.09 (b)
    to motion to dispense with agreement, 10.09 (b)
  report of adoption agency (s. 23) and local authority (s. 22) to deal with, 3.01, 8.09 (b)
  s. 3 of 1975 Act, now s. 6 of 1978 Act, 2.01, 8.05 (k)

Welfare—*cont.*
  single petitioner, dangers of, 3.01, 8.05 (k)
  status quo, maintenance of, 8.05 (k)
  step-parent petition, only one circumstance in, 2.01
  surname given on adoption, 8.05 (k)
  "totality of circumstances" to be considered, 2.01
Wishes and feelings of child,
  curator *ad litem* to report on, 3.01 (c), 8.05 (s)
Withdrawal of petition, 11.02